The Language of Small Business

The Language
of Small Business

A Complete Dictionary of Small Business Terms

Carl O. Trautmann

UPSTART PUBLISHING COMPANY, INC.
The Small Business Publishing Company
Dover, New Hampshire

Published by Upstart Publishing Company, Inc.
A Division of Dearborn Publishing Group, Inc.
12 Portland Street
Dover, New Hampshire 03820
(800) 235-8866 or (603) 749-5071

Neither the author nor the publisher of this book is engaged in rendering, by the sale of this book, legal, accounting or other professional services. The reader is encouraged to employ the services of a competent professional in such matters.

Library of Congress Cataloging-in-Publication Data

Trautmann, Carl O.
    The language of small business: a complete dictionary of small business terms/Carl O. Trautmann.
        p.   cm.
    Includes index.
    ISBN 0-936894-59-8
    1. English language—Business English—Dictionaries. 2. English language—Terms and phrases. 3. Small business—Dictionaries.
    I. Title.
PE1479.B87T73 1994
423'.02465—dc20
                                            94-808
                                              CIP

Cover design by Marcy Stamper, Canterbury, NH.

Printed in the United States of America
10 9 8 7 6 5 4 3 2 1

For a complete catalog of Upstart's small business publications, call (800) 235-8866.

Contents

Acknowledgments

The author wishes to thank many people for their contributions that have made this book possible, providing ideas, facts, definitions and information. I am especially indebted to those family and friends who provided incentive and encouragement in the face of the major task of authoring a book.

Special acknowledgment must go to Gus Berle, Alice Brown and Maurice Frankel, each of whom painstakingly devoted many hours of expert advice by thoroughly reviewing each word, phrase and concept to ensure accurate definitions applicable to the small and start-up business. Without these three key contributors, this book could never have been published.

During recent years, many of the 13,000 volunteers of the Service Corps of Retired Executives (SCORE) have added insight to the author's knowledge concerning the start-up and operation of a small business. As a SCORE volunteer, the author was given an exposure to the small business environment that would otherwise not have been possible. SCORE also provided the opportunity for working beside the U.S. Small Business Administration (SBA). Observing the dedication of SBA and SCOREs toward the success of small business has been an educational, enlightening and rewarding experience.

My wife, Trudy, has been particularly understanding with my personal attention to my Macintosh computer and the considerable amount of time I have devoted to drafting the manuscript for *The Language of Small Business*.

Finally, I am indebted to Spencer Smith, president, and the entire staff of Upstart Publishing Company, Inc. for their faith in the potential economic return from this work.

vii

Preface

The Language of Small Business is the result of many years of difficult and thorough searching for answers to everyday problems of the small business person. Numerous books and articles exist concerning the theory of business and the practical application of business principles, but no other single glossary or dictionary exists that defines the terms as a ready reference for the small business person.

This book provides a ready reference to 2,500 of the most commonly used terms encountered by the start-up entrepreneur, the small business person and the student of business theory. In addition, there are 13 self-help guides to assist the start-up business person. Thus *The Language of Small Business* is a totally functional small business reference book, a comprehensive, single-volume, instant-answer book to just about any problem or question concerning small business principles, practices and concepts.

There are thousands of companies, industries and disciplines concerning small business. Furthermore, the volume of this diversity grows larger every day. Thus there is a widening gap of understanding among small business entrepreneurs, bankers, accountants, government officials, investors and the like. Precise definitions of the terms promotes more effective communication and aids understanding. This book contains the definitions of more than 2,500 small business terms and commonly accepted practices. If you understand these terms, you will be more successful in your small business because you will not be misled by confusion or misunderstandings.

In 1993, more than 800,000 businesses were started in the United States. All of these business start-ups were small businesses. Furthermore, an analysis of about 21,000,000 federal tax returns from businesses showed only 14,000 classified as large businesses. The conclusion: At least 95 percent of all businesses are small businesses. That is, about 21,000,000 businesses in the United States are small businesses. You can become a small business entrepreneur yourself. And, remember, all large businesses began as a small business.

In business, words sometimes have unique or multiple definitions depending on the context in which the words are used. What is more important, idioms, phrases, acronyms and abbreviations have acquired unique definitions that have become commonplace. To the novice or start-up entrepreneur, the onslaught of these definitions can complicate understanding. Often the precise definition is dependent on usage because of the combinations of words, acronyms and abbreviations into business idioms and phrases. In view of this, *The Language of Small Business* provides the solution to understanding.

The computer, advanced communications and high-speed jet aircraft have all added to the rapid development of new business terms. These technological advances have given rise to such terms as "fax," "modem," "spreadsheet," "International Monetary Fund" and "exchange rate." When confronted with these expressions, the small business person has no place to turn for the definitions without asking a knowledgeable person in the field or by doing considerable time-consuming research. Enter, *The Language of Small Business*, which defines these terms and is a single concise reference for rapid and complete understanding.

It is this book's purpose to define the words, idioms, phrases, acronyms, abbreviations and terms of this new technology, while updating the traditional business language specifically oriented to the small and start-up business person. Since the English language is rapidly becoming the universal language of business throughout the world, *The Language of Small Business* provides a base for worldwide use and standardization of the definitions. As users in other world markets consistently apply the definitions, business communication becomes more efficient. With the exception of unique government definitions and unique tax-related terms, all the definitions in *The Language of Small Business* can be applied consistently throughout the world.

The author has made a deliberate attempt to keep the definitions in this book concise and specifically applicable to the start-up business person; that is, any ordinary person with a business idea, the desire to succeed and who wants to start a business. For further study, or if more precise understanding is needed, the reader is encouraged to consult the specialized dictionary from the field in question. Specialized dictionaries exist for all of the many fields of small business activity.

Since the evolution of small business is a constantly expanding and growing field, definitions may change and new terms are frequently introduced. Please use or make a photocopy of the form at the back inside cover to submit your suggested additional terms and definitions. The author welcomes the correspondence and will include applicable definitions in future editions of *The Language of Small Business*. These definitions may also be added to a planned on-line computer database that will be accessible by PC users with modems.

How to Use
This Book Effectively

ALPHABETIZATION: All entries are alphabetized by letter rather than by word so multiple-word terms are treated as single words. For example, **ANNUAL MEETING** follows **ANNUALIZE** as though it were spelled **ANNUALMEETING**, without spacing. Similarly, **OFFICE SUPPLY STORE** follows **OFFICER**. Abbreviations and acronyms appear as if they were text words, for ease of reference. No separate listing of abbreviations and acronyms is used. Numbers in entry titles are listed as if the numbers were spelled out.

When a term has several meanings, most common usage for the small business person usually determines the first subhead listing. Others follow in priority order unless clarity dictates a different order. In some entries, the various meanings of the term may be preceded by simple numerical headings.

CROSS REFERENCES: In order to gain fuller understanding of a term, sometimes it helps to refer to the definition of another term. In these cases, the additional term is capitalized. Such cross-references appear in the body of the definition or at the end of the entry. Cross-references may also refer to related or contrasting concepts to give more information and a fuller understanding of the term of interest. As a rule, a term is printed in capitals, only on its first appearance in the definition. Where a term is fully defined by another entry, a reference rather than a definition is provided.

PARENTHESES: Parentheses are used in definitions for three reasons: (1) to indicate that an abbreviation is used with about the same frequency as the term itself, for example, **FREE ON BOARD (F.O.B.)**; (2) to indicate an entry's opposite is such an integral part of the concept that only one discussion is necessary, for example, **NET INCOME (OR LOSS)**; and (3) to list several items concerning the definition in numerical order but not necessarily related to the frequency of occurrence.

SELF-HELP GUIDES: Several self-help guides enhance understanding of general small business terms. In addition, related helpful information peculiar to the small business person has been included. The self-help guides are as follows:

A. **Marketing and Selling Your Product or Service**: Practical guides that will help to evaluate your market and identify available sources for gathering the information to speed the process of developing your market plan. Understanding the primacy of the marketing concept focuses the owner/manager on the customer. Selling tips enhance the opportunity for success of your small business. Much of this information is free, if you search for it.

B. **How to Write a Business Plan**: A business plan is your pathway to profit. During the writing of your business plan, you will be forced to make each decision necessary for successful start-up. On the other hand, you may prove to yourself that the venture is not worthy of further pursuit. Write the business plan yourself; don't hire someone else to write the plan for you. If someone else writes the business plan, he or she will make vital decisions for you. You alone must make these decisions! To assist you in making these important decisions, Self-Help Guide B will ask the right questions and will lead you through the steps of plan preparation.

C. **Personal Financial Statement**: You must document your personal net worth on a personal financial statement since your personal net worth is fundamental to establishing credit for a start-up business and must be included in your start-up business plan. Those who have net worth can borrow money! When you start a business, you cannot borrow all the money from someone else, such as a bank. You must invest your money in the business.

D. **How to Get a Business Loan**: Borrowing money is not easy to accomplish. Only if you understand the lender's language and your business plan demonstrates that you are investing your own money wisely will you be able to convince a lender that you are a good risk and profitable for the lender's money. A lender has to believe you will safeguard his or her money, make prudent use of it and have the ability to repay. See the lender's criteria for a lending decision under the definition for **ABUNDANCE OF CAUTION** in this book. The loan application, attached to your start-up business plan, should include:

1. *Equity*: The amount of money you are investing in the business;

2. *Assets*: The equipment, materials, working capital and other property needed to start the business, i.e., the collateral for a business loan;

3. *Liabilities*: The amount of money you need to borrow in addition to showing the collateralization; and

4. *Repayment Ability*: A convincing argument that the business will be sufficiently profitable to earn enough money to make the loan payments.

E. **Balance Sheet for a Small Business**: For an established business, a balance sheet documents the financial information in a way that displays the viability (solvency) of the business. At a point in time, the balance sheet shows the value of things owned, how much is owed, and how much of the business is owned by the owners (equity).

F. **Pro Forma Balance Sheet for a Small Business**: For a start-up business, you must prepare a pro forma balance sheet. Prepared for some future date when you plan to start your business, the pro forma balance sheet will display how much you plan to invest in the business (your equity), the things that the business needs to own when it gets started (assets/collateral) and how much borrowed money is needed, if any (liabilities). This pro forma balance sheet must be included in your start-up business plan.

G. **Income Statement for a Small Business**: For any period during the operation of a business, you need to see the financial progress made from the beginning of the period to the end of the period. This information is displayed on an income statement that shows your profit (or loss) for the period. For the period, expenses are subtracted from the income received to show your profit (or loss).

H. **Projected Income Statement for a Start-Up Business**: To plan effectively, you must make forecasts of future sales (income) and future expenses (payments). The result is summarized as a projected income statement. This information is then used to form the basis of your budgets for the future period. The projected income statement must be included in your start-up business plan to show how you will repay creditors and how you will earn a profit on your investment.

I. **Cash Flow Projection**: An analysis of future cash flow for a start-up business will help avoid many financial problems. Furthermore, a cash flow projection (forecast) can make the difference between your success and failure, as well as the difference between growth and stagnation. A cash flow projection is the single MOST IMPORTANT TOOL available to the small business person. The cash flow projection must be included in your start-up business plan since it will show how the money comes to the business (sources of cash) and how the money is to be spent for wages, material purchases and repayments on loans (uses of cash).

J. **Finding Help for a Start-Up Small Business**: Several places provide help for the start-up small business person. Basically, the help is divided into eight categories: governments, not-for-profit organizations, educational institutions, similar businesses, suppliers and customers, business associations, professionals and for-fee consulting services. Particularly, every small business should consider counseling from the Service Corps Of Retired Executives (SCORE). This nationwide organization consists of 13,000 former small business owners and managers who volunteer their time to counsel small businesses. SCORE is sponsored by the U.S. Small Business Administration.

K. **Finding Professional Assistance**: To be successful, your small business must depend on the services of others in the business community. Some of these include your attorney, your accountant, your banker and your insurance representative. This self-help guide provides a means for searching and evaluating these services.

L. **Code of Ethics for the Small Business Person**: Businesses prosper in an environment of ethical standards. By operating with a high standard of ethical conduct, your future as a small business person will be more assured and more rewarding.

M. **A Start-Up Checklist for Small Businesses**: When you start your business, it is very important that you consider all the elements necessary for success. If an item is left out or is not considered fully, you may fail. This comprehensive and practical checklist is designed to help you consider all the factors crucial to a start-up.

A

AA RATING In advertising, media and publishing, the Average Audience Rating.

ABUNDANCE OF CAUTION In banking, a lender's requirement that the borrower's collateral equal more than the asset to be purchased with the loan and that the borrower have enough money invested to insure the borrower cannot back out without significant loss of personal finances. If the borrower has his or her own money invested, the borrower will be more committed to succeed.

ACCELERATED COST RECOVERY SYSTEM (ACRS) An AC-CELERATED DEPRECIATION method of FIXED ASSET write-off as an expense faster than the STRAIGHT-LINE DEPRECIATION method. Sometimes called the 3-5-10 RULE that describes the duration in years of the time periods for depreciating different classes of assets.

ACCELERATED DEPRECIATION Any method of cost recovery of a FIXED ASSET that is faster than using the STRAIGHT-LINE DEPRECIATION method. Traditional rationale supports higher maintenance and repair costs in later years. These costs are offset in the early years by the higher depreciation expense, resulting in a level effect on earnings throughout the useful life of the asset. Sometimes accelerated depreciation is used as a tax shelter because of large up-front write-offs with no reduction of cash flow. See several methods of accelerated depreciation described: AC-CELERATED COST RECOVERY SYSTEM; SUM-OF-THE-YEARS-DIGITS; DOUBLE-DECLINING BALANCE.

1

ACCELERATION CLAUSE   A provision in a NOTE, BOND or MORTGAGE that states that, in the event of a default by the debtor, the entire balance outstanding shall become due and payable.

ACCEPTANCE   In contracting, an agreement by a buyer to accept an offer by a seller, often preceded by negotiation of price, scope, terms and conditions.

In general financial transactions, the free act of assuming a risk. Some examples include: commercial paper issued by a sales finance company; an agreement on a TIME DRAFT promising payment; a BANKER'S ACCEPTANCE; a time draft drawn by the seller of goods on the buyer (a TRADE ACCEPTANCE).

ACCEPTANCE COMPANY   A company that purchases consumer loans (PAPER) from others. When sales are made, small businesses can make loans to customers then sell the loans to an acceptance company to obtain cash, but less cash than waiting for payment. Also known as sales finance company; factoring company. See FINANCE COMPANY.

ACCOUNT   In general, the contractual relationship between buyer and seller under which payment is made at a later time. The term OPEN ACCOUNT is used for commercial transactions whereas CHARGE ACCOUNT is used to describe personal transactions.

In accounting and bookkeeping, an historical record of transactions, as shown on a STATEMENT OF ACCOUNT. Each account is an individual subclassification of 1) an asset; 2) a liability; 3) equity; 4) income; or 5) an expense as represented by ledger pages to which debit and credit entries are chronologically posted to record changes in value. Guidance for typical account types can be found in a CHART OF ACCOUNTS.

In banking, a relationship established at a bank in the name of a client where deposits and withdrawals are made. Usually deposits are on-hand against which withdrawals can be made. Administrative responsibility is handled by an ACCOUNT OFFICER.

ACCOUNT AGING   See AGING.

ACCOUNTANT   A practitioner of ACCOUNTING as a profession after having attained a level of financial knowledge. A person whose work is to inspect, keep and adjust accounts. See also BOOKKEEPER; CERTIFIED PUBLIC ACCOUNTANT.

ACCOUNTANT'S OPINION   A statement signed by an independent public accountant that describes the scope and accuracy of an examination of the financial books and records of a business. Because financial reporting involves considerable discretion, the accountant's opinion is an important assurance of integrity.

ACCOUNT EXECUTIVE   A professional person in a firm who is responsible for a customer's ACCOUNT; the person at the firm who is contacted for discussion about the account.

ACCOUNTING   The system for recording, verifying and reporting financial information. Also, the profession performing these functions. See also ACCOUNT.

ACCOUNTING CONTROL   Procedures and systems used to maintain accurate financial records and to safeguard the assets of the company.

ACCOUNTING CYCLE   The routine steps in processing accounting data during an accounting period. In sequence, 1) occurrence of the transaction, 2) classification of each transaction in chronological order (journalizing), 3) recording the classified data in ledger accounts (posting), 4) preparation of financial statements and 5) closing of nominal accounts.

ACCOUNTING EQUATION   The mathematical formula that defines the relationships of accounting arithmetic. At a given point in time, the BALANCE SHEET reflects the results of the accounting equation, wherein ASSETS equal LIABILITIES plus NET WORTH. To account for changes in financial condition over a period of time, the equation must also consider the INCOME STATEMENT effects of operations, wherein ASSETS equal LIABILITIES plus NET WORTH plus INCOME less EXPENDITURES.

ACCOUNTING FIRM   A business that provides professional financial and accounting services.

ACCOUNTING PERIOD   The normal calendar duration for reporting of financial information. The time for closing accounts when accounting data are summarized into financial statements. In most businesses, this is done monthly, quarterly and annually.

ACCOUNTING POLICIES; ACCOUNTING PRACTICES; ACCOUNTING PRINCIPLES   Basic concepts, assumptions, policies, methods and practices used by a company for maintaining the BOOKS OF ACCOUNT and summarization into FINANCIAL STATEMENTS. The principles should be consistent with GENERALLY ACCEPTED ACCOUNTING PRINCIPLES. In larger companies, accounting policy, practices and principles may each have more precise definitions.

ACCOUNT PAYABLE   See ACCOUNTS PAYABLE.

ACCOUNT RECEIVABLE   See ACCOUNTS RECEIVABLE.

ACCOUNTS PAYABLE   Money owed by the business to suppliers; amounts owed to others (creditors) on an open account for goods and services purchased by a business. Analysts look at the relationship of accounts payable compared to purchases for indications of sound day-to-day financial management. See TRADE CREDIT.

ACCOUNTS RECEIVABLE   Money owed by customers to the business; amounts owed to a business for goods and services sold by the business but not yet collected. A key factor in analyzing LIQUIDITY of a business is the ability to meet current obligations without additional revenues.

ACCOUNTS RECEIVABLE AGING   Classification of customer ACCOUNTS RECEIVABLE according to the date of sale. The aging schedule reveals patterns of delinquency and shows where collection efforts should be concentrated. The longer accounts are left unpaid, the more likely they become uncollectible. Aging evaluations can help prevent losses on future sales, since old customers who fail to pay may begin buying from other sources of supply and will leave bad debts on the aged accounts in your business. See AGING; AGING SCHEDULE.

ACCOUNTS RECEIVABLE FINANCING   Short-term loans made to obtain cash using ACCOUNTS RECEIVABLE as COLLATERAL. The cash received will be less than the amount of the accounts receivable.

ACCRUAL BASIS   An accounting method whereby income and expense items are recognized and entered in the books as they are earned or incurred, even though they may not have been received or actually paid. Many small businesses use the alternative CASH BASIS or MODIFIED CASH BASIS accounting method. Opposed to CASH BASIS.

ACCRUAL METHOD   See ACCRUAL BASIS.

ACCRUALS   See ACCRUED EXPENSE.

ACCRUE   To accumulate over a period of time, such as AC-CRUED INTEREST, ACCRUED EXPENSE or ACCRUED DEPRE-CIATION. As an example, accrued expenses have been incurred but are not yet payable.   See also ACCRUED.

ACCRUED   That which has accumulated over a period of time and is an obligation that must be satisfied at some point in the future.

ACCRUED DEPRECIATION   See ACCUMULATED DEPRECIA-TION.

ACCRUED EXPENSE   A debt that has been incurred or has accumulated over a period of time and must be paid but has not yet been paid.

ACCRUED INCOME   Sales or revenue that has been earned or accumulated over a period of time but has not yet been collected.

ACCRUED INTEREST   INTEREST that has accumulated over a period of time and is obligated to be paid but has not yet been paid. Accrued interest can either be income, such as interest from investments, or it can be an expense, such as payment of interest on a debt.

ACCUMULATED DEPRECIATION   An accounting term for the amount of DEPRECIATION accrued over a period of time.

ACCUMULATED DIVIDEND   Payment to stockholders due to be paid.

ACE   See ACTIVE CORPS OF EXECUTIVES. Also Association of College Entrepreneurs.

ACID TEST; ACID TEST RATIO   See QUICK RATIO.

ACQUISITION   To purchase a business or buy another business. Also, the process of obtaining a loan, obtaining other forms of financing or the purchase of property by the business.

ACQUISITION COST   The amount of money expended to obtain title to property, usually relating to fixed assets.

ACRS   See ACCELERATED COST RECOVERY SYSTEM.

ACTIVE CORPS OF EXECUTIVES (ACE)   A program sponsored by the U.S. Small Business Administration in which business owners and managers who are still working volunteer their time to counsel small businesses. ACE volunteers are one part of the SERVICE CORPS OF RETIRED EXECUTIVES.

ACTUAL   That which has occurred, as opposed to that which was previously expected, budgeted, estimated or planned.

ACTUAL COSTS   The expenses that have been incurred and recorded in the books; as opposed to forecasted or anticipated expenses. Also, production expenses that are incurred by production activities during an accounting period.

ACTUAL PERFORMANCE   In accounting, the financial amounts recorded as a result of operations; demonstrating the manner in which a product operates; the results of decisions.

ADDENDUM   Additional material attached to and made part of a document. Often an addendum is the result of information learned after the original document was prepared.

ADD-ON INTEREST   A method of computing interest whereby interest charges are made for the entire principal amount for the entire term, regardless of any repayments of principal made. The result is an interest charge that is almost double that of the stated SIMPLE INTEREST RATE.

ADJACENCIES   In retail, adjoining merchandise-category areas in store layouts.

ADJUSTED BASIS   The original COST BASIS of property reduced by depreciation and increased by improvements.

ADJUSTING ENTRY   An accounting entry to record an internal transaction on an account that is usually made at the end of an accounting period, such as an allocation or correction of an error.

ADJUSTMENT ASSISTANCE   Financial and technical assistance by a government to companies, workers and communities designed to help them adjust to rising import competition.

ADMINISTRATIVE EXPENSE   Costs associated with staff and supporting personnel who are involved in managing the activities of the business; indirect expenses. As opposed to direct or production personnel expenses.

AD VALOREM EQUIVALENT   In international trade, a "specific" duty imposed as a percentage of the value of the imported goods, usually applied during a tariff adjustment.

AD VALOREM TARIFF   In international trade, a duty (tariff) assessed by customs as a percentage of the value of the imported goods.

AD VALOREM TAX   A tax that is proportionate to the value of the property being taxed, such as sales tax; a tax calculated as a flat percentage of sales price. As opposed to a specific tax per unit based on quantity, such as excise tax per package of cigarettes.

ADVANCE   To give an amount before it is due, such as an advance payment of salary to an employee.

ADVANCE PAYMENT   In international trade, payment for goods by a foreign customer prior to receiving the goods. This method of payment is beneficial to the supplier but is very risky for the foreign customer because the goods may not get shipped as planned, the goods may get lost or the goods could be damaged during shipment.

ADVENTURE CAPITAL   A speculative investment, sometimes by another entrepreneur who was previously successful in a new business venture, sometimes by another business looking for new avenues of growth. Adventure capital is a more risky investment than venture capital. In 1987, it was estimated that about $27 billion was invested as adventure capital, as compared to about $1 billion invested in VENTURE CAPITAL. See also ADVENTURE CAPITALIST; VENTURE CAPITAL.

ADVENTURE CAPITALIST   A speculative investor who invests for the excitement of the venture, based on faith and trust that the vision of the person, new company, product or service will be successful; the decision is not based on solid financial analysis, but with the hope financial rewards will result. An adventure capitalist is more speculative than a VENTURE CAPITALIST. Also see ADVENTURE CAPITAL.

ADVERTISE   The act of providing information to the public concerning products and services for sale.

ADVERTISEMENT   A paid message, in a public medium, designed to influence the purchasing behavior or thought pattern of an audience.

ADVERTISING   Providing information to the public concerning the products and services for sale through written or spoken media, such as newspapers, handbills, television and mail. An enticement to encourage people to buy.

ADVERTISING MEDIA   The public means for distribution of an advertising message. The most common media include newspapers, magazines, radio, television, direct mail and computer bulletin boards.

ADVERTISING SUCCESS FORMULA   The seven essential steps that are the keys to pay-off of advertising money spent: 1) get attention, 2) hold attention, 3) create desire, 4) make the message credible, 5) provide the value, 6) make it easy and 7) cause action now.

ADVISING BANK   In international trade, a bank, operating for the exporter in the exporter's country, who handles letters of credit for foreign banks. An advising bank informs the exporter of the conditions of the letter of credit without necessarily bearing responsibility for payment.

AFFIDAVIT   A written statement that is sworn under oath before a notary public or other official authorized by law to administer an oath.

AFFILIATE   Two companies are affiliated when one owns less than a majority of the voting stock of the other, or when both are subsidiaries of a third company, which is the parent company. See also SUBSIDIARY; PARENT COMPANY.

AFFIRMATIVE ACTION PROGRAM   A program designed to ensure that all parties are being treated equally regardless of color, sex, race, creed, age, disability, etc., particularly so that minorities are not discriminated against.

AFTERMARKET   The sale of goods, services or securities by another company after the original manufacture or original issue.

AGENCY   A legally established relationship (often a business firm) whereby one party (the PRINCIPAL) delegates to another party (the AGENT) the right to act on behalf of the principal in business transactions and to exercise some degree of discretion while acting. For example in the insurance industry, an agency represents an insurance company (the PRINCIPAL).

AGENT   One who is authorized to represent and act on behalf of another person or business (called the PRINCIPAL) in transactions involving a third party. Unlike an employee who merely works for the principal, an agent works in place of the principal. Agents have three basic characteristics: 1) they act on behalf of and are subject to control of the principal; 2) they do not have title to the principal's property; 3) they owe their duty of allegiance to the principal's orders.

AGING   In business, the process of determining the length of time since a financial transaction occurred on an account. A listing of the accounts (an AGING SCHEDULE) showing time periods, past due amounts, customer names, etc. See ACCOUNTS RECEIVABLE AGING; INVENTORY AGING.

AGING RECEIVABLES   See ACCOUNTS RECEIVABLE AGING.

AGING SCHEDULE   A listing of items showing time periods along with amounts, names, titles, actions, etc. Examples: a list of ACCOUNTS according to the length of time they have been outstanding; a list of maintenance actions according to the length of time since the last maintenance was performed. See AGING.

AGREEMENT   An understanding or arrangement between two or more businesses or business people; a CONTRACT. An agreement may be verbal or written; if only verbal, the agreement is subject to a greater amount of misunderstanding.

ALIEN   A person born outside the United States, that has not been naturalized and is not a citizen of the United States.

ALLOCATE   To set funds apart for a specific purpose. Also, to distribute proportionate shares according to a plan.

ALLOCATED COSTS   Expenses that are proportionately assigned to costs that result from a cause/effect basis. Example: Indirect costs are often proportioned to direct costs when establishing a bid posture. Also, expense proportioned to different areas of operation on an operating statement.

ALLOWANCE   In retail, any means by which the seller reduces the effective cost of goods purchased by a retailer. Common allowances are for advertising, freight or markdowns.

ALLOWANCE FOR BAD DEBTS; ALLOWANCE FOR DOUBTFUL ACCOUNTS; ALLOWANCE FOR UNCOLLECTIBLE ACCOUNTS   An account established to record a subtraction from

ACCOUNTS RECEIVABLE, to allow for those accounts that will not be paid.

ALLOWANCES   Deductions from the price of previously sold merchandise for merchandise not received or received in damaged condition.

AMORTIZATION   See AMORTIZE.

AMORTIZATION SCHEDULE   A table for an AMORTIZED ASSET that shows the term, time periods, principal amount, interest rate, payment amounts that are due, payable or paid. See AMORTIZE.

AMORTIZE   Repayment of a loan by installments; an accounting procedure allowing gradual repayment (retirement) of a debt by means of systematic payments of principal and interest over a period of the estimated life of the asset on which the loan is made or secured. For FIXED ASSETS, DEPRECIATION is the allowance for wear-out. For natural resources, DEPLETION is the allowance for the wasting away of the asset.

AMORTIZED ASSET   See AMORTIZE.

AMOUNT   A numerical representation of quantity. In finance, amount usually refers to quantity of money. Also refers to a sum, i.e., "That amounts to —."

ANCHOR   In retail, a large well known store in a shopping mall that usually attracts customers to smaller stores.

ANNUAL   Occurring on a yearly basis; each 12-month period.

ANNUAL BASIS   See ANNUALIZE.

ANNUAL DEBT SERVICE   The amount of money on a total yearly basis required for the payment of interest and principal on a long-term debt. Also called DEBT SERVICE.

ANNUAL INTEREST RATE   See INTEREST; SIMPLE INTEREST.

ANNUALIZE   To normalize data to a yearly basis, usually for comparison with other periods. A statistical technique whereby figures covering a period of less than one year are extended to cover a 12-month period to adjust for seasonal or other variations, called an ANNUAL BASIS.

ANNUAL MEETING   A once-a-year meeting of stockholders where the managers of a company report the year's results; the board of directors stand for election for the next year; and those present provide a forum for discussion or voting on pivotal issues of the company. Usually presided by the Chairman of the Board of Directors or the Chief Executive Officer.

ANNUAL PERCENTAGE RATE   The yearly INTEREST RATE; an expression of the relationship of the total finance charge (interest) to the total amount to be financed (the loan) as required by the Truth-in-Lending Act. See INTEREST; SIMPLE INTEREST.

ANNUAL RATE OF INTEREST   Same as ANNUAL PERCENTAGE RATE.

ANNUAL REPORT   A document prepared annually. The document prepared by a company's management for submittal to the owners (stockholders) summarizing the activities of the business for the previous year.

ANSWERING MACHINE   An electronic device that is attached to a telephone line for the purpose of recording a message from a caller when the telephone is not answered by the called party.

ANTI-DUMPING DUTY   In international trade, a DUTY levied against all entries of a product that was found to have been dumped, sometimes levied retroactively. See DUMPING.

ANTITRUST   Federal laws designed to prevent monopolies and restraint of trade.

ANTITRUST LAWS   See ANTITRUST.

A/P   An accountant's abbreviation of ACCOUNTS PAYABLE.

APPLIED TARIFF RATE   In international trade, the TARIFF rate actually used to determine the amount of DUTY owed on a particular import transaction. Differs from BOUND RATE.

APPRAISAL   The process of formulating and supporting an opinion of value; a written document by a professional appraiser stating the value of an asset; an estimate of the amount for which an asset could be sold. Also, an evaluation of performance, i.e., an employee performance appraisal. See also APPRAISAL REPORT.

APPRAISAL REPORT   The document prepared by an appraiser that presents an estimate of value along with information substantiating the methods, assumptions and conditions of the APPRAISAL. In evaluating personnel, the document contains a review of goals met and critical incidents, (good and bad) influencing the future performance of the individual.

APPRAISER   A person professionally qualified by education, experience and ability to conduct an opinion of the value of real or personal property; one who estimates value. Often an appraiser may be certified by a professional organization, government or other means. Also, a supervisor is an appraiser of the performance of an employee. See APPRAISAL.

APPRECIATION   An increase in value of an asset due to economic or related causes. The opposite of DEPRECIATION.

A/R   An accountant's abbreviation of ACCOUNTS RECEIVABLE.

ARBITRAGE   The difference between interest rates; the simultaneous purchase and sale of debt securities in different markets to profit from the interest rate differentials.

ARBITRATION   A nonjudicial submission of a controversy to selected third parties for settlement of the controversy in a manner provided by law or by agreement among the parties.

ARM'S LENGTH TRANSACTION   A transaction in which the parties are dealing from equal bargaining positions, neither party is subject to the other's control or dominant influence, and the transaction is treated with fairness, integrity and legality. If discovered by a taxing authority, the absence of an arms length transaction may result in additional taxes incurred resulting from transfer at less than fair market value.

ARRANGER OF CREDIT A person who regularly arranges for consumer credit by another person if a finance charge is imposed.

ARREARS The state of being delinquent by not paying a debt when due; past due.

In lending, a loan on which interest is paid at the end of the period; as opposed to interest paid in advance (the beginning of the period).

ARTICLES OF INCORPORATION A document filed with a state of the United States by the founders of a corporation. Upon approval of the articles, the state issues a CERTIFICATE OF INCORPORATION that legally establishes the corporation as a business entity. The two documents together (Articles of Incorporation and Certificate of Incorporation) are sometimes called the CHARTER of the corporation, embodying such information as the corporation's name, officers' names, the incorporator, purpose, amount of authorized shares, and number of directors. The charter and the laws of the state give rise to the powers of the corporation. Rules governing the internal management of the corporation are set forth in the BYLAWS as drawn up by the founders/officers.

"AS IS" Words by a seller in a contract suggesting no further responsibilities on the part of the seller, frequently meaning that no guarantees of any kind are given regarding the property being sold. It is intended to be a disclaimer of warranties or representations.

ASKED Same as ASKING PRICE.

ASKING PRICE The price at which someone who owns something is willing to sell it or where negotiation between seller and buyer can begin to reach agreement on the exchange price for the transaction. Asking price differs from FIRM PRICE in that asking price implies some degree of flexibility for negotiation before reaching the agreed price at sale. As opposed to a BID price made by the prospective buyer to begin the negotiation process.

AS OF The calendar date from which terms begin; the STATEMENT DATE.

ASSESSED VALUE   The value of real property established for the purpose of computing real property taxes. The assessed value may differ from the APPRAISED VALUE and MARKET VALUE.

ASSESSMENT   An official valuation of real property for the computation of real property taxes. Same as ASSESSED VALUE.

ASSET   Anything of value that is owned by a business or an individual. Assets are either financial, such as cash; physical, such as real property; tangible, such as a patent; or intangible, such as goodwill. An asset embodies probable future benefit and the ability to contribute directly or indirectly to future income.

In accounting, assets are listed on the left hand side of a balance sheet statement showing the things owned. Things owed are listed on the right side (liabilities and equity).

ASSET-BASED FINANCING   A loan that is secured by a specific ASSET of a small business, especially ACCOUNTS RECEIVABLE or INVENTORY.

ASSETS   The sum, accumulation or list of each ASSET; the total of all amounts owned. On a BALANCE SHEET, a summary list of the property and things owned.

ASSETS TURNOVER   Same as TOTAL ASSETS TURNOVER.

ASSIGNMENT   The transfer of right, title and interest in the property of one person (the assignor) to another person (the assignee). Assignments are made for things such as sales contracts, mortgages, leases and options. Most contracts consist of rights and duties. Of these, the duties can be delegated or assigned unless prohibited in the contract.

ASSOCIATION   People who join together for a common business purpose, sometimes treated as a corporation under tax law. An association can be a "for-profit" or a "not-for-profit" organization. A poorly drafted partnership agreement could be judged by taxing authorities as an association and taxed as a corporation.

AT PAR   At a price equal to the PAR value of the security; the original issue price of a security.

AT-RISK RULES   Special rules (practices) established by the Internal Revenue Service to restrict leverage opportunity by limiting an individual taxpayer's deductible losses to the amount he or she is "at risk," generally the sum of amounts contributed (invested) plus amounts borrowed and liable for payment from personal assets.

ATTACH   In business language, to seize or get control of. Usually used in the sense of recovering from a bad debt, such as to attach collateralized assets to recoup the money not repaid.

ATTACHMENT   See ATTACH.

ATTORNEY   Any person legally empowered to act as agent for or on behalf of another person; a lawyer. See LAWYER.

ATTORNEY AT LAW   See LAWYER.

ATTORNEY-IN-FACT   A competent and disinterested person who is authorized by another person to act in his or her place.

ATTRACTION PRINCIPLE   The pulling force of a commercial business center due to existing merchandising factors. A shopping center made up of many diverse businesses holds cumulative attraction for customers.

AUDIT   A professional examination and verification (usually by an independent CERTIFIED PUBLIC ACCOUNTANT) of a company's accounting documents and other papers; a review by a disinterested accountant for the purpose of rendering an opinion of fairness.

AUDITED STATEMENT   A FINANCIAL STATEMENT that has been the subject of an AUDIT by an independent CERTIFIED PUBLIC ACCOUNTANT.

AUDITOR   An outside or independent CERTIFIED PUBLIC ACCOUNTANT who examines the financial records in accordance with the GENERALLY ACCEPTED ACCOUNTING PRINCIPLES; a person who performs an AUDIT.

AUDITOR'S CERTIFICATE See ACCOUNTANT'S OPINION

AUDIT REPORT A document that contains the results of an examination by an independent CERTIFIED PUBLIC ACCOUNTANT and usually signed by the accountant; the published results of an AUDIT. An audit report often includes AUDITED STATEMENTS.

AUDIT TRAIL A step-by-step record review by which accounting data are traced to the source. Thereby, the validity and accuracy of accounting data can be verified by reviewing the sequence of events leading to the stated data.

AUTHORIZED SHARES The number of shares of each class of stock that is allowed by the ARTICLES OF INCORPORATION, and that represents the maximum capital investment in the corporation as permitted by the CHARTER. The books of the corporation will show the number of shares ISSUED AND OUTSTANDING, the number of shares of TREASURY STOCK and the number of shares of UNISSUED STOCK comprising the total authorized shares. Also called authorized stock.

AUTHORIZED STOCK See AUTHORIZED SHARES.

AVERAGE COST; AVERAGE COSTING A method of valuing the cost of INVENTORY; a specialized costing method that combines beginning inventory costs with the current-period production costs less the ending inventory. The result is then divided by the equivalent number of units of production to create a measure of AVERAGE COST PER UNIT of output.

AVERAGE COST PER UNIT The approximate expenses incurred to produce a single unit of production as calculated by dividing the total costs incurred by the total number of units produced during an accounting period.

AVERAGE FIXED COST Cost determined by dividing total fixed cost by the number of units of output.

AVERAGE REVENUE Total revenue divided by the number of units sold.

AVERAGE TOTAL COST   The cost determined by dividing total cost (fixed and variable) by the number of units of output.

AVERAGE VARIABLE COST   Cost determined by dividing total variable cost by the number of units of output.

AXIAL GROWTH   City expansion that occurs outward along main transportation routes and provides opportunity for business development.

B

BACKLOG   The sum of unfilled orders, expressed as a dollar value as of the date prepared; the amount of work that must be performed by the business without counting additional orders received after the date of preparation.

BACK-ORDER   Items that are not immediately available for shipment to a customer but will be shipped at a later date. Often occurs when several items are ordered simultaneously but only part of the order is delivered; the remaining items are said to be on back-order.

BACK-TO-BACK LEASE   An agreement made by a landlord as a concession to a prospective tenant, in which the landlord agrees to take over the tenant's existing lease in return for the tenant's agreement to lease existing space in the landlord's commercial building.

BAD CHECK   A check that is uncollectible.

BAD CREDIT RATING   Inability to get credit because of a poor record of paying loans, notes, accounts payable, or other obligations; cause for distrust by a lender for extending credit. See CREDIT RATING.

BAD DEBT   An open account balance or loan that is proved to be uncollectible and is written off.

BAIT AND SWITCH   In retail, an unethical practice (illegal in some locations) of advertising that lures customers into a store to

19

buy a product that is not available and then urges them to buy other products that may be more profitable to the store.

BALANCE   Whatever money amount is left over as a remainder amount, such as the amount still due to be paid.

In accounting, the equality of debits and credits in an account or an expression of the difference between the debits and credits.

When used as a verb, "to balance" means to bring both sides into equality, that is, to make debits and credits equal. A common expression is "to balance the checkbook," meaning to verify that your record reconciles with the statement received from the bank.

BALANCED BUDGET   A budget in which total expenditures equal total revenues, no more and no less.

BALANCE SHEET   A FINANCIAL STATEMENT of an individual or firm showing assets, liabilities and net worth on a given date, usually the close of a month. One way of looking at a business is the value of things owned (ASSETS) listed beside the debts owed to others (LIABILITIES), along with the amount owed to the owners (NET WORTH or OWNER'S EQUITY). Assets are equal to the sum of liabilities and equity. Therefore, a balance sheet is a listing of the items making up the two sides of the equation. A balance sheet shows the state of affairs at one point in time. Whereas, an INCOME STATEMENT shows financial progress over a period of time.

BANK   An official government-chartered establishment for receiving, keeping and lending money. A bank makes it easier to exchange money, for instance, by a check. Also the building that houses the offices of the establishment; to deposit money in or do business with a bank.

BANK ACCEPTANCE   A bill of exchange (DRAFT) drawn by a bank and accepted by it.

BANK ACCOUNT   Money deposited in a bank and subject to withdrawal by the depositor.

BANK CARD   A document issued to a customer of a bank that allows the customer to perform some banking transactions with automated tellers rather than with a human attendant (teller). Not to be confused with a CREDIT CARD.

BANK CHARGE A fee for services performed by a bank; a BANK SERVICE FEE. Also, to purchase an item charged to a credit card issued by a bank.

BANK CHECK Any of several checks issued by a bank, such as a CASHIER'S CHECK, CERTIFIED CHECK or BANK DRAFT.

BANK CREDIT The approval by a bank that a customer can borrow from the bank; a good credit standing with a bank.

BANK DRAFT A bill of exchange (DRAFT) drawn by a bank on another bank. See DRAFT.

BANKER A person who owns or manages a BANK. See BANK.

BANKER'S ACCEPTANCE See BANK ACCEPTANCE.

BANK HOLDING COMPANY A company that owns other banks; a bank for another bank.

BANKING RELATIONS The mutual respect and cooperative trust between a bank and its customers.

BANK LINE See LINE OF CREDIT by a bank.

BANK LOAN Money borrowed from a bank. See also LOAN; DEBT.

BANK LOAN APPLICATION The form used by a bank to evaluate the credit worthiness of a potential borrower. When completing a loan application, provide the maximum amount of detail to permit the loan officer to make a fair evaluation of the need for the money, including equity, collateral and ability to repay the loan.

BANK NOTE Paper money issued by a commercial bank.

BANK PARTITIONS Floor fastened short walls of about five feet in height that are used to divide a large office area into smaller spaces, commonly called cubicles.

BANKRUPTCY   A condition of insolvency by a person or business in which liabilities exceed assets and the debtor is unable to repay amounts owed. Bankruptcy is voluntary when the debtor brings the petition to a court; or the bankruptcy is involuntary when a creditor petitions the court to force insolvency. In both cases, the objective is an orderly and equitable settlement of obligations.

BANK SERVICE FEE   An amount of money paid to a bank in exchange for the bank performing transactions or service functions.

BANK STATEMENT   A document provided by a bank showing the increases in amounts (DEPOSITS) and decreases in amounts (CHECKS and WITHDRAWALS) on the account held for a business during a given period.

BAR CODE   Identification (in the form of stripes or bars) on a product that identifies the manufacturer and the specific product. Of the many types of bar code systems, UNIVERSAL PRODUCT CODE (UPC) and STOCKKEEPING UNIT (SKU) are used for specific types of products in retail trade.

BARGAIN   As a noun, sale of a product for less than its fair market value. When used as a verb, bargain means to negotiate.

BARGAIN SALE   A sale for less than the usual price. See BARGAIN.

BARRIER TO COMPETITION   Any circumstance that makes it difficult for a new business to enter an industry. Examples are the exclusive ownership of a unique resource, economies of scale, patents, licenses and copyrights.

BARTER   Merchandise or services exchanged directly for other merchandise or services without the use of money. Barter is particularly important in international trade when the currency of the foreign country is not readily convertible.

BASE PERIOD   A starting point or time interval for calculating business and economic data.

BASIS   In taxing analysis, the purchase price of an ASSET, plus the value of CAPITAL IMPROVEMENTS, reduced by ACCUMU- LATED DEPRECIATION. All property has a basis for taxing by the IRS.

BASIS POINT   One one-hundredth of one percent when describing changes in interest percentages. Used to describe the amount of change in the market price of bonds and many debt instruments.

BDC   See BUSINESS DEVELOPMENT CORPORATION.

BEGINNING BALANCE   The amount on hand at the start of a period.

BELLY-UP   The state of a company when it becomes illiquid or unprofitable and ceases operation.

BETTER BUSINESS BUREAU   An association of businesses (including many types of businesses) in a given locality that have joined together to promote the improvement, advancement, professionalism and credibility of the businesses in the area.

BIANNUAL   Occurring twice a year; semiannual.

BID   An offer to purchase for a specified amount. As opposed to a willingness to sell at an ASKING PRICE.
    A PROPOSAL by a business to perform work at a price by a date. Often, bids contain very detailed written descriptions of the work to be performed, the methods to be used, etc.

BID AND ASKED   The amount buyers are willing to pay (BID) and the amount sellers expect to receive (ASKED); expressed as two different numbers.

BIDDER'S MAILING LIST   A list complied by a government agency or a business showing firms that wish to receive information on invitations for bids.

BID INVITATION   See INVITATION TO BID.

BID PRICE   The amount of an offer to purchase. As opposed to an ASKING PRICE to sell.

BIENNIAL   Occurring every two years. Sometimes a duration of two years.

BIG BOARD   The New York Stock Exchange.

BIG EIGHT   The eight largest accounting/CPA firms.

BILATERAL AGREEMENT   A formal or informal understanding between two parties.

BILATERAL CONTRACT   A contract in which each party promises to perform an act in exchange for the other party's promise to perform. In other words, a contract cooperatively performed.

BILL   In small business, bill most often means INVOICE; a notification of an amount to be paid for goods or services performed. Also a DUE BILL; a document stating a debtor's obligation to a creditor.
   Other definitions include: 1) paper currency such as a $20 bill; 2) short for a BILL OF SALE, a document used to transfer assets from seller to buyer; 3) short for DUE BILL; 4) short for TREASURY BILL; 5) short for BILL OF EXCHANGE.

BILL OF EXCHANGE   An order by one person directing a second person to pay a third person. In international transactions, a DRAFT. Also called, simply a BILL.

BILL OF LADING   A contract issued to a transportation company (a SHIPPER), listing the goods shipped, acknowledging their receipt and promising delivery to the person or business named. Sometimes called a MANIFEST; WAYBILL.

BILL OF SALE   A written agreement by which one person sells, assigns or transfers to another his or her right or interest in personal property. The document is used to legally sell, assign or transfer title of personal property from a seller to a buyer.

BINDER   An agreement formed by the exchange of EARNEST MONEY, showing good faith to complete the purchase of real property or to show good faith in the execution of a contract. A written document giving immediate insurance coverage until the regular complete policy can be issued. Also, temporary insurance coverage until consideration of other items is completed.

BINDING   A formal agreement that has been consummated by both parties and is legally enforceable, such as a contract.

BLACKLIST   Any list that is published to restrict the activities of the items or the persons listed. As an example, a list of names circulated among employers of persons who are unacceptable because of prejudicial allegations, such as union-organizers.

BLACK MARKET   A market in which goods are traded (illegally) at prices often above a government-imposed ceiling, import quota or other control.

BLANK CHECK   A check that has not yet been written or one without a payee's name, amount and payor's signature. Blank check also commonly refers to freedom inadvertently given to someone else who could spend money without authorization.

BLUE COLLAR; BLUE-COLLAR WORKERS   Shop, construction or factory workers; generally people who work in skilled labor jobs, but also includes unskilled labor jobs. As opposed to WHITE COLLAR, i.e., office workers.

BLUE-SKY   An anticipation or projection of future business that is not realistic—in fact, so imaginary that it is unattainable.

BOARD   In business, short for the BOARD OF DIRECTORS of a corporation. May also refer to other governing bodies of other types of organizations. See BOARD OF DIRECTORS.

BOARD OF DIRECTORS   The governing body of a corporation, authorized and empowered to carry on and control the business affairs in accordance with the CHARTER. Members of the board of directors, termed DIRECTORS, are elected by the shareholders. Powers include appointing senior management, naming committee heads, issuing additional shares, and declaring dividends. Members may include top executives, termed INSIDE DIRECTORS, and members chosen from the business community at large, termed

OUTSIDE DIRECTORS. Directors may own shares of stock in the corporation, but it is not mandatory unless directed by the BY-LAWS. Directors meet several times a year to consider important issues concerning guidance of the corporation and to preside over the ANNUAL MEETING.

BOILERPLATE; BOILERPLATE LANGUAGE   The standard, repetitive language in a contract or document. The wording can be repeated from one contract or document to the next.

BOILER ROOM   A questionable promotional technique whereby multiple "cold pitch" phone calls are made to sell products.

BONA FIDE   Real; actual; in good faith. Without malice or deceit.

BOND   Any interest bearing or discounted security that obligates the issuer to pay the holder a specified sum of money, usually at specific intervals, and to repay the principal amount at maturity; a LONG-TERM DEBT.
   In finance, a bond is the obligation of a person to repay a debt of another person if that person defaults, as in a PAYMENT BOND.
   In insurance, a SURETY or PERFORMANCE BOND is an agreement that the insurance company will become liable (financially responsible) for performance of work or services of a contractor if the contractor fails to perform.

BONUS   An extra payment of money or privilege in excess of the customary salary as an incentive (reward) for performance. Also, in insurance, a dividend to policyholders.

BOOKKEEPER   One who works at keeping a systematic record of business transactions, more specifically, financial transactions. See also ACCOUNTANT and CERTIFIED PUBLIC ACCOUNTANT. An accountant and a certified public accountant have more education and are regarded with higher standing in the accounting profession than is a bookkeeper.

BOOKKEEPING   The act of maintaining written documentation of the financial information in a business. The work of keeping a systematic record of business transactions.

BOOKKEEPING SYSTEM   The particular method of recording transactions (DEBITS and CREDITS) in a company; the accounting techniques applied within a company.

BOOKS   Same as BOOKS OF ACCOUNT.

BOOKS OF ACCOUNT   The financial records of a business. Usually refers to the lowest level of recorded data, before summaries are made.

BOOK-TO-BILL RATIO   A comparison (ratio) of orders received to the invoices mailed.

BOOK VALUE   The value of anything as recorded in the BOOKS OF ACCOUNT of a company. An asset recorded at original cost less accumulated depreciation; the amount recorded on the balance sheet as the value of an asset. The value of the stock in a company at the original par purchase price; the par value of stocks and bonds issued by the company. Book value is contrasted with current MARKET VALUE.

BOOTSTRAP FINANCING   Obtaining money for a proposed use that is from internal sources such as tighter management control, collection of accounts receivable, delayed payments to suppliers, and advanced payments for future sales.

BORDER TAX ADJUSTMENTS   In exporting, the remission of taxes that have been paid on exported goods to ensure that the taxing system within the country does not impede exports. Reduced taxes include indirect taxes, such as sales taxes and value added taxes, but does not include direct taxes, such as income taxes for the company.

BORROW   To take or use something that belongs to another with the understanding it will be returned; especially in finance, to obtain a loan of money from another with the promise to repay.

BORROWED CAPITAL   Money loaned to a business from another. Same as a loan. See LOAN; CAPITAL. As opposed to money invested in the business (EQUITY CAPITAL).

BORROWER   A person or business who owes money to another; a DEBTOR; one who owes money to a LENDER.

BOTTOM LINE   The net income; the last line on an INCOME STATEMENT. The end result of a financial transaction, as a PROFIT or LOSS. See NET INCOME.

BOUND RATE   In international trade, fixed tariff rates for a country that have resulted from negotiations between countries.

BOYCOTT   A refusal to transact business with a person, business or country

BRAINSTORM   An original idea that apparently arises from no organized thought process; a flood of creative ideas. Also, the structured process of BRAINSTORMING for new ideas.

BRAINSTORMING   A structured or formalized process by which participants offer original ideas to solve an existing problem. Often, participants are invited from different disciplines or businesses to stimulate originality and creativity.

BRANCH OFFICE   Any secondary place of business apart from the main office of the business.

BRAND   See BRAND NAME.

BRAND NAME   The name of a single product, a line of products or a company that produces many products. Usually, brand name is highly recognizable by consumers as having high quality and distinctive packaging.

BREACH OF CONTRACT   Violation of any of the terms or conditions of a contract without legal excuse; default; nonperformance.

BREAKEVEN   See BREAKEVEN POINT; BREAKEVEN ANALYSIS.

BREAKEVEN ANALYSIS   An evaluation of the profitability of a product, service or an entire business to determine the level of sales at which income just equals the cost. Income greater than the BREAKEVEN POINT results in a profit; whereas income below the breakeven point results in a loss. See BREAKEVEN POINT.

BREAKEVEN POINT   The amount (volume) of sales needed to cover all expenses (fixed and variable) before any profit is earned. The number of units that must be sold at a specified price to cover all contributing costs. Zero profit; a lower volume causes losses; a higher volume causes profits. Also called a BREAKEVEN.

BREAKEVEN REVENUE   The level of sales dollars required to cover all costs during an accounting period.

BREAKEVEN UNITS   The number of units that must be produced and sold in an accounting period to generate revenues sufficient to exactly cover all production costs.

BROKER   One who acts as an intermediary between parties in a transaction. A broker, for a fee or other consideration, arranges a transaction (a sale) by a seller to the buyer. A license is often required for businesses engaged in brokerage transactions.

BROKERAGE   The aspect of business concerned with bringing parties together for the transaction of business and the execution of contracts. Brokerage involves sales, exchanges and rentals.

BUDGET   A document that lists planned income and expense items along with the dollar value for each. A budget is most useful when, at a later date, actual transactions are compared to the budget for analysis and control of future decisions. Of the many kinds of budgets, a CASH BUDGET shows CASH FLOW, an EXPENSE BUDGET lists expected payments of money, and a CAPITAL BUDGET shows the anticipated payments for CAPITAL ASSETS.

BUILDING   A structure erected on land and used for the conduct of business.

BUILDING CODE   A local law specifying techniques of construction to improve safety, structural integrity or appearance.

BUILDING PERMIT   A written government permission for the construction or improvement of building structures. Also called, simply a PERMIT.

BUILDING RESTRICTIONS   Limitations on the size or types of improvements established by public or private ZONING acts. Also may place limitations on the types of business that may be conducted.

BUILD INVENTORY   To purchase or manufacture more products than the amount sold; add a quantity to INVENTORY; a larger ending inventory than the beginning inventory.

BUILD-TO-SUIT   An understanding or contract in which an owner agrees to develop a property in return for a commitment by the lessee.

BULK TRANSFER   Any large quantity transfer of materials, supplies or inventory by a business.

BURDEN   See OVERHEAD.

BUSINESS   The line of work engaged in; the type of product or service provided; the buying or selling of products or services; commercial trade for a profit. A commercial or industrial establishment such as a store or factory that is engaged in a profit making venture.

BUSINESS ACCOUNT   A commercial credit relationship established by a business in which customers may buy now, take delivery and pay at a later date.

BUSINESS BROKER   A person or firm that arranges, for a fee, the sale of a business from a seller to a buyer; an intermediary who facilitates the transaction of selling a business. See BROKER.

BUSINESS CYCLE   Regularly recurring periods of good and bad times of profitability and cash flow in a business; fluctuations in economic activity, often as a result of seasonal variations or holiday periods. On a national scale, the recurrence of periods of expansion and contraction as measured by the GROSS DOMESTIC PROFIT (GDP).

BUSINESS DAY   The hours when most businesses in a given locality are in operation or open for business. The conventional business day is from 8 A.M. until 5 P.M. Yet individual businesses may have hours that differ from others or a business may choose staggered schedules.

BUSINESS DEVELOPMENT CORPORATION (BDC)   A financing agency or corporation composed of private and public members that pool their resources toward economic growth of a single geographic locality. The objective is to provide financing assistance for companies that cannot obtain financing through normal channels.

BUSINESS ENTITY   Same as a BUSINESS.

BUSINESS EXPANSION   Business growth into new product areas or into new territories. Also the creation of more floor space for operations.

BUSINESS FIRM   Same as FIRM or BUSINESS.

BUSINESS INTERRUPTION INSURANCE   Insurance coverage allowing financial compensation for the loss of income resulting from an act; the obligation to pay lost income that occurs from a forced stoppage of business activity.

BUSINESS LAW   That portion of the LAW that deals exclusively with legal maters of business conduct.

BUSINESS LEAD   See LEAD.

BUSINESS LIABILITY INSURANCE   Insurance coverage for risks wherein the business is legally obligated to pay the damages resulting from an event causing a loss.

BUSINESS LICENSE   A certificate issued under law by a governmental body to a business authorizing the company to engage in a specific business activity; the document for such authorization. Examples include a medical license, license to operate a truck for business and export license.

BUSINESS LIFE INSURANCE   An insurance policy purchased by a business on a PRINCIPAL of the business to protect the business from the loss incurred from the untimely death of a most important person in the business.

BUSINESS LOAN   See COMMERCIAL LOAN.

BUSINESS LOCATION   The geographical vicinity where a business is established. Often, location is an important ingredient in the success of a business, especially a small or new business.

BUSINESS MEETING   See MEETING.

BUSINESS NAME   The name or title given to a company, product or service. The intent is to create an easily recognizable identity for promotion and publicity.

BUSINESS OPPORTUNITY   The vision of an individual or firm that foresees profiting from engaging in a venture. Often this can involve the purchase of an existing business, yet it can also be the start-up of a new small business. New products and changing current operating methods of an existing business often result in a profitable venture for the entrepreneur.

BUSINESS ORGANIZATION   The way the people in a business are structured to work together; the relationship of the various functional parts of a business, such as manufacturing, engineering, marketing and accounting. See also BUSINESS STRUCTURE. The legal form of a business consisting of Sole Proprietorship, Partnership and Corporation.

BUSINESS OVERHEAD EXPENSES   See OVERHEAD.

BUSINESS PLAN   A documented expression of the facts concerning a business with a forecast of the desired future direction. It is like a roadmap or guidebook concerning where the business wants to go. A business plan usually covers one to five years of historical facts and one to five years of projections into the future. The two main uses are for guidance in decision making by the owner-manager and for presentation to a financial institution when applying for a loan. A business plan is especially important for a start-up business because it sets the course of actions necessary for survival of the business. The main elements to include in a business plan are an executive summary with a description of the firm and its future; profiles of the owner and managers; product description; a description of the industry; marketing plans; and a financial plan. See Self-Help Guide B on "How to Write a Business Plan." See also MARKETING PLAN; FINANCIAL PLAN, LONG-RANGE PLAN; STRATEGIC BUSINESS PLAN.

BUSINESS POLICY   The general practice established within a single company or within a single business environment. Often business policy may be unwritten and therefore subject to a wide latitude of interpretation. Written policy is preferred.

BUSINESS RECORD   Any RECORD that provides information on the operation of the business, especially financial information; the written documentation of the happenings in the firm.

BUSINESS STRATEGY   See STRATEGY.

BUSINESS STRUCTURE   In business, the legal form of a business entity, i.e., sole proprietorship, partnership or corporation. Less common business structures also exist, such as, Ltd., Limited Liability Company (LLC) and Professional Corporation (PC).

BUSINESS USE   In accounting, expenditure of money or use of property by a business. As opposed to PRIVATE USE. Do not commingle business use and private use because they are taxed differently. Particular care must be exercised in a situation where the use may be subject to interpretation.

BUSINESS VENTURE   A vision of a new product or a new service as a viable business entity; a start-up business requiring an entrepreneurial spirit.

BUY AMERICAN   A generally accepted practice of purchasing goods that are produced in the United States as opposed to purchasing imported goods. Also, a U.S. government law (and that of some states) requiring certain government procurement contracts to buy only goods produced in the United States.

BUY-BACK AGREEMENT   A provision in a sales contract whereby the seller will reacquire property within a specified period upon the happening of a specified event, usually at the original price.

BUY-DOWN   Money offered by a lender as an inducement that reduces monthly interest in a loan or mortgage payments.

BUYER'S MARKET   A market situation characterized by supply that exceeds demand. Lower prices are often found in order to attract customers. Competition and a large supply of products or services abound, allowing the buyer more control over purchases. Also called SOFT MARKET.

BUYOUT   Purchase of at least a controlling percentage of a company's stock so as to take control of its assets and operations, often the purchase of an entire small company.

BUY-SELL AGREEMENT   An agreement among partners or share-holders in which one party will sell and another party will buy a business interest at a stated price upon occurrence of a stated event, i.e., the death or disability of one participant.

BYLAWS   Rules governing the internal management of an organization, as in a business corporation. Bylaws are drawn up by the founders under the authority of the CHARTER at the time of incorporation. Bylaws cover such points as the election of directors, the appointment of an executive committee, duties of the officers, and how share transfers are made. Bylaws cannot countermand laws of government. Bylaws can usually be amended by the directors themselves.

C

CAFETERIA PLAN A program within a company whereby several types of company benefits are offered to each employee. Thus each employee may select those benefits wanted and those benefits rejected, usually with a maximum total benefit dollar amount.

CALL In banking and lending, to demand repayment of the entire principal amount of a secured loan, usually when the borrower has failed to meet repayment provisions. Same as CALL THE LOAN; DEMAND LOAN.

For bonds, the right to redeem outstanding bonds before their scheduled maturity.

CALLABLE Redeemable by the issuer before the scheduled maturity. See also DEMAND LOAN.

CALL THE LOAN See CALL.

CANCEL To void a negotiable instrument like an order for goods or services; to prematurely terminate a contract or bond. Thus the document is annulled.

Also, evidence of payment, as in a CANCELED CHECK.

CANCELED See CANCEL.

CANCELED CHECK A check that the bank has honored and paid in the amount written to the payee. See CHECK; CANCEL.

C & F A commercial acronym meaning "Cost and Freight"; that is, the invoice price includes all costs and freight-out shipping cost but does not include prepaid transit insurance cost. See also CIF; F.O.B.

CAP   The maximum amount specified on a financial document, such as an amount that would be paid on a contract or the maximum interest rate on an adjustable rate loan.

CAPACITY OF PARTIES   The legal and financial ability of people or companies to enter into a valid contract. Three general broad categories exist: full capacity, limited capacity, no capacity.

CAPITAL   Wealth (money or property) owned or used in business by a sole proprietor or corporation, to produce more wealth. In a start-up business, capital is the amount of money invested by the owner, before borrowing from others. Same as EQUITY; NET WORTH.
   In accounting, most often capital is synonymous with the EQUITY (NET WORTH) of a business; the amount by which ASSETS exceed LIABILITIES. There are, however, really two kinds of business capital, EQUITY and LONG-TERM DEBT. In a broad sense, long-term debt is sometimes considered as capital because the money is totally under the control of the owners rather than under the control of the lender. See CAPITAL STRUCTURE.
   In finance, the total tangible assets of a firm.

CAPITAL APPRECIATION   The difference between the selling price and the acquisition price for a FIXED ASSET; the amount a selling price of a fixed asset is greater than the amount paid for the asset at an earlier time. Same as APPRECIATION.

CAPITAL ASSET   A LONG-TERM ASSET (REAL PROPERTY and PERSONAL PROPERTY), with a life exceeding one year; property that is not usually bought or sold in the normal course of conducting the business. Generally, the same as a major FIXED ASSET, such as land, buildings, equipment, furniture or fixtures. For tax purposes, the IRS publishes a very precise definition of capital asset.

CAPITAL BUDGET   A plan or amount of money to be used for financing major purchases of CAPITAL ASSETS at some future time; a list of planned investment expenditures and the timing of such expenditures. See also BUDGET.

CAPITAL DEPRECIATION The wearing out of a CAPITAL ASSET, often measured by its decline in value. Same as DEPRECIATION.

CAPITAL EQUIPMENT The assets of a company that are used in the production process, such as machinery. Most often capital equipment refers to long-term assets, but it can include short-term assets as well. Such equipment will not be sold in the normal course of business but will be used, worn out or consumed over time as business is conducted.

CAPITAL EXPENDITURE A disbursement of money to acquire or improve a CAPITAL ASSET; the cost of purchasing or improving real property and other tangible property used in the conduct of the business.

CAPITAL FORMATION In a start-up, the assembling of all the moneys (equity and loans) to begin operation. Also, a savings program intended for starting a business or for a future major purchase, such as a CAPITAL ASSET, usually to be used for the production of goods or services.

CAPITAL GAIN The profit derived from the sale of a CAPITAL ASSET; the positive difference between the selling price and the purchase price (or DEPRECIATED BASIS) of a capital asset. See also CAPITAL LOSS.
    For taxing purposes, the IRS precisely differentiates SHORT-TERM CAPITAL GAINS (less than one year) from LONG-TERM CAPITAL GAINS (more than one year).

CAPITAL GAINS TAX A tax paid on the CAPITAL GAIN from the sale of an ASSET. Often, the tax rate is lower than the ordinary income rate, to encourage investment, but the tax rate can be higher.

CAPITAL GOODS Materials or products (goods) used in the production of other products (goods), such as industrial buildings or machinery. Same as CAPITAL ASSET. In government, capital goods include highways and government installations, which form a country's productive capacity.

CAPITAL IMPROVEMENT Any addition or betterment made to a CAPITAL ASSET, usually to extend the useful life of the property or to upgrade to higher quality, size or capacity. Any structural improvement to REAL PROPERTY is a capital improvement.

CAPITAL-INTENSIVE Requiring a large investment in CAPITAL ASSETS (money); a high proportion of FIXED ASSETS, as opposed to LABOR INTENSIVE.

CAPITAL INVESTMENT The amount of money put in (INVESTED in) a business by the owner; the investment of money; EQUITY.

Also, the purchase of a CAPITAL ASSET (FIXED ASSET), such as a building or machinery; also called CAPITAL EXPENDITURE.

CAPITALISM An economic system of government in which 1) private ownership of property exists; 2) CAPITAL ownership can provide income to the owners; 3) relative freedom of competition for economic gain is permitted; 4) the profit motive is basic to economic life. Also called FREE ENTERPRISE SYSTEM.

CAPITALIZATION The par value of all stock plus the face amount of outstanding bonds and loans. See CAPITAL STRUCTURE.

Also, the mathematical procedure for converting income into an indication of value (principal), such as the income approach to an appraisal.

CAPITALIZATION RATE (CAP RATE) The INTEREST RATE that would be used to convert a series of future payments into a single PRESENT VALUE.

CAPITALIZATION RATIO The proportions of a firm's CAPITAL STRUCTURE in its various elements as percentages of LONG-TERM DEBT, BONDS, PREFERRED STOCK and COMMON STOCK. The ratios are useful in evaluating risk and leverage.

CAPITALIZE In accounting, to add to an asset account; a change in the accounting classification of something from an EXPENSE to a FIXED ASSET, such as a CAPITAL EXPENDITURE.

To turn something into one's economic advantage, such as to sell umbrellas on a rainy day.

See also CAPITALIZED VALUE; CAPITAL LEASE.

CAPITALIZED VALUE A schedule of INCOME converted into a PRINCIPAL amount; to CAPITALIZE the income.

CAPITAL LEASE A lease obligation that is converted to a balance sheet entry as an ASSET and a corresponding liability. Generally applies to a lease where the lessee acquires essentially all of the economic benefits and risks of the leased property.

CAPITAL LOSS A loss derived from the sale of a CAPITAL ASSET; the amount by which the proceeds from the sale of an asset are less than the cost of acquiring it. Opposite of a CAPITAL GAIN.

For tax purposes, a capital loss may be used as an expense to reduce income.

CAPITAL MARKET Private and public sources for obtaining CAPITAL, including both debt and equity. Also, the place (market) where buying and selling of these instruments occur.

CAPITAL OUTLAY See CAPITAL EXPENDITURE.

CAPITAL REPATRIATION The transfer of company money or property from a foreign country back to its home country. Some foreign governments restrict this action to prevent a drain of capital or exploitation by the company to its home country.

CAPITAL REQUIREMENTS The permanent financing needed for the normal operation of a business; that is, to finance fixed assets and working capital. Also, the appraised investment in fixed assets plus the normal amount of working capital.

CAPITAL STOCK In accounting, a term used to identify the various classes or categories of equity investment in a corporation, such as AUTHORIZED STOCK, ISSUED AND OUTSTANDING, TREASURY STOCK, and UNISSUED STOCK. Capital stock includes COMMON STOCK and PREFERRED STOCK.

The financial framework of a corporation consists of LONG-TERM DEBT, PREFERRED STOCK, BONDS and EQUITY; the

CAPITALIZATION of the corporation. As contrasted with FINANCIAL STRUCTURE, which includes such additional sources of capital as short-term debt and accounts payable.

CAPITAL SURPLUS   A common umbrella term for the classification of EQUITY other than CAPITAL STOCK and RETAINED EARNINGS, such as: 1) stock issued at a premium over par; 2) proceeds from stock bought back and then resold; 3) a reduction of par value; 4) reclassification of capital stock; 5) donated stock; 6) acquisition of a company that has a capital surplus. Also called PAID-IN SURPLUS; SURPLUS.

CAPITAL TURNOVER   Annual sales divided by equity, a measure of the ability to grow without additional capital investment. Companies with a high profit margin generally have a low capital turnover. Also called EQUITY TURNOVER.

CAP RATE   See CAPITALIZATION RATE.

CARRYBACK   In accounting, a transaction during one period that requires a correction to an earlier period. Opposite of CARRYFORWARD. See also CARRYBACK FINANCING.

CARRYBACK FINANCING   A situation involving purchase of an asset whereby the seller holds a note (lends the money) for part of the purchase price.

CARRYFORWARD   In accounting, a transaction during one period that is recorded in a subsequent period. Opposite of CARRYBACK.

CARTEL   An agreement among a group of businesses or nations in the same field that agree to influence prices by regulating production and marketing practices to secure a national or international monopoly. However, a cartel has less control over an industry than a MONOPOLY. A number of nations, including the United States, have laws prohibiting cartels. TRUST is sometimes used as a synonym for cartel.

CASH   In accounting, an asset on the balance sheet comprising cash on hand, paper currency, coins, bank balances, negotiable money orders and checks; MONEY or MONEY EQUIVALENTS.

To cash a negotiable instrument (as a check) is to convert it into money (paper currency and coins).

CASH BASIS   An accounting method whereby income is recognized when money is received, and expense items are recognized when money is paid, regardless of when material is received or work is done. For alternative methods, see MODIFIED CASH BASIS and ACCRUAL BASIS. Most small and start-up businesses use the MODIFIED CASH BASIS accounting method.

CASH BUDGET   An estimate, for a future period, of cash receipts and cash payments; a CASH FLOW analysis. See BUDGET; CASH FLOW.

CASH CONVERSION CYCLE   The elapsed time required to convert raw materials into finished goods, finished goods into sales and receive the money after the goods have been sold. This cycle is financed by the availability of WORKING CAPITAL and is directly affected by production efficiency, credit policy and other controllable factors. In shorter cycles, working capital is generated sooner requiring fewer borrowed funds. Small businesses should work diligently to keep the cash conversion cycle as short as possible. The cash conversion cycle is directly related to INVENTORY TURNOVER. Sometimes called EARNINGS CYCLE; CAPITAL TURNOVER.

CASH COW   A product or service that provides large revenues and large profit margins associated with low operating costs, often because of product recognition without advertising or because of a technological advantage.

CASH DISBURSEMENT   A payment of money or simply a payment. Usually, the writing of a check to pay for an item previously obligated to be paid, such as loan payment, salary payment or accounts receivable payment. See also DISBURSEMENT.

CASH DISCOUNT   An amount that the originally listed sale price is reduced when the product/service is sold, i.e., payment upon delivery of the product or rendering of the service as opposed to the listed sale price that would be paid if bought on credit. Sometimes, when a short grace period is permitted, price is still reduced for a cash sale, such as two percent discount if paid within 10 days.

CASH EQUIVALENTS   All short-term, highly liquid investments that are readily convertible into cash, e.g., treasury bills.

CASH FLOW   The actual movement of cash within a business: money inflow minus money outflow.

In an accounting sense, an analysis of all the transactions that affect the cash account during an accounting period; the spendable income of a business (cash received less expenses paid) over a given period of time. In the analysis, SOURCES OF CASH are shown along with USES OF CASH. When more money comes in than goes out, we speak of POSITIVE CASH FLOW. Conversely, when more money goes out than comes in, we speak of NEGATIVE CASH FLOW. Companies with assets well in excess of liabilities may nevertheless go bankrupt because they cannot generate enough cash to meet current obligations.

CASH FLOW ANALYSIS   An evaluation of the sources and uses of the money by a business. See CASH FLOW.

CASH FLOW FORECAST   A prediction of future money income and outgo; a CASH FLOW PROJECTION; a CASH FLOW STATEMENT.

CASH FLOW PROJECTION   A prediction of future money income and outgo, forecasted sources of cash and forecasted uses of cash. A regular analysis of CASH needed in the future will help avoid many financial problems. A cash flow projection can make the difference between success and failure, as well as the difference between growth and stagnation. Making a cash flow projection is THE MOST IMPORTANT TOOL available to the small business person. A detailed method of preparing a cash flow projection is presented in Self-Help Guide I.

CASH FLOW STATEMENT   An accounting presentation of the amounts of money coming in over a period of time compared to the amounts of money going out over the same time period; a summary of all cash transactions during a period. See CASH FLOW; CASH FLOW PROJECTION.

CASHIER   A person whose job is the day-to-day receipt and disbursement of cash; a person receiving cash for the sale of merchandise; the person responsible for PETTY CASH.

CASHIER'S CHECK   A monetary bill of exchange (check) drawn by a bank (usually signed by its cashier) upon itself as issuer and payable upon demand. It is like a promissory note executed by a bank. A cashier's check is, however, still subject to a stop payment order by the maker. See CHECK; CERTIFIED CHECK; PERSONAL CHECK.

CASH MANAGEMENT   The utilization of prudent and thrifty methods of money income and outflow; planning for cash expenditures and providing adequate money for payment; using techniques such as CASH BUDGET, CASH FLOW ANALYSIS and EXPENDITURE FORECAST. Cash management seeks to make less cash do more work.

CASH METHOD   See CASH BASIS.

CASH ON DELIVERY (COD)   A transaction requiring that goods be paid for in full by cash or a cash equivalent at the point of title transfer from seller to buyer, most often after delivery by a transportation company. Cash on delivery is most frequent when buyer and seller are separated by geographical location or shipping time. If the buyer refuses the order, seller must bear round trip shipping expenses. Sometimes called collect on delivery.

CASH ON HAND   Specifically, all money, cash and cash equivalents in the business cash registers and safes on the business premises; as opposed to cash in the bank. Same as CASH.

CASH-OUT   A situation where the seller desires quick sale for money without any financing or credit by the seller.

CASH POSITION   See LIQUIDITY.

CASH RECEIPTS   Money received (usually from sales) by a company in whatever form; as opposed to sales on credit.

CASH REGISTER   The machine used in retail businesses for recording transactions of money received as items are sold.

CASH REGISTER TAPE   The paper or magnetic recording of transactions from a CASH REGISTER.

CASH SALES   Goods or services sold for cash money, as opposed to CREDIT SALES.

CASH SURRENDER VALUE   In insurance, the monetary amount that would be paid by the insurer to the policyholder if the policy were canceled. Usually, life insurance companies will permit a loan against the cash surrender value, often at lower than market rates. Cash surrender value of life insurance on the principals of a business (called KEY MAN INSURANCE) is shown on a balance sheet as an asset.

CASH SURRENDER VALUE OF LIFE INSURANCE (CSVLI)   See CASH SURRENDER VALUE.

CASH VALUE   In business, the worth, in dollars, of an asset.
   In insurance, the monetary amount that could be received if the policy were canceled or surrendered; the CASH SURRENDER VALUE.

CASUAL LABOR   Workers employed for temporary periods and for specific jobs or tasks. See TEMPORARY WORKER.

CAVEAT EMPTOR   Let the buyer beware; a sale in an "AS IS" condition. Without inspection the buyer purchases the goods at his or her own risk.

C-CORPORATION   The identification of a type of CORPORATION for legal or tax purposes, distinct from other forms such as CLOSELY HELD CORPORATION or S-CORPORATION.

CENTRAL BUSINESS DISTRICT   A city's downtown area where the main businesses are concentrated, along with government, professional and service activities.

CEO   See CHIEF EXECUTIVE OFFICER.

CERTIFICATE   A formal declaration that can be used to document a fact. In business, finance and investments, certificate is often used in conjunction with other descriptive words. See the specific grammatical business phrase of interest, such as stock certificate or insurance certificate.

CERTIFICATE OF DEPOSIT   A statement from a bank certifying that the named person or firm has a specified sum of money on deposit. The certificate states the date of certificate purchase, payor, payee, amount on deposit, interest rate and due date.

CERTIFICATE OF INCORPORATION   A document of fact as formal declaration of the existence of a corporation as a business entity. The Certificate of Incorporation is issued by the state where the ARTICLES OF INCORPORATION are filed.

CERTIFICATE OF INSURANCE   A document issued by an insurance company verifying coverage of property, specifying the amount of coverage.

CERTIFICATE OF ORIGIN   In international trade, a document attesting that goods were produced in a specific country.

CERTIFIED ACCOUNTING STATEMENT   A BALANCE SHEET or INCOME STATEMENT on which the reviewing independent public accountant has signed his or her name as evidence of the accuracy and integrity of the information. See ACCOUNTANT'S OPINION.

CERTIFIED CHECK   A check for which a bank guarantees payment. When a check is certified, it legally becomes an obligation of the bank, and the funds to cover the check are immediately drawn from the depositor's account. See also CHECK; CASHIER'S CHECK; PERSONAL CHECK.

CERTIFIED COPY   A copy of a document that is signed by the person having possession of the original, declaring it to be a true copy; sometimes attested to by a NOTARY PUBLIC.

CERTIFIED DEVELOPMENT CORPORATION (SBA 504 LOAN PROGRAM)   A private corporation established to provide capital improvement financial assistance to existing businesses whereby the financing is guaranteed by the SBA.

CERTIFIED FINANCIAL STATEMENT   A PERSONAL FINAN-
CIAL STATEMENT or BUSINESS FINANCIAL STATEMENT that
has been reviewed and authenticated by a CERTIFIED PUBLIC
ACCOUNTANT.

CERTIFIED LENDER   A bank approved by the U.S. Small Business Administration (SBA) for making GUARANTEED LOANS
under the CERTIFIED LENDER PROGRAM (CLP).

CERTIFIED LENDER PROGRAM (CLP)   A U.S. Small Business
Administration program whereby banks are pre-approved as
qualified to submit applications for U.S. Government GUARAN-
TEED LOANS. Also see PREFERRED LENDER PROGRAM (PLP).

CERTIFIED PUBLIC ACCOUNTANT (CPA)   A licensed public
accountant by a state. A professional accountant of highest standing who has passed certain exams, achieved a certain amount of
experience, reached a certain age and met all other statutory and
licensing requirements of the state of the United States where he
or she performs the services. See also BOOKKEEPER; ACCOUN-
TANT.

CERTIFIED PUBLIC ACCOUNTING FIRM   A professional corporation that is owned and controlled by a CERTIFIED PUBLIC
ACCOUNTANT and is practicing in the field of accounting.

CERTIFY   To testify in writing; to confirm; to guarantee in writing, as a certified check; to endorse, as with a seal.

CHAIN   A large company with many retail outlets called CHAIN
STORES.

CHAIN OF COMMAND   The proper lines of authority from the
head of an organization, through directors, managers and supervisors to the workers. A good manager will ensure employees and
customers understand the order of authority and the method of
communicating with management.

CHAIN STORE   Any one of a number of retail stores under
common ownership, under common management, selling standardized products and operating under a uniform policy.

CHAIRMAN OF THE BOARD; CHAIRMAN OF THE BOARD OF DIRECTORS The highest ranking position in a corporation; the member of the board of directors who presides over board meetings. However, the chairman of the board may not always have the greatest actual authority; this is reserved for the CHIEF EXECUTIVE OFFICER. Sometimes the title is honorary. In small companies, it is common for one person to hold several titles. See BOARD OF DIRECTORS.

CHAMBER OF COMMERCE An organization of persons and businesses that is interested in promotion of business and the betterment of business operations in a given area.

CHANGE ORDER A contract revision initiated after work has begun on a signed contract, often arising from unforeseen work at the outset of the original contract.

CHAPTER 11 (ELEVEN) A provision of bankruptcy under which a company that has declared bankruptcy can continue to operate, under protection and supervision of the court, while the company develops a way to pay its debts.

CHAPTER 7 (SEVEN) A bankruptcy provision that requires a company to liquidate its assets for the benefit of its creditors under supervision of the court.

CHARGE To record a debt against a person or business account, such as to charge a purchase. Also to specify the price or fee—such as, What do you charge for this product?

CHARGE ACCOUNT An account by a business with a person against which debts are recorded. Charge account means regular trading and transactions, such as purchase of merchandise or services by a person from a business on credit, wherein payment is made at a later date. Similar to OPEN ACCOUNT, which is a commercial account (a business-to-business account). See ACCOUNT.

CHARTER A business charter consists of two documents, the ARTICLES OF INCORPORATION and the CERTIFICATE OF INCORPORATION, both of which are required to establish the existence of a corporation. See ARTICLES OF INCORPORATION.

CHARTERED LIFE UNDERWRITER (CLU)   A life insurance sales agent of highest professional standing who has qualified for the title by completing advanced coursework.

CHARTER PROPERTY CASUALTY UNDERWRITER (CPCU)   A property and casualty insurance sales agent of highest professional standing who has qualified for the title by completing advanced coursework.

CHART OF ACCOUNTS   A listing of typical account names, descriptions and classifications that are used for recording accounting transactions. For a start-up business, the chart of accounts can provide a guideline for selection of those accounts that should be established for recording the financial transactions of the business.

CHATTEL   An item of personal property. Chattels are transferred by a BILL OF SALE. The Uniform Commercial Code regulates the transfer of chattels and the use of chattels as security for debts.

CHATTEL MORTGAGE   A mortgage secured by personal property. Under the Uniform Commercial Code, chattel mortgages have been replaced by security agreements. See SECURITY AGREEMENT.

CHECK   A negotiable instrument authorizing a bank to pay money to the payee (bearer); a monetary bill of exchange often used in lieu of cash money that authorizes a bank to withdraw previously deposited money upon demand from the issuer's account for payment to the payee's account. A check identifies the date of issue, payee name and amount, and is signed by the issuer. A check is considered as cash and is negotiable when endorsed. Types of checks include PERSONAL CHECK, CASHIER'S CHECK; CERTIFIED CHECK.

Also, to review by notation; to witness; to compare or examine for verification of correctness; a mark (√) to show approval.

CHECKBOOK   A document containing BLANK CHECKS that have not been written and CHECK STUBS that record checks that have been written. Thus, the checkbook contains an accurate record of transactions made from the checking account along with a current balance on the account.

CHECKLIST   An orderly compilation of information for ease of comparison with other types of information.

CHECK STUB   A document in some checkbooks for recording payee, amount, date and other information about checks written.

CHIEF EXECUTIVE OFFICER (CEO)   The company officer principally responsible for activities of the company. The officer of a company with the highest ranking executive authority and often, an additional title for the chairman of the board of directors, the president, or other senior officer.

CIF   A commercial acronym standing for "Cost, Insurance and Freight." If the value of a shipment is expressed in CIF terms, the invoice as shipped includes all costs, prepaid insurance and freight-out shipping costs. See also C & F. As opposed to F.O.B.

CIRCULAR E   See EMPLOYER'S TAX GUIDE.

CLAIM   To demand or ask for, as rightfully belonging or due to the person or business that makes the claim; assert one's right to title or benefit; a statement of fact that may be called into question.
   In insurance, a statement by a policyholder as to the amount of money due resulting of a covered loss.

CLAIM CHECK   A document given by a business to a customer as a receipt for customer goods received by the business. For example, a customer can reclaim goods after repair has been made.

CLAIMS MADE; CLAIMS MADE FORM   A method for determining whether or not insurance coverage is available for a specific claim. A claim made during the term of the liability insurance policy is reimbursed by the insurance company, up to policy limits, regardless of when the event occurred that caused the claim. See also OCCURRENCE FORM.

CLASS OF STOCK   In a corporation, the ARTICLES OF INCORPORATION will identify the authorized class of stock (COMMON STOCK or PREFERRED STOCK), which is used as the means for acquiring EQUITY on the corporation.

CLAUSE   A single statement, condition or provision specified in a contract.

CLEAN DRAFT   SEE DRAFT.

CLEAR   In banking, withdrawal of funds from the account of the issuer and payment of those funds to the holder of the check. When a check is said to have "cleared," the payee has received the amount specified and the bank has deducted the specified amount from the account of the account holder.

In finance, not encumbered; an asset not used as security for a loan; an asset free of debt. Comparison of the details of a transaction to assure accuracy or agreement of the parties. To make a profit, such as "after expenses we cleared an amount of net profit."

CLERICAL   Relating to routine administrative, office or accounting work; the work of a CLERK.

CLERK   A retail store employee; an office worker who keeps records, types letters, does filing or posts accounting entries.

CLIENT   A customer of a professional service, such as legal, accounting, advertising or consulting.

CLOSE AN ACCOUNT   All entries for a period are completed or the account is terminated.

In banking, to withdraw all funds on deposit from the bank.

CLOSE CORPORATION; CLOSED CORPORATION   A CORPORATION owned by a few people, all or most of whom are directly involved in the conduct of the business, usually members of the management family. Differs from a CLOSELY HELD CORPORATION in that shares are not for sale to the public nor are shares held by outside investors, and there is no public market. Also called PRIVATE CORPORATION; PRIVATELY HELD CORPORATION. See also CORPORATION.

CLOSED SHOP   A company that hires only union labor, a company that requires union membership as a condition of employment.

CLOSELY HELD CORPORATION   A CORPORATION owned by relatively few people, all or most of whom are directly involved in the conduct of the business, with few shares of stock held by outside investors. Differs from a CLOSED CORPORATION because enough shares of stock are publicly held to provide a basis for trading. Shares held by the controlling group are not likely to be available for purchase by the public. See also CORPORATION.

CLOSING   An accounting definition of the time when the books are completed for a specific period of time and summarized into financial statements for the company. After this date, no other entries are permitted for the period. Also, the final conclusion of other transactions, such as real estate purchase.

CLP   See CERTIFIED LENDER PROGRAM.

CLU   See CHARTERED LIFE UNDERWRITER.

COD   See CASH ON DELIVERY.

CO-ENTREPRENEURS   Two owners of a start-up venture, often used when referring to an unmarried couple but not limited to that. See MOM & POP BUSINESS.

COGS   See COST OF GOODS SOLD.

CO-INSURANCE   Sharing of an insurance risk; a provision in an insurance policy or contract requiring the insured party maintain some amount and type of insurance to protect another party from certain provisions of the policy or contract if a loss occurs. Co-insurance is prudent when one company cannot underwrite the entire risk or when more that one company is working on the same project.

Also, co-insurance can apply to a situation wherein you insure for 100 percent and your business assumes co-insurance for 20 percent (20 percent FLOOR or 20 percent DEDUCTIBLE); thus, your insurance premium is much less because you have assumed only 20 percent of the loss.

COLA   See COST OF LIVING ADJUSTMENT.

COLD CALL   A telephone call or personal visit to a potential customer without prior introduction, letter or leads. Prior to the cold call, the potential customer may have no knowledge of the product or service offered for sale.

COLD CANVAS   A series of COLD CALLS that entirely covers a particular location or a specific segment of potential customers.

COLLATERAL   Assets given as security for a loan; something of value (an ASSET) pledged to a lender as security for a LOAN or DEBT. If the BORROWER fails to repay (DEFAULTS on) the loan according to the terms, the LENDER has the legal right to seize the collateral and take legal title to the property. The borrower can sell the collateral to repay the loan.

COLLATERALIZED LOAN   A loan secured by COLLATERAL; a loan on which an asset has been pledged. See COLLATERAL.

COLLATERALIZED MORTGAGE   A loan secured by an asset, such as real estate, against which the loan is made. See COLLATERAL.

COLLECTION   Receipt of money from a customer for goods or services previously sold; conversion of ACCOUNTS RECEIVABLE into cash.

Referral of past due accounts to a specialist for collection of the amount due on a loan or account receivable, such as a collection agency.

In banking, the presentation of a negotiable instrument, such as a check or draft, to the place at which it is payable, and receiving cash or a cash equivalent.

COLLECTION ACCOUNT   An account established to receive periodic payments on a debt or obligation and make disbursements from the account as requested by the payee.

COLLECTION AGENCY   A firm that specializes in accepting past due accounts (loans or accounts receivable), locating the debtor and obtaining the funds from the debtor.

COLLECTION FLOAT   The time between a sale made (the extension of credit for a sale) and receipt of the money. It is prudent to set an interest rate for this period at a rate greater than the normal return on assets. Both internal and external factors affect the FLOAT period. Internal factors (controllable by the firm) include fast order entry, invoicing, billing and follow-up until paid. External factors include speed of payment by the customer, distance and speed of collection in cash by the firm. See FLOAT.

COLLECTION PAPER   All the documents (commercial invoices, bills of lading, etc.) submitted to a buyer for the purpose of receiving payment for goods delivered.

COLLECTIVE BARGAINING   The process by which labor and management negotiate mutually acceptable wages and other conditions of employment.

CO-MAKE   See COSIGN.

CO-MAKER   See COSIGNER.

COMMERCE   Trade; the buying and selling of goods and services, especially when done on a large scale, such as between cities, states or countries.

COMMENCEMENT OF WORK   The noticeable beginning of work on a contract as determined under local law.

COMMERCIAL   A business-to-business relationship. As opposed to a business-to-person relationship.

COMMERCIAL ACCOUNT   An ACCOUNT that is for the transaction of business with another company, as opposed to a PERSONAL ACCOUNT for the transaction of business with a person.

COMMERCIAL BANK   See BANK.

COMMERCIAL COUNTERFEIT   A product that is a copy of an original product to such a degree that it deceives the buyer into believing the product to be produced by the original manufacturer.

COMMERCIAL CREDIT COMPANY   A company engaged in making loans to other businesses. Unlike a bank, a commercial credit company does not receive deposits; it obtains financing from banks and others sources. Businesses that do not qualify for bank credit often can obtain a loan from a commercial credit company. See also: 1) a CONSUMER FINANCE COMPANY, which makes small loans directly to individuals; and 2) an ACCEPTANCE COMPANY, which purchases consumer loans (PAPER) from others.

COMMERCIAL FINANCE COMPANY   See COMMERCIAL CREDIT COMPANY.

COMMERCIAL INVOICE   See INVOICE.

COMMERCIAL LOAN   A LOAN made by a COMMERCIAL BANK to a business. As opposed to a PERSONAL LOAN, which is made to a person. About 95 percent of all commercial loans are made to small businesses.

COMMERCIAL MORTGAGE   A MORTGAGE on real estate for the purpose of buying, constructing or enlarging business property.

COMMERCIAL PAPER   Short-term loans with maturities ranging from two days to nine months issued by banks and companies. to obtain cash. Usually commercial paper is unsecured and discounted, although some bear interest. Some may be long-term.

COMMERCIAL PROPERTY   A classification of real estate used for business purposes. Commercial property usually must be zoned for the specific type of business operation. As opposed to property that is for residential, farm or industrial use.

COMMINGLE; COMMINGLED FUNDS   See COMMINGLING.

COMMINGLING   In finance and accounting, to mix or mingle financial information from two or more separate entities. For example, business financial records must be kept separate from personal financial records. To commingle business and personal money is illegal.

COMMISSION   The compensation paid to an employee, agent or broker based on performance. For example, a salesman may be paid a percentage (a commission) of the amount of products sold, or a third-party broker receives a commission when a transaction is consummated between two other parties.

COMMITMENT A pledge or promise to perform a certain act, such as to execute a contract agreement or to adhere to certain quality standards.

COMMITMENT FEE An amount paid to another party to secure a loan or guarantee a performance; an amount paid to a lender to reserve credit availability at a future time.

COMMODITIES Generally, commodities refer to bulk goods such as food, grains, metals and all types of raw materials. Yet, broadly defined, commodities may refer to any type of good.

COMMODITY AGREEMENT An agreement on the price at which COMMODITIES will be bought and sold, often an agreement between exporting and importing countries.

COMMON SHARES Same as COMMON STOCK.

COMMON STOCK A unit (share) of ownership of a public corporation; the term applies to the most junior form of ownership. The person owning shares of common stock (SHARE-HOLDER) is entitled to the four basic rights of ownership: 1) proportionate share of the corporation's undivided assets; 2) one vote for each share at the annual meeting; 3) paid dividends from corporate earnings as declared by the Board of Directors; 4) PREEMPTIVE RIGHT to subscribe to additional stock offerings before they are available to the general public. See STOCK; SHARE.

COMMUNITY PROPERTY Property and income accumulated by a married couple and belonging to them jointly together in a 50%/50% relationship for each spouse. The two have equal rights to the income and assets as well as the appreciated value of the assets.

COMMUNITY PROPERTY STATE A state of the United States wherein the law of the state requires all property of married couples to be defined as COMMUNITY PROPERTY.

COMPANY   An organization engaged in buying and selling products or services, including all business types (proprietorship, partnership and corporation). Often, company is used interchangeably with corporation. See also FIRM.

COMPARATIVE ADVANTAGE   A concept of trade theory wherein a country or region should produce those goods and services that can be produced most efficiently and at least cost to achieve a favorable competitive and profitable posture over other countries or regions. Most often comparative advantage applies to products or services in international trade but applies equally well to INTRADE and EXTRADE.

COMPENSATING BALANCE   The average balance required by a bank to make credit available; funds deposited with a bank as an inducement to extend a line of credit or make a loan.

COMPETITION   The existence of many businesses engaged in the same business or trade vying for the same customers. See PERFECT COMPETITION.

COMPETITIVE   The act of vying for success in a business; more than one company engaged in an area of business activity attempting to obtain the available potential sales.

COMPETITIVE ADVANTAGE   Technological superiority, higher quality, better distribution availability or lower cost that attracts buyers.

COMPETITIVE BID   One of several proposals to accomplish a scope of work; a BID in COMPETITION with other companies.

COMPETITIVE WAGE RATE   A payment to employees for work that is generally equivalent to the payment made to others performing similar work.

COMPLETED CONTRACT METHOD   A procedure for computing payments on a contract whereby payment is made only after the entire job is satisfactorily completed. As opposed to PROGRESS PAYMENTS.

COMPLETION BOND A type of insurance that guarantees accomplishment (completion) of work on a contract. See PERFORMANCE BOND.

COMPOUND INTEREST An accumulation of INTEREST where each interest payment is added to the investment amount, rather than paid in cash to the investor. In succeeding periods, the interest amount is increased because of the amount of accumulated prior interest on which later interest is also calculated; interest earned on prior interest paid. As opposed to SIMPLE INTEREST. Interest can be compounded (multiplied by itself) annually, monthly, daily or on any other regular basis.

COMPOUND INTEREST RATE The annual percentage value used for calculations of COMPOUND INTEREST; as opposed to SIMPLE INTEREST RATE.

COMPOUND TARIFF A TARIFF for a good that combines both a SPECIFIC TARIFF plus an AD VALOREM TARIFF.

COMPUTER See PERSONAL COMPUTER.

CONCESSION To relinquish one contract provision in place of another provision. During the negotiation process, some small areas of a contract (the concessions) may be relinquished in order to secure a more lucrative larger total contract order.
   A franchise right granted by a government agency (also at a sports stadium, airport or other entity) for the conduct of business on the premises.

CONDITIONS Provisions in a contract that clearly describe the manner or method of accomplishment; the environment under which the contract must be executed.

CONFIRMED LETTER OF CREDIT An international LETTER OF CREDIT that is issued by a foreign bank and validity is verified (confirmed) by a U.S. bank. Thus payment from the buyer to the seller is assured.

CONGLOMERATE A firm that produces a wide variety of largely unrelated goods and services or a company with a wide variety of dissimilar subsidiaries and other controlling rights. The only apparent tie is the profit motive.

CONSIDERATION   An act or the promise thereof that is offered by one party to induce another to enter into a contract; money or property that is given in exchange for something from another.

CONSIGNMENT   Delivery of merchandise from a seller to a buyer under agreement whereby the buyer intends to resell the merchandise. After the merchandise is sold by the buyer, payment is made to the first seller.

CONSOLIDATE   To unite, combine or incorporate into a more concise business operation; the collection of several financial matters into a single account, i.e., consolidate the books or accounts. Also to merge several businesses into a larger business or conglomerate.

CONSULAR INVOICE   A document, required by some foreign countries, that describes the goods shipped, showing information such as the consignor, consignee and value of the shipment as certified by a consular official of the foreign country. The consular invoice is used by customs officials to verify the value, quantity and nature of the shipment.

CONSULTANT   An expert specialist, person or company called on, for a fee, to provide professional or technical advice, information, opinions, knowledge or services.

CONSULTING   The process of providing professional or technical expert knowledge or guidance to a small business. A fee is usually charged by the CONSULTANT for the service provided. Also, seeking such professional or technical advice, i.e., consulting a lawyer.

CONSUMER   A person or business that buys goods or services for his or her own needs, not goods purchased for resale. As opposed to PRODUCER who purchases goods for the production of other goods or WHOLESALE who purchases for resale.

CONSUMER FINANCE COMPANY   A company that makes small loans directly to individuals. See FINANCE COMPANY.

CONSUMER GOODS   Goods or services purchased for personal, household, or business use and to be consumed or used up; goods that are not to be resold. Includes items such as food, clothing, utilities, entertainment and supplies; as distinguished from CAPITAL GOODS. See CONSUMER.

CONSUMER LOAN   Money borrowed by a customer (consumer), usually to finance the purchase of a product or service at the time of the sale. See also PERSONAL LOAN.

CONSUMER PRICE INDEX (CPI)   A measure of change in consumer prices, revised monthly by the U.S. Bureau of Labor Statistics. Prices are calculated as products reach the consumer; consisting of components such as cost of housing, food, transportation and insurance. CPI measures the consumer effects resulting from inflation and reduced purchasing power. Also called cost-of-living. The equivalent for manufactured goods is the PRODUCER PRICE INDEX.

CONSUMMATE   To bring to a completion, such as a jointly-signed contract that would consummate a deal.

CONTINGENCY   A provision placed in a contract that requires the completion of a certain act or the happening of a particular event before some part of the contract is binding.

CONTINGENT LIABILITY   A potential obligation of a grantor; a debt that is not now the responsibility of a person or business but could be due and payable under some circumstances, such as a cosigner on a note by another. The cosigner must repay the note if the maker fails to repay. Also an open bank line of credit that could be obligated if a draft is signed.

In business, many items are considered contingent liabilities, such as pending lawsuit, judgment under appeal, disputed claim, delinquent or contested taxes, environmental hazard, lien waiver, lien and long-term commercial property lease i.e., items posing potential financial liability in the event of an adverse outcome.

CONTRACT   An agreement whereby services, rights or acts are exchanged for payment. To be valid, a contract must be mutual and freely accepted by both competent parties and cover legal and moral transactions. In business, a contract identifies the services to be performed, the provider, the recipient, the amount of payment, the date of completion and other provisions and clauses.

CONTRACT COMPLETION   The time when all activity associated with a CONTRACT has been accomplished; all work is done and all bills have been paid. Payment may not yet have been received for the completed work.

CONTRACT LABOR   Service by a person who is paid in accordance with the terms of a contract. See CONTRACT.

CONTRACTOR   A company that works for others under the terms of a CONTRACT. See also INDEPENDENT CONTRACTOR.

CONTRA-ENTRY   In double-entry bookkeeping, a corresponding credit entry for each debit entry and vice versa.

CONTRIBUTED CAPITAL   Same as CAPITAL INVESTMENT.

CONTROL   To regulate the financial affairs of the business; to exercise authority over the conduct of the business; to verify by comparison with duplicate register, such as payments and accounts.

CONTROL ACCOUNT   An account that summarizes the total of related items from other accounts; a summary account. Several SUBSIDIARY ACCOUNTs may be summarized into a control account.

CONTROLLABLE EXPENSES   Those things over which decisions can be exercised concerning the amount of money to be paid out.

CONTROLLER   A company executive who is responsible for the firm's financial affairs, including budget, accounting and auditing.

CONVERTIBLE SECURITY   A bond or preferred stock that may be exchanged for common stock.

COOLING-OFF PERIOD   A kind of grace period provided by law or by contract during which a party to a contract can legally withdraw from the contract; a right of recession.

In management and labor relations, a period after expiration of a labor contract to allow the participants to regroup and reconsider their respective positions. Labor cannot strike and the company cannot lock-out the employees.

COOP   A common abbreviation for COOPERATIVE. See COOPERATIVE.

COOPERATIVE   An organization owned by its members who agree to combine their resources to achieve greater results than they could achieve individually. Most common in agricultural products but also in some real estate ventures. Commonly, any group of people or businesses with common interests that join together to gain the advantage of pooled buying or selling.

COOPERATIVE ADVERTISING   ADVERTISING that involves two or more participants in which all participants benefit. Two main types exist: 1) a retailer in cooperation with a manufacturer or a supplier; and 2) an advertisement that benefits a group of peers, such as merchandisers in a shopping mall. Cooperation exists in areas such as preparation, media, distribution and payment.

COPYRIGHT   The exclusive right granted by law for a specified period of time to an author to publish, produce, sell and profit from a literary work, computer program, drama or musical. Copyright provides legal protection for unauthorized duplication or reproduction of an original work. A copyright can be registered with the federal government, but registration is not mandatory for the protection granted.

CORPORATE CHARTER   See CHARTER; also ARTICLES OF INCORPORATION.

CORPORATE IMAGE   The perceived public vision of the type, market and quality of a company and its products or services.

CORPORATE INCOME TAX   By law, the amount paid to the federal government (and most states) by a corporation, calculated on the amount of profits (NET INCOME). Federal income taxes are required to be paid by corporations on FORM 1120.

CORPORATE INCOME TAX RETURN   The federal government FORM 1120 used for computing and reporting the amount of income taxes due to be paid by the corporation. Many states also require corporate income tax returns.

CORPORATE RESOLUTION   A summary of a specific action taken by the board of directors of a corporation as recorded in the minute book.

CORPORATE RETURN   See CORPORATE INCOME TAX RETURN. Also see RETURN ON INVESTMENT.

CORPORATE VEIL   Legal protection provided to the owners of a corporation from payment of corporate debts with personal funds; isolating personal finances from the corporate finances. Only corporate assets can be used to repay corporate debts.

CORPORATION   A legal entity, chartered by a state of the United States or by the federal government that in a business sense is separate and distinct from the persons who own it, as an artificial business person. A corporation can own property, engage in contracts, incur debts, pay taxes, sue or be sued. A corporation: has limited liability whereby owners can only lose the amount invested; can expand ownership by sale of additional shares of stock; can easily transfer ownership through the sale of shares of stock; continues to exist beyond the life of individual owners; has centralized management in a board of directors, president, secretary and treasurer. Corporations are subject to regulation in the state where incorporated and in the states where they do business. Special corporate income tax rates apply; dividends are paid to shareholders from earnings of the corporation; see DOUBLE TAXATION. In a broad sense, corporation includes all types of corporations. In a specific reference, a corporation is synonymous with C-CORPORATION. See also CLOSED CORPORATION; CLOSELY HELD CORPORATION; S-CORPORATION.

CORRESPONDENCE   Business communication by exchange of letters, faxes, and other written material, including both transmitted and received items.

CORRESPONDENCE FILE   A place for storage of CORRESPONDENCE; a collection of stored letters, faxes and other correspondence.

CORRESPONDENT   In general, a preparer or recipient of correspondence. See also CORRESPONDENT BANK.

CORRESPONDENT BANK   A financial institution that regularly performs services for another financial institution in markets inaccessible to the first financial institution. In correspondent banking, a depository relationship usually exists that compensates for expenses and facilitates transactions.

C.O.S.   See COST OF SALES.

COSIGN   To sign (a promissory note) in addition to the maker, thus becoming fully responsible for the obligation if the maker should default; to sign jointly.

COSIGNER   The person who COSIGNs a note for another, thus the cosigner must repay the obligation if the maker does not repay the note.

COST   An expenditure or the amount expended for a product or service. In marketing, the price.

COST ACCOUNTING   The process by which dollar amounts (costs) are traced directly to the project, job or unit that caused them to be incurred as expenditures.

COST BASIS   The original price (cost) of an asset, usually the purchase price. Often cost basis is commonly used to mean ADJUSTED COST BASIS, i.e., the original purchase price reduced by depreciation and increased by improvements.

COST-BENEFIT ANALYSIS   An analytical tool used to measure the results (benefits) compared to the required expenditure (cost) that may result from a decision.

COST CONTROL   The analysis of anticipated expenditures (costs) coupled with decisions (control) whether to incur or not to incur the expenditure. A knowledge of cash available is necessary to determine the ability to pay the expenditure.

COST OF CAPITAL   The expenses incurred either when acquiring money through borrowing from creditors (interest) or obtaining investment capital from owners (dividends). Sometimes also includes the administrative and selling acquisition expenses.

COST OF GOODS SOLD (COGS)   The sum of expenditures for materials and labor necessary to produce the products/services sold. Also known as DIRECT COSTS, they include the clear-cut cost factors of factory output; as opposed to INDIRECT COSTS or OVERHEAD COSTS, which are less clear-cut factors.

In accounting, the beginning inventory plus purchases minus ending inventory equals the cost of goods sold.

COST OF LIVING; COST OF LIVING INDEX   See CONSUMER PRICE INDEX.

COST OF LIVING ADJUSTMENT (COLA)   Money added to the base wage to compensate for inflation.

COST OF SALES   Same as COST OF GOODS SOLD.

COST PER SQUARE FOOT   The average amount of expenditures by a business to maintain the building area of operation. Costs include rent, utilities, repairs, improvements and other expenses.

COST-PLUS   See COST-PLUS CONTRACT.

COST-PLUS CONTRACT   A contract agreement wherein the purchaser agrees to pay the cost of all labor and materials plus an amount for contractor overhead and profit (usually as a percentage of the labor and material cost).

COST RECOVERY   A form of deduction for DEPRECIATION of real and personal property used in a trade or business or held for the production of income; an expense on an income statement called depreciation. See DEPRECIATION.

COTTAGE INDUSTRY   The collection of small businesses that operate from homes (cottages), generally producing goods or supplies that may be offered directly for sale to the retail market.

COUNSEL   To confer with, discuss with or advise another person. Counsel is frequently used collectively for a group of counselors. In law, a lawyer or a conference with a lawyer.

COUNSELOR One who confers with, discusses with or advises another person. In law, a LAWYER.

COUNTEROFFER A new OFFER made in response to an offer received. This has the effect of rejecting the original offer received and placing the counteroffer on the table for consideration.

COVENANTS Conditions placed in a loan or in a credit agreement by a lender to protect its position as a creditor of the business that is borrowing the money.

In real estate, a restriction on the use or non-use of property.

COVERAGE In insurance, the types of risks and the amount of financial protection if a loss should occur; the types and amount of financial reimbursement purchased under an INSURANCE POLICY.

In business, the territory or market served by a business.

In advertising, the breadth or extent of the distribution.

CPA See CERTIFIED PUBLIC ACCOUNTANT.

CPCU See CHARTER PROPERTY CASUALTY UNDERWRITER.

CPI See CONSUMER PRICE INDEX.

CREDIT In business, loans, bonds, charge-account obligations and open-account balances with other commercial firms, credit is the ability to borrow or the amount of money borrowed. In other words, one's financial confidence or trust in another.

In accounting, an entry, or the act of making an entry, in the financial books of a firm that increases a liability, owner's equity or income, or an entry that decreases an asset or an expense. The corresponding entry appears as the DEBIT.

CREDIT ACCOUNT An authorized ACCOUNT by a seller that permits a purchaser to take possession of the goods and remit payment at a later date.

CREDIT AND COLLECTIONS The combined functions of lending money to and receiving money from customers; temporarily lending money to a customer for the purchase of goods or services. A CREDIT is extended at the time the goods or services are

sold. The receipt of payment at a later date is called COLLEC-
TION.

CREDIT BALANCE   In general, an accounting balance in the
customer's favor. See also CREDIT.

In business, money deposited and not withdrawn from a bank
account; a repayment of a debt in excess of the amount owed with
an amount remaining that is due and payable to the remitter.

CREDIT CARD   A document issued to a customer of a bank
establishing a credit account that allows the customer to charge
purchases and make cash disbursements from the account. A credit
card is different from a BANK CARD even though the credit card
may be issued by a bank.

CREDIT CRUNCH   A scarcity of funds to be borrowed; a time
when some businesses with good credit risk cannot borrow at any
price. Short-term interest rates are unusually high.

CREDITOR   A person who owes money to another person; a
LENDER. The other person is known as the DEBTOR.

CREDIT POLICY   The practice and approval process within a
company for accepting or denying credit to customers.

CREDIT RATING   The ability to pay debts that have been incurred; a formal evaluation of the credit history of a person or
business and its capability of repaying obligations. Several firms
perform credit rating evaluations, including TRW (for private
persons) and DUN & BRADSTREET (for commercial businesses).

CREDIT REPORT   A document including the detailed credit history of a person or business, used to determine credit worthiness.

CREDIT RISK   The chance that a debtor will not repay.

CREDIT SALES   Goods or services that are sold but the customer
has not yet paid for them; as opposed to CASH SALES.

CRISIS MANAGEMENT   A description of a situation where
little planning had been accomplished necessitating that the

majority of effort is spent responding to unforeseen events. As opposed to management control with a plan of activity that anticipates the events and plans actions to be followed when the events occur.

CROSS FOOT An accounting term meaning to add the rows across a page to the right (cross) and to add the columns down the page (foot). The sums in the right-hand column can then be added down to a total for the entire page. Likewise, the sums in the bottom row can be added across to obtain a total for the entire page. If performed correctly, the two answers will equal the same value, verifying the accuracy of the arithmetic.

CROSS-PURCHASE AGREEMENT A type of BUY-SELL AGREE-MENT whereby each shareholder agrees to buy a proportionate share of each other's stock if the conditions of the buy-sell agreement occur.

CRUNCH NUMBERS Performance of many mathematical calculations, such as the calculations necessary to summarize accounts and finalize totals into an income statement and a balance sheet.

CSVLI Abbreviation for CASH SURRENDER VALUE OF LIFE INSURANCE. See CASH SURRENDER VALUE.

CUMULATIVE The sum of subsidiary amounts over a period of time.

CURRENCY In reference to money, usually paper money; sometimes paper money plus coins.
   In lending, a measure of the timeliness of debt repayment. As opposed to ARREARS.

CURRENT Something that is happening now in business, such as current month or current contract.
   In financing, such as with a loan, a current loan is one that has been paid on time and is not past due.

CURRENT ASSET Cash or other assets that are likely to be converted into cash, usually within a year, through sale, exchange or expense during the normal course of business. Examples include cash, inventory and accounts receivable. Also called LIQUID ASSET.

CURRENT ASSETS The sum of each CURRENT ASSET as shown on a BALANCE SHEET. See also FIXED ASSETs.

CURRENT LIABILITIES The sum of each CURRENT LIABILITY as shown on a BALANCE SHEET.

CURRENT LIABILITY Debt, loan, trade credit or other obligation due for payment within one year.

CURRENT RATIO Current assets divided by current liabilities; a measure of the ability of a small business to pay short-term debts from readily available funds. A high current ratio will allow safe operation of a small business whose cash flow is less dependable. Also see QUICK RATIO.

CURRENT YIELD The RATE OF RETURN on an investment at the present time expressed as an annual percentage. Also, the annual interest on a bond divided by the market price.

CUSHION An amount of money added to a bid for unforeseen occurrences such as delays, poor weather and bidding mistakes. This concept is also applied to a budget or an asset purchase.

CUSTOMER The person or business that buys from a business; a purchaser of goods or services.

CUSTOMER BASE For a business, its total list of customers, total number of potential customers or group of customers with specific classification characteristics. Such customer-base identification allows more accurate targeting of marketing objectives.

CUSTOMER PROFILE The precise definition of the characteristics of the aggregate buyers of a specific product or service. Also, the characteristics of buyers of the entire line of products of a company.

CUSTOMHOUSE BROKER A person or business licensed by the U.S. government to enter and clear goods through CUSTOMS.

CUSTOMS   An agency of the federal government charged with enforcing IMPORT and EXPORT regulations, and charged with collection of duties. See also CUSTOMS DUTY.

CUSTOMS DUTY   A tax, levy or fee imposed at the point of entry on goods imported into a country. Same as TARIFF; IMPORT DUTY.

D

DAILY Those events that occur each and every day.

DAMAGES Unsalable merchandise for which reimbursement is sought from the supplier or the transporter.
  In insurance, the physical and financial cost of a loss.

DATE Usually, the exact year, month and day. A single day on which a legal contract is signed or an event occurs.

DATED, OR "AS OF" The calendar date from which terms begin.

DATE OF INVOICE The calendar date affixed to the INVOICE document. This date cannot be prior to shipment. The terms of the sale originate from the date of the invoice.

DAY A single calendar day; a period of time equal to 24 hours, one seventh of a week and one 365th of a year.

DAY-TO-DAY The events or actions that tend to occur frequently, such as each day, or that could occur on any given day.

DBA An abbreviation for the phrase "doing business as"; used to identify a fictitious name or trade name as a business name.

DDB See DOUBLE-DECLINING-BALANCE DEPRECIATION METHOD.

DEAL   A buy/sell transaction; a business relationship; a business opportunity; a consummated business contract; a business agreement.

To perform a business transaction.

DEALER   A business that purchases goods or services for resale to consumers; a buyer or seller; a business engaged in trade. The element of inventory risk experienced by a dealer distinguishes a dealer from an agent or sales representative.

DEBENTURE   An unsecured long-term note as evidence of a debt.

DEBIT   In accounting, an entry, or the act of making an entry, in the financial books of a firm that increases an asset or an expense or an entry that decreases a liability, owner's equity or income. The entry appears on the lefthand side of an accounting statement. The opposite of a debit is a CREDIT.

DEBIT CARD   Similar to a CREDIT CARD, but deducts the transacted amount directly from a bank account immediately at the time of the transaction.

DEBT   Debt refers to money borrowed. Money, goods or services that one party (DEBTOR) is obliged to repay to another (CREDITOR) in accordance with an expressed or implied agreement. Debt may be secured or unsecured. See also LOAN.

DEBT COVERAGE RATIO   The ratio of annual net income to annual debt service.

DEBT-EQUITY RATIO   The relationship of borrowed capital versus owned capital. The relationship of money owed by a firm to others (DEBTs) to the amount of money owed to the owners (EQUITY). The ratio serves to assess long-range financial stability.

DEBT FINANCING   The payment, in whole or in part, for a capital investment with borrowed monies. As opposed to EQUITY FINANCING by investing one's own funds.

DEBT INSTRUMENT   A document containing a written promise to repay, such as BILL, NOTE, BOND, BANKER'S ACCEPTANCE, CERTIFICATE OF DEPOSIT or COMMERCIAL PAPER.

DEBTOR A person or business that owes money to another; a BORROWER. The other person is know as the CREDITOR.

DEBT RATIO A comparative analysis designed to determine the ability to incur debt. Three common measures are used: 1) total debt to total assets, 2) total debt to net worth and 3) total debt to current debt.

DEBT SCHEDULE A list of the payments of principal and interest necessary to repay a given debt instrument or combination of debts.

DEBT SERVICE Paying the amount owed on a debt; the amount of money required for the payment of current interest and principal on a long-term debt. Also called ANNUAL DEBT SERVICE when the term is for a total year.

DEBT-TO-EQUITY RATIO See DEBT-EQUITY RATIO.

DEBT WARRANT The right of a debt holder to purchase common stock at a specified price in exchange for the outstanding debt.

DECLINING-BALANCE METHOD An ACCELERATED DEPRECIATION method of FIXED ASSET write-off that is faster than the STRAIGHT-LINE DEPRECIATION method in the early years of life on the asset.

DEDUCTIBLE In insurance, the amount of loss borne by the owner before insurance coverage begins to compensate for the loss.

In taxation, the act of taking a deduction.

DEDUCTION An expense allowed by the IRS as a subtraction from income in computing the income that is taxable.

An adjustment (subtraction) from an invoice allowed by a seller for a discrepancy or shortage.

DEED A written document containing the transfer of or contract for property; most commonly conveying the legal title to real estate from one party to another; evidence of property ownership.

DEED OF TRUST　A legal document in which title to property is transferred to a third-party trustee as security for an obligation owed by the borrower to the lender. Most often used in real estate.

DEFAULT　The nonperformance of a duty or obligation that is part of a contract; a breach of contract. Sometimes occurs when a borrower or lessee does not remit a payment of money when due.

DEFAULT JUDGMENT　A court order in favor of the plaintiff resulting from the defendant's failure to answer a complaint or appear in court to defend the action.

DEFENDANT　The person being sued by the plaintiff in a lawsuit; the person charged with the wrong and from whom recovery is sought.

DEFERRED　In accounting, a situation whereby a payment may be due but has been assigned for payment at a later date.

DEFINED BENEFIT PENSION　A type of PENSION in which a worker is guaranteed a specific amount of retirement income.

DEFINITION OF SMALL BUSINESS　See SMALL BUSINESS DEFINITION.

DEFLATION　A decline in prices for goods and services; the price for a product is lower as measured today than at a time in the past. Generally, the effects of deflation are opposite to those produced by INFLATION, with two differences: 1) prices of things that increase with inflation do not always decrease with deflation, such as union wage rates and 2) while inflation usually stimulates output and employment, deflation usually causes a rise in unemployment and decline in output. Deflation should not be confused with DISINFLATION, a slowing of the rate of inflation (slowing the rate at which prices are rising). See INFLATION; DISINFLATION.

DELIVERY　Transportation of goods by the seller to the buyer from the seller's location to the location designated by the buyer;

the legal act of transferring ownership; the exchange of a document like a contract from the preparer to the recipient.

DELIVERY INSTRUCTIONS   The document that describes the nature of a shipment and precise conditions that need to be known for transportation of the shipment.

DEMAND   An economist's term describing the amount of a product or service people are willing to buy at each price; as opposed to SUPPLY. The aggregate desires to purchase a product or service. Also an urgent requirement or claim for financial remuneration.

DEMAND CURVE   Graphic representation of DEMAND.

DEMAND DEPOSIT   A deposit from which funds may be withdrawn on request (demand) and from which funds may be transferred to another party by means of a check.

DEMAND LOAN   A loan with no set maturity date that can be called for repayment of the amount in full when the lender chooses. Interest payments are usually required at fixed intervals. See also CALL.

DEMAND SCHEDULE   A numerical tabulation of the quantitative relationship between quantity demanded and price. See DEMAND.

DEMOGRAPHICS   Population statistics that are arranged to isolate socio-economic factors of potential customers. Demographic information that is available from most government bodies is very useful to a small business for marketing, advertising and other related matters.

DEMONSTRATE   Show by the use of samples or models to show the usability and functioning of products that are for sale.

DEMONSTRATION   The act of showing; using samples or models to show the usefulness and functioning of products that are for sale.

DEPLETION   An accounting charge for the use of natural resources, such as oil, gas or timber. Similar to DEPRECIATION of real property.

DEPOSIT   Cash, checks or drafts placed with a financial institution, such as a bank, for credit to a customer's account. Banks differentiate between, a DEMAND DEPOSIT, such as a checking account, which can be withdrawn at any time; and a TIME DEPOSIT, such as a CERTIFICATE OF DEPOSIT, which has a specified maturity date when cash can be withdrawn.

Money paid initially by a purchaser as part payment on a contract as evidence of intention to complete the contract and protect the seller in the event the contract is not completed. Also called EARNEST MONEY.

Sums paid as security to protect the selling party for services delivered, but not paid, such as utilities or rentals.

DEPOSIT IN TRANSIT   A DEPOSIT that has been made ready for the bank or has been mailed to the bank, but has not yet been entered in the bank records for the business account.

DEPOSIT SLIP   A record of a DEPOSIT transaction with a financial institution, such as a bank.

DEPRECIATE   See DEPRECIATION.

DEPRECIATED BASIS   See ADJUSTED BASIS; BASIS.

DEPRECIATION   An accounting term for the cost recovery of REAL PROPERTY and PERSONAL PROPERTY; the EXPENSE deduction on an INCOME STATEMENT allowing for gradual wearout of a FIXED ASSET; AMORTIZATION of a fixed asset. The duration of the depreciation period approximates the useful life of the asset. Commonly used methods of depreciation include STRAIGHT-LINE DEPRECIATION; ACCELERATED DEPRECIATION; ACCELERATED COST RECOVERY SYSTEM; DECLINING-BALANCE METHOD; SUM-OF-THE-YEARS-DIGITS METHOD.

DEPRECIATION EXPENSE   The amount of cost recovery of a fixed asset that is entered as a subtraction (an expense) on an INCOME STATEMENT.

DEPRECIATION LIFE   An approximation of the useful life (in years) of an asset used for calculation of depreciation amounts to be applied as an expense to an income statement. See DEPRECIATION.

DEPRECIATION RECORD   The document that describes the method, DEPRECIATION LIFE, and amount of depreciation. See DEPRECIATION.

DEPRECIATION SCHEDULE   A document displaying the period-by-period amount of DEPRECIATION to be entered in the income statement worksheets. See DEPRECIATION.

DESK   The article of office furniture used for performing various business related tasks.

DESKTOP PUBLISHING   Method of producing publications and advertising materials within a small business office by means of a personal computer with special software, as opposed to hiring layout and printing professionals.

DESTINATION CONTROL STATEMENT   In exporting, the destination statement that is displayed on the outside of an export shipment, as required by the U.S. government.

DEVELOPMENT ASSISTANCE 7(j) PROGRAM   See SECTION 7(j) PROGRAM.

DILUTED EARNINGS   A situation whereby additional shares of stock were sold to other investors causing the earnings to be spread over a broader base. Thus fewer earnings are available for each share unless earnings grow proportionately more than the number of new shares issued.

DIRECT COST   An EXPENSE (cost) that is incurred only because of a specific contract, job or project being accomplished. Without that specific contract, the expense would not normally be incurred. In cost accounting direct costs are usually tabulated according to the specific jobs to evaluate profitability. As opposed to INDIRECT COST.

DIRECT LABOR   Personnel assigned to the production process whose payroll expenditures are easily traced to the units of output and are included in the COST OF GOODS SOLD. As opposed to INDIRECT LABOR, or supporting personnel.

DIRECT LOAN   Money borrowed directly from the federal government. Special conditions apply.

DIRECT MAIL   Marketing goods directly to the consumer through the mail as opposed to marketing through a retail store.

DIRECT MARKETING   Sale of products by a producer to customers by the use of mail rather than middlemen such as wholesalers and retailers. Also commonly used for business-to-business sales.

DIRECT MATERIALS   Raw materials and other purchases that become a part of the units produced and incur expenditures that are easily traced to the units of output and included in the COST OF GOODS SOLD. As opposed to INDIRECT MATERIALS, such as office supplies.

DIRECT METHOD MARKET ENTRY   A form of exporting whereby the exporter retains responsibility for shipping the product but may or may not retain responsibility for sales, regulations, marketing and final distribution.

DIRECTOR   A member of the BOARD OF DIRECTORS. Also a title for one who directs; one who controls the operation of a business. See BOARD OF DIRECTORS.

DIRECT TAX   A tax levied on income, such as INCOME TAX. The opposite of INDIRECT TAX.

DISABILITY   A physical condition of a person that prevents the person from performing certain normal functions required for work. Under the Americans with Disabilities Act (ADA) employers must not discriminate against disabled persons. Businesses must provide reasonable accommodations in the workplace for disabled workers and customers.

DISABILITY CLAUSE   The portion of an insurance policy (the clause) entitling a policyholder who becomes permanently disabled to cease premium payments yet still retain insurance coverage under the policy.

DISADVANTAGED A person who has a disability or is economically depressed due to race, color, sex, etc. A business owned by such a person is called a SMALL DISADVANTAGED BUSINESS.

DISADVANTAGED BUSINESS See SMALL DISADVANTAGED BUSINESS.

DISASTER LOAN Physical or financial assistance by a government to individuals and businesses that have suffered losses due to natural disaster.

DISBURSEMENT Money paid out or expended in the discharge of a debt, as in an accounting process, distinguished from a distribution from earnings. Examples include a draw on a construction loan, advances on salary, discharge of a debt payment and payment of an invoice.

DISCLOSURE STATEMENT A complete report of information about a loan, provided by a lender to a borrower, such as interest rate, fees and charges. Required by the Truth-in-Lending Law. Also a full explanation of the facts about a situation.

Also, a complete listing of the facts, warranties, dangers, hazards, problems or truths. for manufactured products, services performed, real estate transacted or other transaction.

DISCOUNT The amount by which the current amount is less than the original amount; the difference between the face value and the cash value; a percentage off; the current amount is a percentage less than the original amount. In retail merchandise sales, a discount is the percentage off the original selling price in exchange for quick payment. In discount financing of a loan, the interest is deducted in advance.

DISCOUNTED CASH FLOW The PRESENT VALUE of a future income stream where each cash payment is reduced by a DISCOUNT (INTEREST) amount at a DISCOUNT RATE. The measure weighs dollars received early with more value than those dollars received later. Two common methods are INTERNAL RATE OF RETURN and NET PRESENT VALUE. Also known as PRESENT VALUE ANALYSIS.

DISCOUNT FACTORING   A method of financing (FACTORING) wherein accounts receivable are exchanged for cash and the cash is received prior to the average maturity date of the accounts. The amount of cash received is determined by face value of the receivables less cash discounts, an allowance for estimated claims, returns and carries an interest rate typically two percent to three percent above the bank prime rate based on daily balances. See FACTORING.

DISCOUNTING   In marketing, selling at a lower price than the usual price or the price previously offered.

DISCOUNT POINT   A loan fee that is charged by a lender and is paid up-front in order to make a lower interest rate on the loan. The fee usually covers the administrative cost of making the loan. One discount point is equal to one percent of the loan amount.

DISCOUNT RATE   The INTEREST RATE used to calculate the PRESENT VALUE of a future cash flow stream. Also see NET PRESENT VALUE; CAPITALIZATION RATE.
    In banking, the interest rate charged by the Federal Reserve to member banks for loans made to the banks. This rate provides a floor for establishing the interest rate banks charge to customers.

DISCRETIONARY FUNDS   Money available for investment; money in excess of that required for basic needs; money for unbudgeted items. Money that has no predetermined need at the time it is identified; a decision later will determine the use of the money spent.

DISCRIMINATION   The act of unfavorably treating a particular group or class of people; failure to treat all people equally.

DISINFLATION   A decrease in the rate of inflation (slowing the rate at which prices are rising). Disinflation is often seen in a recession when sales drop and retailers are not always able to pass the higher prices to consumers. See DEFLATION.

DISPLAY   To show a product that is for sale. In an overall sense, a selection and arrangement of products for sale that can be viewed by the public.

DISTRIBUTION   That part of the marketing function involved with getting the product from the factory to the customer.

DIVESTITURE   Required sale of some assets of a company.

DIVIDEND   A proportionate payment of earnings to shareholders for each share of stock in money or equivalent as declared by the Board of Directors.

DIVIDEND CHECK   The money payment of a DIVIDEND in the form of a check.

DIVIDEND YIELD   The annual DIVIDEND paid on a share of stock divided by the price paid for the share.

DIVISION   A grouping of departments in a large business, usually organized along product or functional lines. The act of separating into two or more parts.

DOCK RECEIPT   In exporting, the document (RECEIPT) from the seller or seller's agent at the point of shipment that acknowledges receipt of goods by the transportation company.

DOCUMENT   Paperwork in general, usually with an official significance such as contracts, conveyances and other legal instruments.

DOCUMENTARY DRAFT   A DRAFT to which the appropriate documents are attached, such as title to goods.

DOCUMENTARY LETTER OF CREDIT   A LETTER OF CREDIT for which the issuing bank stipulated that certain documents must accompany the draft.

DOING BUSINESS AS   See DBA.

DOME LEDGER   Standardized forms of bookkeeping that provide a ready-made system for recording transactions.

DOMESTIC   Having to do with the home or housekeeping; of a house or family. Sometimes a shortened form of DOMESTIC EMPLOYEE.

DOMESTIC EMPLOYEE   A person who is hired to perform work or services in the home or for a family, i.e., house cleaning, care for a child or drive a car to run errands. A servant, maid or cook.

DOUBLE-DECLINING-BALANCE DEPRECIATION METHOD (DDB)   One of the methods of ACCELERATED DEPRECIATION permitting twice the annual depreciation write-off as the STRAIGHT-LINE METHOD.

DOUBLE-ENTRY   A system of keeping ACCOUNTING records (BOOKKEEPING) in which every transaction is listed twice (once for source of the transaction and once for disposition). The entries are called DEBIT and CREDIT. This method provides assurance of accuracy and conformity with the underlying accounting equation: ASSETS equal LIABILITIES plus EQUITY.

DOUBLE-ENTRY ACCOUNTING   See DOUBLE-ENTRY.

DOUBLE INDEMNITY   An insurance policy rider that pays double the amount of the face amount of the policy under specific conditions, such as death.

DOUBLE TAXATION   Effect of law whereby dividends are taxed as earnings to a corporation and then taxed again as personal income to the owner (shareholder) when distributed as dividends.

DOWN PAYMENT   The amount of cash paid by a purchaser of a FIXED ASSET at the time of purchase. Down payment includes EARNEST MONEY (a good-faith intention to complete the purchase) previously paid. The terms are not synonymous.

DOWNSIDE RISK   A "worst case" situation of the gradation of risk in which an investor will lose money in a business venture if the venture fails.

DOWNSTREAM   The direction of goods from the producer toward the consumer; the flow of funds from the originator toward the user. The opposite of UPSTREAM.

DO YOUR HOMEWORK   See HOMEWORK.

DRAFT   A signed, unconditional written order prepared by one party (DRAWER) who instructs another party (DRAWEE) to pay a specified sum to a third party (PAYEE). Payee and drawer are often the same party. A draft is called a BILL OF EXCHANGE in foreign transactions. A CLEAN DRAFT is without supporting papers. A DOCUMENTARY DRAFT includes papers or documents attached. A SIGHT DRAFT is payable on demand. A TIME DRAFT is payable either on a definite date or at a fixed time after sight or demand.
    Also to prepare a preliminary document, such as a contract.

DRAFT ON FOREIGN BUYER   An exporter may receive payment by presenting a check written against the buyer's account. The bank will agree to pay the value when it matures or to forward it to the buyer's foreign bank to hold until payment by the buyer.

DRAW   An advance payment of money, such as partial payment (similar to salary) made to a partner from a partnership in anticipation of earnings at the end of the period, or payment to a commissioned salesman in anticipation of the consummation of a sale.

DRAWDOWN   The amount actually borrowed from a total amount available for borrowing, i.e., from a LINE-OF CREDIT.

DRAWEE   See DRAFT.

DRAWER   See DRAFT.

DRAW MONEY   See DRAW.

DRAW-UP   To prepare a preliminary document, such as a contract.

DROP DEAD DATE   The final date when the option being considered is no longer available.

DROPSHIP   Delivery of a product or service to a location other than the ordering location.

DUAL PRICING   Selling identical products in different markets for different prices. May be unethical or illegal.
    In exporting, often a reflection of export subsidies or dumping.

DUAL-SOURCING   Having two suppliers for the same product or service to ensure a continuous supply at a favorable price.

DUE BILL   A document stating a debtors' obligation to a creditor. See also BILL; INVOICE.

DUE DATE   The calendar date agreed upon or planned for an occurrence, like payment on the first of each month.

DUMPING   In international trade, a practice wherein the price of an exported product is less than the cost to produce the product. Dumping is often employed by a country to lock up a market and gain a future monopoly for the product.

DUN & BRADSTREET   A MERCANTILE AGENCY that provides credit information on businesses, including CREDIT RATINGS, CREDIT REPORTS, collection statistics and financial ratios.

DUPLICATE   An exact copy; the process of making an exact copy; to reproduce a copy of a document.

DURABLE POWER OF ATTORNEY   A POWER OF ATTORNEY that goes beyond the death of the person who signed the power, giving certain power to another person.

DUTY   In general, an obligation to perform an act.
   In international trade, a TARIFF on imported goods. See TARIFF; CUSTOMS DUTY.

E

EARLY PAYMENT To provide money (to pay) on a date sooner than the specified date.

EARNED INCOME The amount received for goods or services delivered; income (especially wages and salaries) generated by providing goods and services.

EARNED SURPLUS See RETAINED EARNINGS.

EARNEST MONEY The cash deposit paid by a prospective buyer toward the total purchase price of a FIXED ASSET as evidence of a good-faith intention to complete the transaction. See also BINDER; DOWN PAYMENT; MONEY PUT DOWN.

EARNINGS Profits derived from a business enterprise. See PROFIT.

EARNINGS AFTER TAXES PROFIT available to the owners of the business.

EARNINGS BEFORE TAXES Corporate profits after bondholders' interest has been paid but before taxes have been paid. Same as PROFIT BEFORE TAXES.

EARNINGS CYCLE The elapsed time required to convert raw materials into finished goods, finished goods into sales and receipt of money for goods sold. Since profit (sales less expenses) is built into selling price, the cash conversion cycle is sometimes called the earnings cycle. See CASH CONVERSION CYCLE.

EARNINGS PER SHARE (EPS)   The proportionate amount of a company's profit (EARNINGS) for each outstanding share of common stock.

EARN OUT   A clause in a contract between a large company that is buying the entire business of a small company. The clause may specify the small entrepreneur will realize additional money from the sale if the small company earnings exceed a specified amount after the buyout has occurred.

EBIT   An acronym for EARNINGS Before Interest and Taxes. This calculation is sometimes made by the small business person in order to determine the earnings that would have resulted if the business had been financed entirely by equity without any outstanding loans.

EC   See EUROPEAN COMMUNITY.

ECONOMETRICS   The use of sophisticated analysis and modeling techniques to describe in mathematical terms, the relationship of economic factors such as labor, capital, interest rates and government policy, then the testing of changes in economic scenarios.

ECONOMIC   Of or having to do with the management of income and expenditures in a business; thriftiness.

ECONOMIC FACTORS   The basic elements affecting financial matters such as labor, interest rates, government policy, management and taxation.

ECONOMIC INDICATORS   Key statistics showing the direction of the economy, such as unemployment rate, inflation rate, consumer price index and gross domestic product.

ECONOMIC LIFE   The estimated period of time over which an asset will be used; the period of time used for depreciation. Also called SERVICE LIFE; USEFUL LIFE.

ECONOMIC RESOURCES   See FACTORS OF PRODUCTION.

ECONOMICS   The educational science that studies the system of producing, distributing and consuming wealth and evaluates contributing factors such as labor, finance, management, capital and taxation.

ECONOMIST A professional person who practices the art and science of ECONOMICS.

ECONOMIZE To avoid waste or needless expenditure; to reduce expenditures; to manage in a thrifty manner.

ECONOMY The prudent and careful management of income and expenses by a business to avoid waste.

The overall aggregate financial activity within a governmental unit and the system of producing, distributing and consuming wealth.

ECONOMY OF SCALE Decrease in the long-term average total cost of production due to lower cost per unit for larger quantity produced; the efficiency of producing larger quantities.

EEOC See EQUAL EMPLOYMENT OPPORTUNITY COMMISSION.

EFFECTIVE INTEREST RATE The actual (true) rate or yield of a loan regardless of the value stated in the debt instrument.

8(a) [EIGHT A] See SBA 8(a) PROGRAM.

ELAIN See ELECTRONIC LICENSE APPLICATION INFORMATION NETWORK.

ELASTIC PRICE A situation in the marketplace where a change in price will cause a change in DEMAND. As opposed to INELASTIC PRICE. See PRICE ELASTICITY.

ELECTRONIC BANKING The use of computers, wires and telephone lines (electronic equipment) to perform transactions with a bank or with others through a bank. Thus electronic banking avoids using checks and currency.

ELECTRONIC LICENSE APPLICATION INFORMATION NETWORK (ELAIN) A U.S. Department of Commerce, Bureau of Export Administration, computer-based system that allows on-line acceptance of export license applications for most overseas destinations.

ELECTRONIC MAILBOX   The address on a computer network where people pick up messages sent by other computer users.

ELECTRONIC RETAILING   Use of interactive computer technology to present a sales message and consummate the sale.

E-MAIL   Short for Electronic Mail, a means of communicating through computers.

EMBARGO   In international trade, a restriction or prohibition on exported or imported products.

EMBEZZLE   To steal or take the property of another for one's own use; particularly, a business theft by an employee. Often, it is the trusted employee who is discovered to be stealing (embezzling). The following three ways protect a business from theft (embezzlement): 1) select with care the people who are the best risk, 2) set up business procedures that make the practice difficult and 3) purchase insurance or bonding against a loss that may occur. Use all three, not just one or two.

EMPLOYEE   A person who does work for an employer under a verbal or written understanding where the employer gives direction as to what jobs are done, when jobs are done and, to some degree, how jobs are done. Care must be taken not to classify employees as INDEPENDENT CONTRACTORS. To the small business firm, the result may be crucial because withholding is required of employees but not for independent contractors. See INDEPENDENT CONTRACTOR.

EMPLOYEE BENEFITS   Things like health care insurance that are paid in part or in full by a company and not considered part of the employee's salary or wages; free to the employees and paid by the company.

EMPLOYEE LEASING   A personnel management scheme whereby an Employee Leasing Firm hires the employee and pays the wages, withholding and benefits. Then the employee is leased to a small business under contract. Benefits to the small business include lower personnel costs, better employee benefits, avoidance of most employee reporting, less paperwork and reduced employer liability.

EMPLOYEE LEASING FIRM   A business established for the sole purpose of providing employees to other businesses. See EMPLOYEE LEASING.

EMPLOYER   A person or company that engages other people (EMPLOYEES) to perform work under a verbal or written agreement.

EMPLOYER'S TAX GUIDE   A publication by the U.S. government (and some states) that explains basic information concerning employment and employee-related taxes. This publication is especially helpful to the small business person and is free. Also called CIRCULAR E.

EMPLOYMENT RATE   The numerical value of employed persons as a percent of the TOTAL WORKFORCE.

ENDING BALANCE   The amount on hand at the end of a period as a result of operations during the period.

ENDORSE   To sign one's name on the back of a document, such as a check; a signature on the back of an ownership document, such as a title for an asset. A signature on the back of an ownership document that transfers ownership of the asset to another party. Also, a recommendation or affirmation from a celebrity endorsing a product or service.

ENDORSEMENT   The act of signing one's name or evidence of the signature, thus transferring title of a negotiable instrument.

ENDORSER   The person who signed his or her name; the individual to whom the signature belongs.

END USER   The customer; the consumer.

ENTERPRISE   A business firm; most often a newly-formed venture.

Also in business, to show creativity, innovation or originality in a new concept or idea.

ENTERPRISE CENTER   Same as ENTERPRISE ZONE, except perhaps smaller, such as in a building.

ENTERPRISE ZONE   A geographical area, building or location established by a government for the encouragement of start-up businesses, often with free or reduced prices for services (lower rent, shared meeting rooms, office equipment or secretarial service) to permit the business to get started more easily.

ENTITY   For business definition, see LEGAL ENTITY.

ENTREPRENEUR   A person who undertakes the risks of starting a new business. Most often involves a new product or new service. Usually carries the connotation of creativity, vision, self-starting or venturesome. The founder of a business.

ENTREPRENEURIAL SHOCK   The psychological realization by a start-up business person that the "work-for-yourself" idea is accompanied by difficult decisions and disappointments. Entrepreneurial shock often occurs when a start-up business person has worked in the corporate environment and was not exposed to all the complications of operating a business.

EPS   See EARNINGS PER SHARE.

EQUAL CREDIT OPPORTUNITY ACT   Federal legislation passed in the mid-1970s prohibiting discrimination in granting CREDIT, based on race religion, sex, ethnic background, or whether a person is receiving public assistance or alimony. The FEDERAL TRADE COMMISSION enforces the act.

EQUAL EMPLOYMENT OPPORTUNITY COMMISSION (EEOC)
An agency of the federal government established to ensure fair employment practices and prevent discrimination because of race, religion, sex, ethnic background or disability.

EQUILIBRIUM PRICE   A term used in analytical economics to define the quantity at which the price of a supply of goods matches the demand price in a specific market or for a specific product or service. Thus it is the market price at which sales occur. For a manufacturer, the price that maximizes a product's profitability.

EQUIPMENT   Physical goods used in a business, such as machinery or furniture. Equipment is used in a business during the production of income. As opposed to real estate, material or supplies. In accounting, equipment is treated as PERSONAL PROPERTY.

EQUIPMENT EXPENSE   Money paid for the acquisition, installation operation and maintenance of personal property (equipment) used in the production of income. Sometimes an allowance for the depreciation of equipment that is shown on an Income Statement.

EQUITY   In business, the owner's investment in the business; the amount owned by the owners; the owner's interest or value remaining after payment of all debts and charges.

In a start-up business, the amount of money provided by the owner at the outset; often in conjunction with the amount borrowed as a loan. Normally, with greater owner's equity, the business is more stable. Same as NET WORTH in a business.

In banking, the difference between the amount received from the sale of assets and the claims against the assets. Also an estimate of this difference prior to sale.

In investment, ownership interest possessed by common and preferred shareholders in a corporation—stock ownership as opposed to bonds and loans that are liabilities.

In general, fairness. For example, law courts try to be equitable in their judgment when splitting up corporations or estates.

EQUITY BUILD-UP   Adding to the amount of ownership interest in a business (EQUITY or NET WORTH) by accumulation of retained earnings.

In the financing of real property, the gradual reduction of outstanding principal due on a mortgage that results in an increase in the ownership amount, usually through periodic payments, which decrease the amount of the loan.

EQUITY CAPITAL   The initial investment in a start-up business; money invested in a business by the owner. As opposed to money loaned to the business (BORROWED CAPITAL). See EQUITY; CAPITAL.

EQUITY FINANCING   In a corporation, raising money by issuing and selling shares of common or preferred stock or taking on a partner in a partnership, as opposed to incurring debt or borrowing (DEBT FINANCING). Obtaining needed additional money to operate or expand a business by surrendering part of the ownership of the business in exchange for the invested capital. Small businesses must exercise care in obtaining money in this manner because control of the business could be lost, or earnings may be reduced (diluted) by payments to the other owners.

EQUITY TURNOVER   See CAPITAL TURNOVER.

EQUIVALENT UNITS OF PRODUCTION   A measure of the number of production units being manufactured including completed units and partially manufactured units. Partial units are stated proportionally in terms of completed units; for example, 1000 half completed units would be stated as 500 equivalent fully completed units.

ERISA   Employee Retirement Income Security Act enacted to safeguard "the interest of participants in employee benefit plans and their beneficiaries . . . by establishing standards of conduct, responsibility and obligations" for fiduciaries of such plans.

ERRORS AND OMISSIONS INSURANCE   A form of INSURANCE that covers liability for mistakes, negligence or errors, as well as unintentional things left out, judgmental omissions or other factors. However, it does not cover fraudulent behavior. This type of insurance can be purchased by businesses engaged in buying and selling activities involving contracts.

ESCALATOR CLAUSE   A statement in a contract that provides for increasing one amount in proportion to a change in another amount. For example, in a labor contract, wage rates of employees may be periodically increased to keep pace with the rising cost of living.

ESCROW   Money set aside or deposited with a neutral third party that is to be used later for a specific purpose.

ESOP   Employee Stock Ownership Plan, which gives to an employee shares of stock in the company as a deferred compensation benefit.

ESTATE TAX   A tax by a government on the value of property transferred at death.

ESTIMATE   To calculate in advance the value or cost of producing a product or performing a service, based on a description, performance requirements and assumptions. Also, the document stating the amount of such calculations.
   In business this often means the same as a BID.

ESTIMATED TAX   A preliminary accounting approximation (ESTIMATE) of taxes due during a period of time. May be required by law to make partial payments toward the total amount due at the end of the accounting period.

ET AL.   A Latin abbreviation adopted into English meaning "and others."

ETHICS   Moral standards or codes of conduct.

ETHNIC GROUP   People belonging to the same race having a common heritage of language, culture and customs. See DISCRIMINATION.

EUROPEAN COMMUNITY   The alliance formed by several European countries to minimize the business and economic barriers between the countries, thus permitting freedom of people movement and freedom to conduct business across country borders.

EXCHANGE RATE   The price at which the money of one country is converted into the money of another country.

EXCISE TAX   A federal or state tax on the sale or manufacture of a commodity, usually a luxury item. Examples: alcohol and tobacco.

EXCLUSIVE AGREEMENT   An agreement between two parties (businesses) that restrict purchase, sale or use of competing products such as the geographical territory each party may control for a specific business interest.

EXECUTE   To make a document legally valid, such as by signing a contract or acknowledging receipt of an order.

EXECUTIVE   A top-level member of the management team of a company; one with the title of PRESIDENT, VICE-PRESIDENT, SECRETARY or TREASURER.

EXECUTIVE SUMMARY   A brief synopsis of a document that highlights the important facts, issues and conclusions. The executive summary usually precedes the body of the document.

EXEMPTION   A subtraction from income allowed by the IRS in computing the income that is taxable.

EXHIBIT   A display; a trade show where a public offering by many companies and products in one location attracts a large potential base of customers.

EXIMBANK   See EXPORT-IMPORT BANK.

EXISTING BUSINESS   A business that is not a start-up, often used when purchasing the business of another. Also, the product line of business currently engaged in.

EXPANSION   An increase in the capacity of a business, such as more operating space, additional inventory or new product line.

EXPENDITURE   Money paid out for purchase of goods or services.

EXPENDITURE FORECAST   An estimate of future EXPENDITURES; planning for the times when bills are due to be paid; a written plan of expenses.

EXPENSE   Money paid out or identified for payment at a future date. Financial costs of material purchases, wages paid, fees and charges. Also a cause of spending; a drain on business finances. Money paid out for the purchase of goods or services.

EXPENSE BUDGET   An estimate of money to be paid out in a future period. See BUDGET; EXPENSE.

EXPENSE RATE   A measure of efficiency in a business, especially measuring the efficiency of operating expenses (overhead) in relation to sales; divide operating expenses by gross sales and express as a percent. When comparing similar periods, it shows trends of increasing or decreasing overhead expenses.

EXPENSE REPORT   A document that records the money paid to an employee for incidental items and the cost of travel or trips while conducting business.

EXPENSES   An accounting term for the sum of all money paid out for goods and services during a given period of time; they are the cost of goods and services used up in the process of obtaining revenue. They are sometimes referred to as "the cost of doing business" Expenses deducted from INCOME result in a PROFIT or LOSS for the business during a given period. See INCOME STATEMENT.

Sometimes used interchangeably with the portion of overall expenses entitled OPERATING EXPENSES (OVERHEAD), especially when determining percentage relationships to sales.

EXPENSE STATEMENT   An accounting presentation of the money paid out over a period or a forecast of the money to be paid out in a future period.

EXPIRED POLICY   An INSURANCE POLICY (or other business policy) that no longer is in force, one on which the term has concluded or a policy that has been canceled.

EXPORT   To sell products or services for delivery to a customer in another country. Opposite of IMPORT.

EXPORT BROKER   A person or company that brings together, for a fee, buyers and sellers from different countries but does not take part in actual overseas sales transactions.

EXPORT DECLARATION   A federal government document listing products or services that have been sold and delivered to another country.

EXPORT DOCUMENTS   Of the many export documents that may be used, the ten most commonly used are ocean bill of lading, delivery instructions, letter of credit, commercial invoice, insurance certificate, dock receipt, export declaration, consular invoice, certificate of origin and transmittal letter. Each of these documents is defined in this dictionary.

EXPORTER   A company that sells and delivers goods to a destination in a foreign country. See EXPORT.

EXPORT-IMPORT BANK (EXIMBANK)   A U.S. government-sponsored bank that provides loans to finance exports by companies unlikely to find a commercial lender for the products to be exported. Eximbank also guarantees commercial loans to exporters, with loan rates below current market rates.

EXPORTING SERVICE COMPANY   A company that provides some type of EXPORT consulting services.

EXPORT LICENSE   A U.S. government document, required for all exporters that permits the LICENSEE to engage in the EXPORT of designated goods to certain approved destinations.

EXPORT MANAGEMENT COMPANY   A private company that serves as the EXPORT department for several manufacturers, soliciting and transacting export business on behalf of its clients in return for a retainer, salary or commission. See also EXPORT TRADING COMPANY.

EXPORT QUOTA   A restraint by the U.S. government on the quantity of an item that may be exported. See also EXPORT RESTRAINT.

EXPORT RESTRAINT   A restriction by the U.S. government on exports to a specific country. See also EXPORT QUOTA.

EXPORT SUBSIDY   Any form of government payment or benefit that is given to an exporter or producer contingent upon the export of goods.

EXPORT TRADING COMPANY   A private company that provides EXPORT services for manufacturers. It provides more services than an EXPORT MANAGEMENT COMPANY including taking title of goods.

EXPOSURE   In finance, the maximum amount of financial liability attributable to an incident; the greatest amount of loss following a specific event.

In marketing, the number of people who will potentially be able to see or hear the advertisement.

EXTENDED COVERAGE   In insurance, additional financial protection for hazards not covered by the basic policy.

EXTERNAL AUDIT   A detailed financial review of the books of a company by an independent auditor, accountant or CPA.

EXTERNAL SOURCES OF WORKING CAPITAL   See WORKING CAPITAL.

EXTRADE   To sell goods or services for delivery to a customer in another city, county or state in exchange for money; i.e., to sell to a customer that is located in a government entity different from the home government entity. Similar to EXPORT but within a single country. Also, the outward movement of such goods or services from a city, county or state. By selling outside the seller's locality, money is brought into the seller's locality in exchange for the goods or services that were delivered. The influx of these monies causes an economic expansion of the entire seller's locality that is several times greater than the amount brought in due to the economics of scale. Opposite of INTRADE.

F

FACE VALUE The amount printed on a security, such as the amount printed on paper currency, a stock certificate, bond or a mortgage. It is the nominal value. In some situations, face value is also called PAR VALUE.

FACSIMILE See the abbreviated common usage term FAX.

FACTOR A firm that purchases accounts receivable in exchange for cash in a factoring transaction. See FACTORING.

In estimating, a standard or accepted common numerical value or relationship that is used to develop an ESTIMATE.

FACTORING A method of obtaining cash through the sale of accounts receivable or transfer of title of accounts receivable. The amount of cash received is usually less than the value of the accounts receivable on the company books, allowing for payment to the FACTOR. In this method of financing, the purchaser, often a FACTORING COMPANY, becomes the principal (not an agent) for collection of the amounts due. The receivables are sold without recourse, meaning if the receivables are not collectible, the FACTOR cannot go back to the seller for reimbursement or file suit. In NOTIFICATION BASIS FACTORING, the seller's customers remit directly to the factor. In NON-NOTIFICATION BASIS FACTORING, the seller handles the collections and remits the funds to the factor. See also DISCOUNT FACTORING; MATURITY FACTORING.

FACTORING COMPANY A firm that specializes in financing of accounts receivable for other companies for a fee. See FACTORING; ACCEPTANCE COMPANY.

FACTORING HOUSE   See FACTORING COMPANY.

FACTORS OF PRODUCTION   An economist's term for the key elements contributing to production; namely, land, labor, capital and management. Also called economic resources.

FACTORY   A manufacturing plant; a place where goods (products) are produced or manufactured. At a factory, raw materials or parts are purchased and converted into a new product (finished goods) through the application of labor (work).

FACTORY PRICE   The price charged for items on the first sale after producing them at the manufacturing plant.

FAILURE   For a business, failure is the same as BANKRUPTCY; a business that ceases to operate.

FAILURE RATIO   Of a given total of small businesses that begin operations, the percent that cannot survive; the percent that out of business because they could not make a profit. Opposite of SUCCESS RATIO.

FAIR MARKET VALUE   The most probable selling price of an item if offered for a reasonable period of time in a competitive market under average conditions.

FAIR RETURN   In small business management or when investing in a small business, a RETURN ON INVESTMENT comparable and competitive with other investments. For instance, if more can be earned by depositing an investment into a savings account, a person shouldn't waste his or her time struggling with the problems of owning a small business.

In product pricing, the price of an article as determined by the intersection of the AVERAGE TOTAL COST CURVE with the DEMAND CURVE.

FALSE ADVERTISING   Advertising that contains blatantly false or misleading information.

FAMILY BUSINESS   A business owned and controlled by the members of a single family.

FASB See FINANCIAL ACCOUNTING STANDARDS BOARD; a private organization that sets the public accounting rules and practices for American businesses.

FAX A means of transmitting written information by telephone. At the origin (sender), the written paper is electronically copied, then transmitted by wire and decoded onto a piece of paper at the receiving end. Thus the received copy is an exact reproduction of the original. Short for FACSIMILE.

FDIC See FEDERAL DEPOSIT INSURANCE CORPORATION.

FEASIBILITY STUDY An analysis of a potential business op-portunity with emphasis on attainable income, probable expenses and recommendations for the most advantageous marketing ap-proach.

FEATHERBEDDING A practice of requiring an employer to hire more workers than are necessary for the work to be done; con-tinuing to employ workers for jobs that are obsolete.

FED See FEDERAL RESERVE SYSTEM.

FEDERAL Relating to the government of the United States of America. As opposed to STATE, LOCAL or foreign government.

FEDERAL DEPOSIT INSURANCE CORPORATION (FDIC) A federal agency that guarantees (with limits) funds on deposit by member banks and the banks' depositors and assists with bank-ing regulation enforcement for monetary stability.

FEDERAL INSURANCE CONTRIBUTIONS ACT (FICA) A fed-eral government program (law) wherein mandatory contributions are made by employees for old age and survivor financial assis-tance. Also know as SOCIAL SECURITY.

FEDERAL RESERVE SYSTEM An agency established in 1913 to regulate the monetary and banking system of the United States that regulates money supply, supervises the printing of money at the mint, acts as a clearing-house for transactions among banks, sets reserve requirements for member banks and examines member banks' financial records to ensure they meet reserve requirements. Common nickname is "the Fed."

FEDERAL SAVINGS AND LOAN ASSOCIATION   A federally chartered institution with a primary responsibility to accept people's savings deposits and provide mortgage loans for residential housing.

FEDERAL SAVINGS AND LOAN INSURANCE CORPORATION (FSLIC)   A federal agency established in 1934 to insure deposits in member savings institutions.

FEDERAL TAXES   Any of the many types of taxes paid to the U.S. government.

FEDERAL TAX IDENTIFICATION NUMBER; FEDERAL TAX I.D. NUMBER   The number assigned by the Internal Revenue Service to a corporation or a partnership and used for recordkeeping purposes.

FEDERAL TRADE COMMISSION (FTC)   A federal agency established in 1914 to foster free and fair business competition and prevent monopolies and activities in restraint of trade. The FTC administers both antitrust and consumer protection legislation.

FEEDER INDUSTRIES   Small industrial companies that provide parts or services to a major manufacturer.

FICA   See FEDERAL INSURANCE CONTRIBUTIONS ACT.

FICTITIOUS NAME   In business, a name other than the name of the person under which the business is registered. Most state laws require obtaining a fictitious name certificate or a trade name registration. Mandatory for a sole proprietorship if doing business in a name other than that of the owner. The certificate does not give exclusive use of the name to the certificate holder. A fictitious name is registered with the Secretary of State in the state in which business will be transacted and includes the address of the business as well as the names and addresses of the owners.

FIDELITY BOND   Insurance that covers employees who handle money, are entrusted with negotiable securities or are responsible for valuable assets. Such bonded persons are required by the bonding insurance company to carry out their duties and responsibilities effectively and honestly. Also called a SURETY BOND.

FIDUCIARY   A relationship that implies a position of trust or confidence wherein one person is usually entrusted to hold or manage property or money for another.

FIFO   See FIRST-IN, FIRST-OUT.

FILE   To store a document in an orderly manner to permit ease of retrieval at a future time; a cabinet for document storage.
    To place an original document on public record, such as a legal document. To submit a tax return for payment of taxes.

FILE 13   The waste basket; the trash can.

FINANCE   To obtain money, credit or capital for a business; also to supply money, credit or capital for a business; the money resources of a business; the managing of money. Also, a field of study at a University concerning the science of money management, credit, cash flow and similar subjects.

FINANCE CHARGE   The total of all costs in making a loan as imposed by a creditor and payable by the borrower; the cost of credit.

FINANCE COMPANY   A company engaged in making loans to individuals or businesses. Unlike a bank, a finance company does not receive deposits; it obtains financing from banks and other sources. Three general categories are: 1) CONSUMER FINANCE COMPANIES that make small loans directly to individuals; 2) sales finance companies (also an ACCEPTANCE COMPANY) that purchase consumer loans (PAPER) from others; 3) commercial finance companies (a COMMERCIAL CREDIT COMPANY) that make loans to other businesses. Businesses that do not qualify for bank credit often can obtain a loan from a COMMERCIAL FINANCE COMPANY. Businesses can make loans to customers and sell the loans to an ACCEPTANCE COMPANY.

FINANCE FEE   When making a loan, the amount charged by the lender for costs incurred in making the loan; a loan origination fee; a mortgage service charge.

FINANCIAL   Those matters of a company that relate to money. Transactions of the business affecting the FINANCIAL CONDITION of the business.

FINANCIAL ACCOUNTING   The process of financial recordkeeping, data collection, financial statement preparation and analysis for use by business owners, managers, creditors and the government.

FINANCIAL ACCOUNTING STANDARDS BOARD (FASB)   An independent self-regulatory organization responsible for establishing and interpreting GENERALLY ACCEPTED ACCOUNTING PRINCIPLES.

FINANCIAL ANALYSIS   The evaluation of accounting (financial) data and interpretation of the results to determine the company's financial condition and performance.

FINANCIAL CONDITION   The stated financial solvency of a person or business; a personal NET WORTH statement; the value of money and property owed compared to the value of money and property owned.

FINANCIAL DATA   Information relating to the financial affairs of a business.

FINANCIAL INSTITUTION   Organizations that obtain money through deposits then lend the money to earn an income, such as a bank.

FINANCIAL LIABILITY   Being responsible for paying debts or obligations of a business, even under severe adverse financial circumstances. See also LIABILITY; FINANCIAL.

FINANCIAL PLAN   A document that describes a business owner's expectations about money income and outgo for a period in the future and the expected future financial results.

FINANCIAL RATIOS   Measures developed for planning and control that focus on key relationships between different classifications of accounting data such as liquidity, profitability and performance. Small businesses use these ratios to compare different time periods, projects or their business to similar businesses in the same industry.

FINANCIAL STATEMENT A written document describing the NET WORTH, EARNINGS or other monetary relationship of a person, or business; a record of financial information and financial status. The most common of the many types of financial statements are the BALANCE SHEET, the INCOME STATEMENT and the CASH FLOW STATEMENT.

FINANCIAL STRUCTURE The composition of the right side of a BALANCE SHEET, including CURRENT LIABILITIES, LONG-TERM DEBT AND EQUITY. It is distinguished from CAPITAL STRUCTURE, which includes only long-term debt and equity.

FINANCING The process of obtaining equity or borrowing money for a start-up business. Also refers to the money to be borrowed; a loan; a note.

FINANCING STATEMENT A document filed to establish a creditor's security interest in personal property (required by the Universal Commercial Code, form UCC-1); evidence of personal property as security for a debt.

FINISHED GOODS In a manufacturing company, those products that have completed the production process and are available for delivery (sale).

FINISHED GOODS INVENTORY An accounting of FINISHED GOODS.

FIRE; TO FIRE; BE FIRED The situation of an employee who is discharged for poor performance or an infraction of company rules. As compared with LAID OFF.

FIRE INSURANCE INSURANCE coverage for risk of loss due to a fire, usually for real property and personal property.

FIRM A general business noun describing a COMPANY and applies to all forms of business organization (corporation, partnership or proprietorship). See also COMPANY.

Also means steady or unyielding; solidity with which an agreement is made or understanding has been achieved; assurance of completion of the agreement or understanding; not subject to negotiation, as in a FIRM AGREEMENT.

Used as a verb in business means an agreement that is solid and not subject to negotiation; a legally binding commitment.

FIRM AGREEMENT   An AGREEMENT that carries the force of unyielding conditions; an understanding between two or more parties whether verbal or written, as in a contract that is not subject to negotiation. See AGREEMENT.

FIRM COMMITMENT   In lending, a written confirmation of a loan, whereby a lender will make a loan to a borrower with specific conditions such as loan amount, time period, interest rate and collateral. The firm commitment provides information to the borrower to allow processing of other activities while awaiting preparation and execution of the loan document.

FIRM ORDER   A confirmed written or verbal ORDER not subject to cancellation.

FIRM PRICE   An amount specified in an offer to sell that is not negotiable. As opposed to ASKING PRICE that is subject to negotiation before reaching final agreement on the price at which the transaction occurs.

FIRM QUOTE   An offer to sell products or services at a stated price. The seller will not negotiate a lower price; the seller will not sell for less than the quoted price or later ask a higher price. The final price of an offer that the seller is not willing to change.

FIRST-IN, FIRST-OUT (FIFO)   A method of accounting for inventory whereby the material is assumed to be sold in the chronological order in which it was received. Items purchased first are assumed to be sold before items purchased at a later date. See also LAST-IN, FIRST-OUT.

FIRST MORTGAGE   The senior loan on real estate; the mortgage recorded first. In case of default, the first mortgage holder would be paid before payment to any other creditor secured on the property, such as a SECOND MORTGAGE.

FIRST STAGE In VENTURE CAPITAL, the initial financing of a start-up business or a new venture. See SEED MONEY.

FIRST STOP SHOP An office established by many state governments and other agencies that provide a complete package of information for the start-up business person, including counseling, handout literature and important contacts needed for establishing a business.

FISCAL YEAR (FY) A 12-month accounting period of business operations beginning at any date, usually starting and ending on a different day from a calendar year (January 1st). Fiscal year is used for accounting, corporate management and taxing purposes. As an example, the fiscal year of the U.S. government begins October 1st. Sometimes a fiscal year contains 13 periods of four weeks' duration or other subdivision of a year.

5 Cs; 5 Cs OF CREDIT; 5Cs OF LENDING A judgment method of evaluating a borrower's creditworthiness; Character, Capacity, Capital, Collateral and Conditions.

503 LOAN; 503 LOAN PROGRAM See SBA 503 LOAN.

504 LOAN; 504 LOAN PROGRAM See SBA 504 LOAN.

FIXED ASSET An accounting term that describes tangible property, used in the operation of a business such as buildings, machinery, fixtures, furniture and equipment. But fixed assets do not include items normally consumed in the course of business operation or production.

FIXED COST Any cost that occurs as time passes regardless of the volume of production or sales, such as rent, real estate taxes, insurance, office staff or interest. Such an expense does not vary with volume of sales or production. As opposed to VARIABLE COST.

FIXED EXPENSES See FIXED COST.

FIXED INCOME An income that is received on a regular periodic basis and is in a constant amount, such as a retainer which is paid on an open account. As opposed to VARIABLE INCOME, which depends on the amount of products or services sold during the period.

FIXTURE   An article used in business to facilitate the buying or selling process, such as counters or racks.

FLEXTIME   Variable working hours that can be chosen by an employee to fit his or her personal preference.

FLOAT   In banking, the time between the issuing of a check and payment of the check by the bank. In general, the farther away the paying bank is from the deposit bank, the longer it will take for the check to clear. During this period the writer collects interest or has access to the funds.

In lending, to make a loan; to extend credit to a borrower.

FLOOR PLAN   A loan using merchandise that is on display as collateral, such as automobiles on the display room floor.

FLOOR PLAN INSURANCE   Coverage by an insurance company for the merchandise that is on display (the display room floor). Usually, coverage is for the lender in the amount of the loan. Example, insurance coverage for automobiles in the dealer's showroom.

FLOOR SPACE   Within a building, the area available to the business for operation of the business.

FLOW   A quantity per unit of time, such as a production rate per day. Also, the general trend of cash movement.

FLOWCHART   A process planning tool used to symbolically represent the steps involved in a program, process or production.

F.O.B.; f.o.b.   An abbreviation for "Free On Board"; the FACTORY PRICE of products (goods) at the point of shipment from the factory. More specifically, title is transferred from the seller to the buyer at the point of shipment. The transportation company is an agent of the buyer, and shipping charges are borne by the buyer. The definition varies in some situations, such as in exporting.

FOOT   An accounting term meaning to add a column of numbers downward on a page; thus the answer is at the foot of the page.

FORECAST   To estimate or calculate expected business results in advance. To plan the business course for the future. A document that sets down the plan. See BUSINESS PLAN; BUDGET.

FORECASTING   The process of making (beforehand) a FORE-CAST, plan, estimate or prediction of future events.

FOREIGN TRADE ZONE (FTZ)   A location where imported goods may be kept for a limited period of time, free of duty, until shipped to an American destination.

FORFEITURE   The loss of a right to something as a result of nonperformance of an obligation or condition.

FORGERY   The illegal act of making a false signature or counter-feiting documents.

FORM   A printed document with blank spaces to be filled in.

FORM OF BUSINESS   See BUSINESS STRUCTURE.

FORM 940 & 941   The federal government document used to report withholding taxes.

FORM 720   The federal government document used to report manufacturer's and retailer's excise taxes.

FORM 1040   The federal government document used to report income tax due for a person. See INDIVIDUAL INCOME TAX RETURN.

FORM 1099   The federal government document used to report income paid (more than $600) to a person or an independent contractor for work done, as opposed to FORM W-2 for reporting wages of employees. See INFORMATIONAL RETURN.

FORM 1120   The federal government document used to report income tax that must be paid by a corporation. Several variations of the form exist for the various corporate structures. See CORPO-RATE INCOME TAX RETURN.

FORM 1165   The federal government document used to report earnings (INCOME) for a partnership. See INFORMATIONAL RETURN.

FORM K-1   The federal government document used to report the proportionate share of partnership earnings to each person who participates in the partnership. See INFORMATIONAL RETURN.

FORM SE   The federal government document used to report earnings from a sole proprietorship (a self-employed person).

FORM UCC-1   A FINANCING STATEMENT document required by the Uniform Commercial Code.

FORM W-2   The federal government document used to report the amount of wages paid to an employee during a calendar year.

FOUR A   The American Association of Advertising Agencies; a trade association for advertisers that advises its members on topics such as ethics, fairness in advertising and other matters.

401(k) PLAN   A tax provision that encourages company-sponsored investment programs on which tax is deferred; often the employee contribution is accompanied by an employer contribution for the benefit of the employee.

FRANCHISE   The right under which a person or company (FRANCHISEE) may market a product or provide a service, as granted by the proprietary owner (FRANCHISOR). The contract, defining the terms and conditions, between franchisor and franchisee is called a FRANCHISE AGREEMENT. Often a franchise is exclusive for a specified area.

FRANCHISE AGREEMENT   See FRANCHISE.

FRANCHISEE   See FRANCHISE.

FRANCHISE OPERATION   Conducting business as a franchisee or the total overall sense of being identified with doing business as a franchisee, as opposed to independent. See FRANCHISE.

FRANCHISOR   See FRANCHISE.

FRANCHISE TAX   By state law, amounts paid to a state for operation of a business under a FRANCHISE AGREEMENT.

FRAUD   Any form of deceit, trickery, breach of condition or misrepresentation by which one party attempts to gain some unfair or dishonest advantage over another. Unlike negligence, fraud is a deceitful practice or a misstatement of a material fact.

FREEBIE   Something given free of charge by a business to attract or retain customers, such as a trinket or knick-knack.

FREE ENTERPRISE; FREE ENTERPRISE SYSTEM; FREE EN-TERPRISE ECONOMY   See CAPITALISM.

FREE ON BOARD (F.O.B.)   See F.O.B.

FREE TRADE   An agreement between two or more countries that promotes business by removing tax barriers; thus stimulating companies to conduct business in each other's country.

FREE TRADE ZONE   A designated and secured area, legally outside of a country's customs territory, where a trader may store, repack, manufacture or sell goods without paying customs duties or internal revenue taxes unless the product is moved to a customs territory.

FREIGHT BILL   See BILL OF LADING. Also, the document specifying the cost of transporting goods and requesting payment.

FREIGHT FORWARDER   A service company that handles, for a manufacturer, all the transactions and documents needed for shipment of goods.

FREIGHT OUT   Shipping expenses for delivery of merchandise to the customer. Freight out is usually included in the price of the merchandise and is therefore passed on to the customer.

FREQUENCY   The average number of times an event occurs or an activity is repeated.
   In advertising, the average number of times an audience is exposed to an advertisement during a given period of time.

FRINGE BENEFITS   See EMPLOYEE BENEFITS.

FRINGES   See EMPLOYEE BENEFITS.

FRONT END   The beginning of an activity, such as marketing in a business, as opposed to product manufacture and delivery.

FRONT-END LOADED   Better terms at the outset of a deal than in a later phase, used as an inducement to buy; an up-front charge.

FRONT MONEY   The initial payment on a deal, usually a large purchase; in venture capitalism it is called SEED MONEY.

FSLIC   See FEDERAL SAVINGS AND LOAN INSURANCE CORPORATION.

FTC   See FEDERAL TRADE COMMISSION.

FTZ   See FOREIGN TRADE ZONE.

FULFILLMENT OF CONTRACT   See CONTRACT COMPLETION.

FULL POWER OF ATTORNEY   A POWER OF ATTORNEY that bestows total power of the signer to another person.

FUTURE VALUE   The worth, at some later date, of an investment made today, including the amount of interest that could be earned at an appropriate COMPOUND INTEREST RATE. That is, the future worth (FUTURE VALUE) is equal to the present worth (PRESENT VALUE) plus the amount of accumulated interest that would be earned. Also applies to a stream of future payments with the interest amount calculated for each payment. See also PRESENT VALUE; INTERNAL RATE OF RETURN; TIME VALUE OF MONEY; INWOOD TABLE.

FV   See FUTURE VALUE.

FY   See FISCAL YEAR.

G

GAAP   See GENERALLY ACCEPTED ACCOUNTING PRIN-CIPLES.

GAIN   An increase in value; the profit received upon the sale of an asset.

G&A   An acronym for General and Administrative expenses, an alternate expression for some OVERHEAD expenses, often used in businesses dealing with governments.

GARNISHMENT   The legal means for a creditor to obtain the rights to a debtor's personal property that is in the hands of a third party (the garnishee), thereby returning to the creditor that which is owed.

GATT   See GENERAL AGREEMENT ON TARIFFS AND TRADE.

GDP   See GROSS DOMESTIC PRODUCT.

GENERAL AGREEMENT ON TARIFFS AND TRADE (GATT)   A treaty among most countries of the world that provides a forum for negotiating mutual reductions in trade restrictions.

GENERAL CONTRACTOR   A construction or other type of company that enters into contracts for the performance of work and hires employees and subcontractors to accomplish the work. In several layers of contracting relationships, the general contractor is at the top, totally responsible for all work performance to the customer. Also called a PRIME CONTRACTOR.

GENERAL JOURNAL   In a small business, the only JOURNAL that records the transactions of the business; a record of accounting transactions in chronological order. See JOURNAL.

GENERAL LEDGER   The formal listing of accounts (LEDGER) containing all the financial statement accounts of a business and, thus, comprising the TRIAL BALANCE. CONTROL ACCOUNTS summarize the entries made in the separate SUBSIDIARY LEDGER accounts.

GENERAL LIEN   The right of a creditor to have all the debtor's property sold to satisfy a debt. Unlike a specific lien against certain property, a general lien is directed against the individual debtor and attaches to all his or her property.

GENERALLY ACCEPTED ACCOUNTING PRINCIPLES (GAAP) The conventions, rules and procedures defined by the FINANCIAL ACCOUNTING STANDARDS BOARD (FASB) as proper accounting practices.

GENERAL PARTNER   A person or firm that agrees to share ownership of a business with full personal liability for the debts of the business; one of two or more partners who are jointly and severally responsible for the operation of the partnership including the debts of a PARTNERSHIP. The general partner's liability is unlimited.

GENERAL PARTNERSHIP   An association of two or more people or firms that carry on a business for profit. See PARTNERSHIP.

GIVEAWAY   Something given free or sold cheaply to attract customers.

GLOBAL MARKETING   Selling the same product in the same way everywhere in the world. As opposed to INTERNATIONAL MARKETING that tailors a product and the marketing program to fit the country where sales are anticipated. Sometimes the two terms are used interchangeably.

GNP   See GROSS NATIONAL PRODUCT. For most uses, GNP has been replaced by GDP, GROSS DOMESTIC PRODUCT.

GOAL   In business, a predetermined objective to be achieved. For ease of determining success, goals must be quantifiable so that achievement can be compared later.

GOING PUBLIC   A securities industry phrase used when a private company first offers its shares of stock for sale to the public. The firm's ownership thus shifts from a few private shareholders to a base which includes stock offerings for everyone. At the moment of going public, the stock is called an INITIAL PUBLIC OFFERING.

GOOD CREDIT RATING   An excellent record of paying loans, notes, accounts payable or other obligations; credit worthy; trust by a lender for extending credit. See CREDIT RATING.

GOODS   PRODUCTS or MERCHANDISE that are available for sale.

GOODS AND SERVICES   The total line of a business in terms of products (merchandise) and labor provided to customers.

GOODWILL   An intangible salable asset, such as reputation or location of a business, which makes the business worth more to a buyer than the BOOK VALUE; the expectation of continued public patronage. Although goodwill may be listed on a balance sheet as an asset, the stated value may be different than the salable market value.

GOVERNMENT PROCUREMENT   The purchase of goods and services by the U.S. government. Many opportunities are created for small businesses to sell products and services that fill the needs of the government.

GRANDFATHER CLAUSE   A provision in a law or regulation exempting some specified transactions that occurred before the date of enactment from being subject to the law or regulation.

GRANT   The act of conveying or transferring title to real property, as by a deed; a gift according to legal procedure.
    A person or a business may obtain a grant. Also, a not-for-profit organization may receive a grant, i.e., a gift, from either a public or private source, that may be tax deductible to the grantor.

GRANTEE   One who receives a GRANT; the person who receives from the GRANTOR a conveyance of real property; the receiver of a gift.

GRANTOR   One who gives a grant; the one who executes a deed conveying property title to the GRANTEE; the one who gives property.

GRANTOR RETAINED INCOME TRUST (GRIT)   An irrevocable trust established for the purpose of transferring ownership of a business to children or heirs.

GREEN CARD   A document issued by the U.S. government that authorizes an alien to work legally for a firm in the United States.

GRIT   SEE GRANTOR RETAINED INCOME TRUST.

GROSS   In finance, same as GROSS INCOME as opposed to NET INCOME.

GROSS DOMESTIC PRODUCT (GDP)   The total value of goods and services produced in the economy of the United States in a period of a year, including U.S. profits from foreign investments; published quarterly. The GDP growth rate is the primary indicator of United States economic status; GDP measures consumer purchases, government purchases, investments and the total value of exports. Supersedes GROSS NATIONAL PRODUCT.

GROSS INCOME   The gross revenue or SALES of a business over a period.

GROSS MARGIN   Gross margin is gross profit expressed as a percent of net sales; also called GROSS PROFIT RATE.

GROSS NATIONAL PRODUCT (GNP)   See GROSS DOMESTIC PRODUCT for the currently used indicator. GNP is the total retail value of the goods and services produced by the labor and assets of citizens in the United States economy in a period of a year; published quarterly.

GROSS PROFIT   NET SALES less the COST OF GOODS SOLD. The PROFIT before OVERHEAD (operating expenses) has been deducted. Sometimes, commonly used to mean the same as GROSS MARGIN. See also NET PROFIT.

GROSS PROFIT RATE A measure of profitability of a business; a measure of the ability to pay overhead since all costs associated with obtaining and selling are subtracted out; divide GROSS PROFIT by GROSS SALES and express as a percent. When compared to other periods, it measures the efficiency of the purchasing and marketing functions. Same as GROSS MARGIN.

GROSS SALES Total sales at invoice values, not reduced by customer discounts, returns, allowances or other adjustments. See also SALES; NET SALES.

GROSS WORKING CAPITAL Total cash and cash equivalents (CURRENT ASSETS); used when discussing cash flow as opposed to discussing assets. See also WORKING CAPITAL; NET WORKING CAPITAL.

GROUP BENEFITS FRINGE BENEFITS purchased by the company for all employees (the group) and apply to each employee in the group.

GROUP COVERAGE Insurance purchased by a company that applies equally to all employees (the group).

GROUP INSURANCE A type of insurance coverage offered by insurance companies wherein the policy written covers all the people in the similar risk category, called a group. Thus an employer can purchase an insurance policy that covers all the employees employed by the firm. Group insurance commonly carried by employers includes hospitalization, health and life.

GROWTH In business, growth generally refers to a situation where one amount of money or financial condition will be larger at a future time.

GUARANTEE To take responsibility for payment of the debt of another person if the other person fails to repay. A guarantee is a CONTINGENT LIABILITY of the grantor.

GUARANTEED LOAN A loan made by a bank upon which the Small Business Administration has insured partial reimbursement to the bank in the event the borrower fails to repay. Also called INSURED LOAN. See also LOAN GUARANTEE; PREFERRED LENDER PROGRAM; CERTIFIED LENDER PROGRAM.

GUARANTOR   The person or firm that makes or gives a GUARANTY; one who promises to uphold a guaranty.

GUARANTY   A promise that merchandise will perform as claimed. A guaranty differs from a warranty in that a warranty is absolute assurance to the effect that failure to perform may void the basic contract. A guaranty merely provides that the guarantor will be liable. Sometimes used interchangeably with product WARRANTY. See also GUARANTEE.

GUESTIMATE   A rough approximation; an estimate with less certainty or accuracy than an estimate. A guestimate often applies to an approximation of a financial amount.

H

HANDLING FEE An amount charged for physical labor associated with processing a product or in processing paperwork; a processing charge or fee.

HANDS-ON A management style wherein the manager or owner of a business participates in the day-to-day operation of the business.

HARD CURRENCY Currency in which there is widespread confidence. It is the currency of an economically and politically stable country, such as the United States. As contrasted with SOFT CURRENCY.

Gold or coins as contrasted with paper currency. Sometimes paper money is considered soft money.

HARD DOLLARS Payment in cash or cash equivalent. Hard dollars are considered as money in hand. As opposed to a loan or a promise of payment that is money to be received in the future. Contrasts with SOFT DOLLARS.

HARD MONEY See HARD CURRENCY.

HARDWARE A line of products used in construction and mechanical trades, including tools, equipment and supplies.

Computers and accessories; the mechanical equipment in which SOFTWARE is recorded.

HAZARD INSURANCE INSURANCE coverage for a loss resulting from physical damage to property (usually for real property) due to hazards such as fire, flood and wind storm.

119

HEAVY INDUSTRY   A basic INDUSTRY that converts raw materials into finished goods or that manufactures equipment. Heavy industry consists of factories, mills, manufacturing plants and other businesses that require ample property to accommodate their nature and function. The term connotes noise, pollution, heavy truck traffic, vibration, fumes and other annoyances.

HIDDEN RISK   A risk associated with a business venture that is not apparent without considerable investigation and knowledge. In business, there are always unknown factors that can affect the profitability of the business. Therefore, the business entrepreneur should constantly evaluate all phases of business activity to minimize the amount of hidden (unknown or unforeseen) risk.

HISTORICAL COST   Actual costs, as opposed to projected or forecasted costs; expenditures recorded in the books of account.

HOLDING COMPANY   A company that owns, directs or controls the operations of one or more other corporations and subsidiaries; a corporation organized to hold the stock of other corporations; a conglomerate. A holding company usually does not have business of its own. See also SUBSIDIARY; PARENT COMPANY.

HOME OFFICE   For a business, a location within your residence that is used exclusively for business purposes. Special tax considerations may apply. Also, the headquarters office of a large business that has several other office locations.

HOMEWORK   The preparatory work done before a business discussion with a client, customer or associate that is necessary to act effectively on the alternatives as they arise. Often used in conjunction with a new situation that is encountered, wherein having done a complete job of homework preparation, you can deal with any situation that arises.

HOMEWORKER   A worker who has contracted with a company to perform the tasks in the worker's home rather than on the premises of the company; one who works in the COTTAGE INDUSTRY.

HOOK   In marketing, the specific technique that attracts customers and provides an opportunity for the sale.

HOUR   A period of time equal to one 24th of a day; 60 minutes.

HOURLY   An event or activity occurring in increments of one (1) hour. Also, a rate of pay on the basis of each hour worked; a classification of an employee who is paid an HOURLY WAGE.

HOURLY EMPLOYEE   An employee who is paid for each hour of service. As distinguished from an employee who is paid a SALARY.

HOURLY WAGE   An amount paid to an employee for each hour of service. As distinguished from a SALARY.

HOUSE AGENCY   Any service performed by a part of a large company that otherwise would be purchased from another company, such as an advertising "agency" established within a company that handles advertising only for that company or an in-house travel agency.

HURDLE RATE   In budgeting for capital expenditures, the RATE OF RETURN that must be exceeded for the investment to be viable. Above the hurdle rate, the investment should be made; but below the hurdle rate, the investment should not be made. See DISCOUNTED CASH FLOW; INTERNAL RATE OF RETURN.

I

IFB   See INVITATION FOR BID.

ILLIQUID   In finance, a business condition charterized by insufficient CASH FLOW (INCOME) to meet current and maturing obligations. Also, assets that cannot be easily converted into cash, such as real estate and specialized machinery. Illiquid assets may take a long time to sell, and the price at which others are willing to buy is often less than the market value or book value of the asset.

IMF   See INTERNATIONAL MONETARY FUND.

IMPLIED CONTRACT   An unwritten contract inferred from the actions of the parties. Such an agreement is created by neither words nor writing, rather it is inferred from the actions of the parties.

IMPORT   The purchase of goods or services from another country in exchange for money. Also, the inward movement of such goods.

IMPORT DUTY   See CUSTOMS DUTY.

IMPORT LICENSE   A document granting permission from the U.S. government for a person or company to IMPORT specified goods.

IMPORT SUBSTITUTION   A U.S. government policy that encourages companies in the United States to produce goods that are now imported.

IMPREST   Designation of a fund, such as a PETTY CASH FUND, that is replenished in exactly the amount expended from it.

IMPUTED INTEREST   Interest implied by law; an interest rate set by a governmental body that overrides an agreement of the parties, generally for taxing purposes.

INCOME   An accounting term defining the money received by a business in a given period of time as a result of operating the business; the goods and services sold. Also called REVENUE; SALES. Sometimes used to mean PROFIT or EARNINGS as a shortened form of NET INCOME.

INCOME PRODUCING ASSET   An item that is a vital ingredient to the operation of the business, such as an airplane for an airline or high-speed machinery for a manufacturing company.

INCOME STATEMENT   A detailed statement of income, expenses and taxes for a business, revealing the operating position of the business over a period of time. Thus the income statement displays whether the business has made a profit during the accounting period or sustained a loss during the accounting period. The income statement and the BALANCE SHEET at the end of an accounting period, together, constitute the primary FINANCIAL STATEMENTS for a company. Also called OPERATING STATEMENT; PROFIT & LOSS STATEMENT; P&L.

INCOME TAX   By law, the amount paid to a government (federal, state or local), calculated on the amount of earnings (INCOME) less expenses and deductions. Federal income taxes are required to be paid by individuals (FORM 1040) and corporations (FORM 1120). Separate income tax reporting is not required for a sole proprietorship, since the amount of earnings is reported by the individual on SCHEDULE C, FORM 1040 and also entered on the front of FORM 1040 as a profit or loss. Income taxes are not required for partnerships since PARTNERSHIPS prepare an INFORMATIONAL RETURN (FORM 1165) to report income to the individual on FORM K-1.

INCORPORATE   The act of forming a corporation by preparing the necessary articles of incorporation and filing them with the appropriate state governmental business-registration division.

INCORPORATION The process by which a company receives a state CHARTER allowing it to operate as a CORPORATION. The act of incorporation must be acknowledged in the company's name, using the word "incorporated," the abbreviated "Inc." or other acceptable variation. In the incorporation process, ARTICLES OF INCORPORATION are filed by the founders with the state. The state then formally recognizes the new corporate entity by issuing a CERTIFICATE OF INCORPORATION. Together, these two documents comprise the corporate CHARTER.

INCUBATION INVESTMENT Money put into a new business struggling for survival.

INCUBATOR A facility for encouraging entrepreneurs to start a business by housing, in one location, low-cost services such as rent, secretarial and business counseling. Incubators often promote development by new firms or firms attempting to market a new high technology product or service. Financing of incubators may be by state or local government as well as private financing.

INDEBTED Under legal obligation to repay; a debt to another.

INDEPENDENT CERTIFIED PUBLIC ACCOUNTANT; INDEPENDENT PUBLIC ACCOUNTANT See CERTIFIED PUBLIC ACCOUNTANT OR PUBLIC ACCOUNTANT. The word independent is added to emphasize that the professional work is performed by an unbiased source and is fair.

INDEPENDENT CONTRACTOR A person or company retained to perform work for another, often under a written contract, whereby control is subjected to the end result and not as to how the work is performed. As opposed to an EMPLOYEE who receives direction on what, when and, to some degree, how to do a job.

Care must be used in the classification of workers as either employees or independent contractors. What distinguishes them is the degree of control the employer has over the activities being performed. Specific definitions of employee and independent contractor exist in IRS publications. After the fact, the IRS can determine that a person was actually an employee. Serious tax consequences may apply if incorrect classification is made. See EMPLOYEE; CONTRACTOR.

INDEX   A statistical measure expressed in terms of numbers or percentages with a base value at a point in time so that future values are relative to the base value.

INDEXING   A method of correlating the price of one item to that of another item or to an economic factor (the INDEX), such as the CONSUMER PRICE INDEX.

INDIRECT   See OVERHEAD.

INDIRECT BUSINESS TAXES   Sales, excise and business property taxes.

INDIRECT COST   See OVERHEAD.

INDIRECT EXPORTING   A situation where a small company desires to export its products but does not have the ability to do so. Therefore, the company hires an intermediary company to handle all phases of exporting, including shipping.

INDIRECT LABOR   Personnel assigned to tasks other than producing products. Indirect labor is included as part of OPERATING EXPENSES. As opposed to DIRECT LABOR.

INDIRECT MATERIAL   Materials, purchases and supplies used in the operation of the business, not directly associated with production and are part of OPERATING EXPENSES. As opposed to DIRECT MATERIAL.

INDIRECT OVERHEAD   See OVERHEAD.

INDIRECT TAX   A tax levied on commercial transactions rather than on income. Such indirect taxes include sales tax, excise tax, and value-added tax. Opposite of DIRECT TAX.

INDIVIDUAL INCOME   The earnings, wages, salary, dividends and interest of a person.

INDIVIDUAL INCOME TAX   By law, the amount paid to the federal government (and most states) by a person, and is calculated on the amount of earnings (INCOME) less some expenses and deductions. Individual income taxes are required to be paid by persons on an INDIVIDUAL INCOME TAX RETURN, FORM 1040.

INDIVIDUAL INCOME TAX RETURN   Federal government FORM 1040 used for reporting the amount of income taxes due to be paid. Many states also require individual income tax returns.

INDUSTRY   A collective description of all businesses with similar types of products or services, such as manufacturing industry, service industry, paper industry and banking industry.

INDUSTRY AVERAGE   The normal or nominal value for all the companies in an industry. A company owner should compare the values from its company to those for all companies in the industry (the industry average) as a measure of the financial health of the company. Trade associations, publishers and some firms collect, analyze and publish these statistics.   ROBERT MORRIS & ASSOC. and DUN & BRADSTREET specialize in this information.

INDUSTRY POOL   Joining of companies to improve profits by reducing competition. In the United States, such pools are generally unlawful, violating ANTITRUST LAW. See CARTEL; PRICE FIXING.

INDUSTRY PRACTICE   A commonly accepted method of operation within a business similar to other businesses in the same line of work or industry. Practices may differ in other industries.

INELASTIC PRICE   A situation in the marketplace where a change in price will not affect DEMAND. As opposed to ELASTIC PRICE. See PRICE ELASTICITY.

INFANT INDUSTRY   A new industry; a line of business, products or services that has not been available for a very long time. Usually, a fragile area of economic activity.

INFLATION   A rise in prices for goods and services; the price for a product is higher as measured today than at a time in the past. Moderate inflation is a common result of economic growth and therefore perceived as good for society.

INFORMATIONAL INCOME TAX RETURN; INFORMATIONAL RETURN; INFORMATIONAL TAX RETURN   A federal government document used to provide data to others that may have tax consequences. FORM 1165 is used to report earnings (INCOME) for a partnership; although the partnership itself pays no tax, the proportionate share of the earnings is reported to each partner on FORM K-1. FORM 1099 reports amounts paid to contractors, interest paid and other amounts.

INFORMATION FOR BUSINESS TAXPAYERS   See PUBLICATION 583.

INFORMATION HIGHWAY   The concept of a communications network that can deliver vast amounts of information directly to consumers' homes and businesses. Transmission means consist of cable, telephone lines, fiber optic lines and microwave.

INITIAL PUBLIC OFFERING (IPO)   A company's first offering of stock for sale in the market to anyone (the public) who wishes to buy, reflecting the expectations for the company's future growth. From that point on, the shares of stock have a market value controlled by supply and demand for the shares. See GOING PUBLIC.

INJURY   Physical harm to an individual person.
In business and insurance, the financial loss to a company inflicted by an event.

INNER CITY   An urban area that is generally recognized as a central business or commercial part of the city.

INSIDE DIRECTORS   Members of a BOARD OF DIRECTORS who are also top corporate executives. See BOARD OF DIRECTORS.

INSOLVENCY   A state of bad financial condition wherein debts and obligations cannot be repaid when due or a business that ceases to operate. As opposed to SOLVENCY. See also BANKRUPTCY; CASH FLOW.

INSTALLMENT NOTE   A PROMISSORY NOTE providing for payment of the principal in two or more definite stated amounts at different times. SEE INSTALLMENT SALE.

INSTALLMENT SALE A sale of a large dollar value item wherein the payments are made over a period of time, usually also incurring an interest charge. Sales are recorded in the books as payments are made, as opposed to the entire amount recorded at the time of delivery. Title of the property is usually retained by the seller (as collateral) until all payments are made.

INSTITUTIONAL LENDER Any organization (financial institution) that lends money for an interest fee and whose loans are regulated by law, such as a bank, an insurance company or a savings and loan organization. These organizations may lend money that was received from depositors as opposed to a private lender who lends his or her own money.

INSTRUMENT A legal document in which some contractual relationship is given formal expression or by which some right is granted. For example: notes, contracts or agreements. See also NEGOTIABLE INSTRUMENT.

INSUFFICIENT FUNDS; NON-SUFFICIENT FUNDS (NSF) An action by a bank whereby the bank refuses payment of a check that has been presented for payment. This usually means that the issuer of a check did not have enough money in the account to honor payment of the check. The check is boldly stamped NSF, returned to the payee's bank where the amount of the check is debited from the payee's account, a fee is charged to the payee and the NSF check is returned to the payee.

INSURANCE Indemnification against (reimbursement for) financial loss resulting from a specific risk, hazard or peril.

In a broad sense, insurance transfers risk from individuals to a larger group that is better able to pay individual losses from a pool of money collected from all members of the group.

INSURANCE AGENCY A group of insurance agents representing one or more specified insurance companies. The agency sells insurance policies offered only by those companies.

INSURANCE AGENT A person who is authorized to represent an insurance company and acts on behalf of the insurance company, such as a salesperson for an insurance company. See AGENT.

INSURANCE BROKER   A person or firm that represents and sells for more than one insurance company. An insurance broker often, has knowledge of several insurance companies' policies and reputations, allowing selection of the optimum policy for an individual business situation. See BROKER.

INSURANCE CERTIFICATE   See CERTIFICATE OF INSURANCE.

INSURANCE CLAIM   A request by the INSURED for reimbursement from the INSURER following a loss; a LIABILITY CLAIM.

INSURANCE COMPANY   A business engaged solely in the protection against financial loss; a business as an INSURER. See INSURER; INSURANCE POLICY.

An insurance company may be a source of money for a small business to borrow using real property as collateral since the insurance company desires to earn interest income.

INSURANCE COVERAGE   The amount of INSURANCE purchased to protect a financial risk, hazard or peril. See INSURANCE POLICY.

INSURANCE PLAN   A document or estimate of the amount of insurance needed in a small business for the desired coverage.

INSURANCE POLICY ˌA document describing risks, hazards or perils of an individual or business (the INSURED) covered by the INSURER (INSURANCE COMPANY) including the conditions of coverage, amount of coverage and PREMIUM to be paid for such coverage.

INSURANCE POOL   A group of INSURERS who share the premiums and losses in order to spread the risk of unique situations. Thus a group of insurance companies can take on larger risks than any individual company could bear alone, thus permitting small insurance companies to collectively compete with larger companies.

INSURANCE PROTECTION   The act or fact of having purchased an insurance policy. Assurance of financial reimbursement for a loss.

INSURED   The person or business covered by insurance; the POLICY HOLDER; the one who purchased the insurance policy. See INSURANCE POLICY; POLICY HOLDER.

INSURER   The one who insures against financial loss—e.g., an INSURANCE COMPANY.

INTANGIBLE   Something that cannot be seen, touched or evaluated. As opposed to TANGIBLE. See INTANGIBLE ASSET.

INTANGIBLE ASSET   Something owned, other than physical property, that represents an advantage to a company in the marketplace. Such assets include copyrights, patents, trademarks, goodwill, computer programs, organization costs, licenses, leases, franchises, exploration permits, import/export permits, customer lists and know-how. The value of these items generally cannot be substantiated but represent assets on the company's balance sheet. See ASSET; TANGIBLE ASSET.

INTELLECTUAL PROPERTY   Trade secrets; information that is proprietary to a company; assets owned by the business that are patented, copyrighted or trademarked.

INTEREST   The cost of using money borrowed from another; expressed as a rate per period of time, usually one year and more precisely called the ANNUAL INTEREST RATE or ANNUAL RATE OF INTEREST. See also SIMPLE INTEREST; COMPOUND INTEREST.
   Also the share, right or title in property, expressed as "an interest in the property."

INTEREST CHARGE   The amount of INTEREST payment due in terms of money, as opposed to a percent.

INTEREST EARNED   An amount of INTEREST credited to an account but may not yet have been recorded to the account.

INTEREST EXPENSE   An income statement entry that means payment of interest to another party.

INTEREST IN ADVANCE   In lending, a loan on which interest is paid at the beginning of the period; as opposed to paid INTEREST IN ARREARS (the end of the period).

INTEREST IN ARREARS   In lending, a loan on which interest is paid at the end of the period; as opposed to paid INTEREST IN ADVANCE (the beginning of the period). Also means interest due and payable but not yet paid.

INTEREST INCOME   An income statement entry that means receipt of interest from another party.

INTEREST RATE   The percentage value that is multiplied by the PRINCIPAL of a LOAN to determine the amount of money (interest) due or paid in a given period of time.

INTERIM FINANCING   A short-term loan obtained for a short period, when money is needed, prior to securing a long-term loan. Example: a construction loan to finance construction of a building.

INTERMEDIATE TERM   A term (period of time) longer than short-term but not long-term. The length of intermediate term depends on the context. Most common small business usage is in banking for loans of more than one year but less than ten years.

INTERNAL RATE OF RETURN (IRR)   The discount rate at which the present worth of future cash flows is exactly equal to the initial capital investment. In capital budgeting, it is called the HURDLE RATE. The advantage of using internal rate of return as a measurement of an investment's worth is that all types of investments can be analyzed or compared on an equivalent basis and in an objective manner. The results, however, are no better than the projections made by the preparer since risk factors and assumptions may outweigh the mathematical calculation.

INTERNAL REVENUE CODE   The body of statutes relating to the federal tax laws and administered by the Internal Revenue Service (IRS).

INTERNAL REVENUE SERVICE (IRS) The agency of the federal government charged with interpreting, administering and enforcing the federal tax laws (INTERNAL REVENUE CODE).

INTERNAL SOURCES OF WORKING CAPITAL See WORKING CAPITAL.

INTERNATIONAL MARKETING Using a marketing program and selling products, both of which are tailored to fit the country where sales are anticipated. As opposed to GLOBAL MARKETING wherein the same product is sold in the same way everywhere in the world.

INTERNATIONAL MONETARY FUND An international organization, with members from most countries in the world, whose purpose is to lower trade barriers and stabilize currencies. While helping developing countries pay their debts, they usually impose tough guidelines aimed at lowering inflation, cutting imports and raising exports.

INTERNATIONAL TRADE Buying from or selling to a business in another country. See EXPORT; IMPORT.

INTERNET An enormous international computer information network that links government agencies, universities, corporations and individuals. Thus individuals can tap information from any of the sources on-line.

INTRADE To purchase goods or services from a supplier in another city, county or state in exchange for money, i.e., to purchase from a supplier that is located in a governmental entity different from your governmental entity. Also, the inward movement of such goods into a city, county or state. Similar to IMPORT but within a single country. Opposite of EXTRADE.

IN TRIPLICATE To make three copies, often by pen or pencil, using carbon paper or similar paper.

INVENTORY The collective quantity of goods, property or products on hand in a company; an itemized list or catalog of goods.

Also the value of such goods or products. In manufacturing, inventory includes raw materials, work in process, finished goods and supplies. In retail or wholesale, inventory includes the products available for sale and may include supplies and personal property. Also, the act of counting the quantity of products on hand, called taking inventory or inventorying.

INVENTORY AGING   An accounting procedure used to evaluate the purchase dates of the inventory on hand and inventory turnover rate.

INVENTORY COMPOSITION   The mix of various products; an identification of those items which sell fast and those which sell slower. In manufacturing, inventory composition can involve identification of raw materials, work-in-process and finished goods.

INVENTORY CONTROL   The process whereby the company knows where everything is located at all times and efficiently moves inventory (materials) from one station to another as needed. Accountability of goods on hand can prevent loss or theft.

INVENTORY FINANCING   Loans collateralized by unsold inventory. The loan is repaid when the goods are sold.

INVENTORY TURNOVER; INVENTORY TURNOVER RATE   A measurement of the rate at which products are purchased by a business then resold to customers. Inventory turnover is often expressed as the ratio of annual sales divided by ending inventory. Small companies should compare their inventory turnover with industry averages. A low turnover rate might indicate excess stock is on hand, tying up cash, indicating sluggish sales, ineffective buying or vulnerability to falling prices.

INVEST   The process of acquiring ownership in a company; to purchase equity interest in a company. The objective of investing is to obtain income from the profits made in the business.

INVESTMENT   The use of CAPITAL to create more money as a financial gain with the connotation that safety of principal is important. As opposed to SPECULATION that involves greater risk.

INVESTMENT BANKER   A firm, acting as an underwriter or agent, which serves as an intermediary between a company that issues securities and the investing public.

INVESTMENT COMPANY   A firm that invests in the equity of other companies and may sell shares to the public.

INVESTMENT INTEREST   The amount of interest paid as a result of a purchase; the amount of interest necessary to make an investment worthy of purchase.

INVESTMENT POOL   A combining of the resources of several persons or companies for a common purpose, such as to finance a large research project.

Also, a group of investors who contribute to a common investment purpose; as an investment club. Care must be exercised not to gain control of a market by manipulating prices, which is illegal.

INVESTMENT TAX CREDIT (ITC)   A federal government tax provision for reduction of tax liability as an incentive to encourage investment in a specific financial transaction. One such incentive for the small business is the reduction of tax liability when the business purchases new equipment.

INVESTOR   Any person who provides equity capital to a company; a person who INVESTS; a person who buys shares of stock in a company in return for anticipated company profitability and payment of dividends to the investor.

INVISIBLES   The non-merchandise areas of trade, such as freight, insurance and most types of services and investments.

INVITATION FOR BID (IFB)   An announcement of contract work open for submission of BIDS. The IFB documents the specific requirements of the intended purchase.

INVITATION TO BID (ITB)   A request by a buyer for a BID from a seller to perform work or provide a service.

INVOICE   A notification of amount due for goods that were delivered or services that were performed. The invoice is prepared by the seller and submitted to the purchaser. In small business an invoice is most often called a BILL.

INVOLUNTARY BANKRUPTCY   A legal proceeding of bankruptcy when a creditor brings the petition to a court to force insolvency of a person or business. The objective is an orderly and equitable settlement of obligations of the debtor so the creditor can be paid. See BANKRUPTCY; VOLUNTARY BANKRUPTCY.

INWOOD TABLE   A set of interest tables, commonly used by appraisers, for computing the PRESENT VALUE for an annuity. See NET PRESENT VALUE; INTERNAL RATE OF RETURN.

IPO   See INITIAL PUBLIC OFFERING.

IRR   See INTERNAL RATE OF RETURN.

IRS   See INTERNAL REVENUE SERVICE.

ISSUED AND OUTSTANDING   The term used on a BALANCE SHEET to identify those AUTHORIZED SHARES of stock in a corporation that have been sold (issued) to the owners. The sale of the stock acquires Capital investment in the corporation. Shares of stock repurchased by the corporation are not outstanding and are called TREASURY STOCK. Issued and outstanding is the opposite of UNISSUED STOCK. See AUTHORIZED SHARES.

ISSUED STOCK   See ISSUED AND OUTSTANDING.

ITB   See INVITATION TO BID.

ITC   See INVESTMENT TAX CREDIT.

J

JIT   See JUST-IN-TIME.

JOBBER   A wholesaler, especially one who buys in small lots from manufacturers and importers for resale to retailers. Also, a middleperson who arranges purchases between manufacturer and retailer, thereafter delivery is made directly to the retailer.

JOB COST   A financial accounting system that traces and assigns all production (DIRECT) costs to the product, product line, job or project for which the cost was incurred. Thereby, the expenditures directly attributable to the job are known and identifiable. Conversely, all non-production costs (OVERHEAD, INDIRECT) are excluded from the job cost.

JOB SHOP   A manufacturing business that produces products per order after a signed sales contract is executed, as opposed to production of products for warehousing until a customer orders them. A job shop produces outputs in small batches to customer specifications, and these specifications can differ from customer to customer.

JOINT AND SEVERAL LIABILITY   A legal expression meaning all people jointly are liable and/or each person individually is liable for repayment of a debt or obligation. Thus, each individual who signed the obligation could be required to repay the entire obligation.

JOINT TENANCY   Owning property by two or more persons; upon the death of one, the survivor takes title to the entire property.

JOINT VENTURE   A business association of two or more businesses or persons whereby they work together on a single project; similar to a GENERAL PARTNERSHIP, but limited in either scope or duration or both, such as in working on one project together. Investment in a plant, facility or project with another firm. Taxed as a PARTNERSHIP.

In international trade, often a joint venture is mandated by national laws that prohibit majority ownership by a foreign firm.

JOINT VENTURER   One of the member companies or persons engaged in a JOINT VENTURE.

JOURNAL   In accounting, the record of original entry where financial transactions are initially recorded. In a DOUBLE-ENTRY accounting system, a listing of all transactions in chronological order with notation of the accounts to which they belong. Also, the process of making the notations in the journal records for DEBITS and CREDITS.

Sometimes refers to the financial newspaper with the name *The Wall Street Journal*.

JOURNALIZE   To make entries in the JOURNAL; to classify and record transaction data in the journal.

JUNIOR LOAN   A loan that would not be paid in a liquidation situation until all SENIOR LOANS were paid first. See SUBORDINATE.

JUST-IN-TIME (JIT)   A production and inventory method popularized by the Japanese whereby materials and supplies are delivered to the production site at the precise time they are needed rather than being stockpiled in a warehouse at the production site for a future need.

K

KEOGH PLAN   A federal tax law designed to encourage self-employed business people to set aside money for retirement by giving a substantial tax advantage; similar to an IRA, but for a small self-employed business owner and others who do not have a company pension plan.

KEY MAN INSURANCE   Insurance purchased by a company that financially protects the business from the death or disability of a most valuable owner or high level employee.

In accounting, the cash surrender value of such insurance is shown as an asset. See CASH SURRENDER VALUE.

KEY PERSONNEL   The people in a business whose performance is vital to success; those who control business operations.

KICKER   A deal sweetener; an amount added to a deal to induce the potential buyer or lender to consummate the deal.

K.I.S.S.   Keep It Simple Stupid; an acronym used to suggest the elimination of unnecessary work and complications.

KITING   An unlawful procedure whereby a check is written on an account that does not have enough money to pay the check. Most often, the intent is unlawful reliance on a long float period that allows time for money to be deposited to cover the check.

L

LABOR   Human effort expended in return for pay or wages. Generally, labor refers to factory production as opposed to office work. Also the general classification of BLUE COLLAR workers.

LABOR CONTRACT   An agreement between the suppliers and employers of LABOR; most often between a UNION and a COMPANY.

LABOR COST   Expenditures made by personnel employed in the firm including both direct labor and indirect labor. As opposed to MATERIAL COST.

LABOR-INTENSIVE   Work that requires a large number of workers, or where labor costs are much more significant than material costs or capital costs. As opposed to CAPITAL INTENSIVE, whereby a large amount of machinery or inventory is controlled by a few workers.

LABOR POOL   The collective group of workers with the skills needed to perform the desired work.

LABOR SURPLUS AREA   Locations designated by a government as having high unemployment, usually on a county-by-county basis. Often the government will encourage business start-up in "labor surplus areas" in order to reduce the amount of unemployment.

LABOR UNION   An organization of workers with common skills established to protect the welfare, interests and rights of its members, primarily by collective bargaining.

LAG   To follow; to be sluggish; as opposed to LEAD.

LAG TIME   The period of time from the start of work (or production) to the completion of the work. See also LEAD TIME.

LAID OFF   An employee who is discharged from employment because the employer does not have enough work to pay the employee. As opposed to an employee who is FIRED for poor performance or an infraction of company rules. See also FIRED.

LAN   See LOCAL AREA NETWORK.

LAND   The surface of the earth including all natural things thereon, such as trees, water, minerals under the surface and air rights above the surface. The term REAL PROPERTY includes the land plus other artificial things attached to the land, such as buildings.

LANDLORD   The LESSOR of real estate; a person or company that rents land and buildings to another. See LEASE.

LAST-IN, FIRST-OUT (LIFO)   A method of accounting for INVENTORY that assumes the last item purchased is the first item put into production and thus ties the COST OF GOODS SOLD to the cost of most recent purchases. In contrast to the FIRST-IN, FIRST-OUT method. In a period of rising prices, LIFO results in a higher cost of goods sold, a lower profit, lower taxable income and less inventory value on the BALANCE SHEET.

LATE CHARGE   Same as LATE PAYMENT PENALTY.

LATE PAYMENT   To remit money (to pay) on a date after the specified date when payment is due.

LATE PAYMENT PENALTY   An additional charge for paying after a date; a SERVICE CHARGE.

LAUNCH   Introducing a new product to market, including advertising, promotion and distribution; sometimes also includes some amount of product design and manufacture.

LAUNDERING   Processing illegal money through accounts of an apparently legitimate business to make the money appear legal. Often associated with drugs or other crime.

LAW   The rules of conduct established and enforced by authority, legislation or custom of a given community, state or other group; any one of such rules. The branch of knowledge dealing with such rules; jurisprudence.

LAWFUL INTEREST   The maximum interest rate permitted by law, with any amount above the rate being usurious. It is different from the LEGAL RATE OF INTEREST. See INTEREST, USURY.

LAW OF DEMAND   The economic theory that the lower the price of a good, the greater will be the desire for purchasing that good and, conversely, the higher the price, the smaller will be the desire to purchase. See DEMAND.

LAW OF DIMINISHING RETURNS   In business, as more units are produced, the cost or the benefit (profit) from each additional unit becomes smaller. This characteristic also applies in many other situations, i.e., the benefit decreases as more things occur.

LAW OF SUPPLY   The economic theory that suppliers will provide larger quantities of a good at higher prices than they will at lower prices. See SUPPLY.

LAWSUIT   An action to secure justice between private parties at law or in equity; a case before a civil court.

LAWYER   A person who has been trained in the law, has passed an examination and is licensed by a state to practice law, a person who advises others in matters of the law or represents them in lawsuits. See LAW; ATTORNEY.

LAYOFF   A situation where an employer discharges one or more employees for lack of work (LAID-OFF), not because of employee poor performance or an infraction of company rules.

LEAD   In business, information from a business associate advantageous to your business, such as a potential new customer. Sometimes called a business lead.

Generally, to be ahead of others; to be in the forefront; the opposite of LAG.

LEAD TIME   The interval of time before an activity can begin; the duration of time from ordering a product to the time when the product is received; can also apply to the duration of time from idea to salable product or other similar situation.

LEARNING CURVE   The observed phenomenon of a continuing decrease in the time required to perform an operation (or a series of operations) with each successive repetition. When described in a mathematical relationship (the learning curve), the cost to produce later units is less than the cost to produce earlier units because of worker proficiency, better work station layout, redesign with fewer parts and similar factors. The time to perform a task decreases with practice and knowledge gained.

LEASE   A contract granting use of property (real estate, equipment or other fixed asset) for a specified period for a payment. The owner of the property is called the LESSOR; the user is called the LESSEE; and the payment is called RENT. For a legally valid lease, the lessor grants the right of possession to the lessee, but retains the right to retake possession at the end of the lease term. Also used as a verb to use (to LEASE) the property.

LEASE FINANCING   Renting equipment as opposed to purchase or the purchase of equipment by one company for the sole purpose of leasing the equipment to a second company.

LEASEHOLD IMPROVEMENTS   Improvements to rented property that are made and paid for by the lessee but become the property of the LESSOR at the expiration of the lease term. These improvements include remodeling for efficiency or appearance.

LEASE-PURCHASE AGREEMENT   A lease of real estate or equipment whereby part of the lease cost may be applied to purchase of the property at a later date.

LEDGER   In accounting, the book of final entry, in which a record is kept of money and all other transactions affecting the financial status of the business. The ledger accounts are established to categorize the transactions according to classifications established by the business. The entries in the ledger are called DEBITS and CREDITS. Periodically, summaries of the ledger are accumulated into FINANCIAL STATEMENTS of the company.

LEDGER ACCOUNT   An ACCOUNT in the LEDGER of a business; a classification of a specific category of transactions of the business.

LEGAL   Pertaining to the LAW; any action that is acceptable under the law.

LEGAL COUNSEL   A LAWYER.

LEGAL ENTITY   A person or organization that has the legal standing to enter into a contract and may be sued for failure to perform. Usually refers to a corporation that is an artificial person in the eyes of the law.

LEGAL MATTER   Any subject requiring justice under the LAW.

LEGAL RATE OF INTEREST   The rate of interest prescribed by state law that will prevail in the absence of any agreement establishing the rate on an instrument. The USURY limit is referred to as the lawful interest. It is different from LAWFUL INTEREST.

LEGAL STRUCTURE   The types or methods of business organization. Three main types are: SOLE PROPRIETORSHIP, PARTNERSHIP and CORPORATION, although other types of legal structures also exist. Several factors should be considered in selecting the proper legal structure, including ease of starting the business; complexity of operating the business; financial liability of the owner(s); opportunities for growth; federal, state and local tax laws; factors peculiar to a particular business. See also SOLE PROPRIETORSHIP; PARTNERSHIP; CORPORATION.

LEGAL TECHNICALITY   A precise point of the LAW; usually requiring interpretation by a LAWYER; sometime requires a court decision for precise and accurate definition.

LEND   In business, the process whereby the owner of money allows use of the money by another person or business in exchange for paymentof a fee, called INTEREST.

LENDER   In business, an individual or firm that allows use of its money by a BORROWER with the expectation of being repaid; usually with INTEREST and in a specified time; a CREDITOR.

LENDING   The process of making a loan.

LESSEE   The person who takes possession of leased property, also called RENTER. In real estate leases, this person is called the TENANT. See LEASE.

LESSOR   The owner; the person who owns real property that is used by another under the terms of a lease. In real estate leases, this person is called the LANDLORD. SEE LEASE.

LETTER OF CREDIT   An agreement or commitment by a bank for a business customer wherein the bank will honor drafts or other demands for payment from third parties upon compliance with the conditions specified in the letter of credit. A guarantee of payment upon proof of completion of the terms and conditions of the agreement.

In international trade, a common and trusted method of payment between banks for exports.

LETTER OF INTENT   Any document that expresses a desire to take, or not to take, an action. Sometimes the commitment of one party who issues the letter of intent, contingent on actions by another party. After satisfactory negotiations have been completed on a merger of two companies, a letter of intent is signed by both companies that forms a preliminary agreement on the merger. Also, an expression of willingness to invest, develop or purchase without incurring any firm legal obligation to do so.

LEVERAGE   The impact of borrowed funds on investment return; the employment of a smaller investment to generate a larger rate of return through borrowing. High leverage means the owner has made a small investment and the lender has made a large loan.

LEVERAGED BUYOUT The purchase of a company by using a small investment and a large loan. The new owner would gain control with a small amount of invested capital because he or she is able to secure a large loan for the balance of the amount needed.

LEVY To assess; to seize or collect. To levy a tax is to assess the property value and set a rate for taxation. To levy an execution is to seize the property of a person legally in order to satisfy an obligation.

LIABILITIES The sum, accumulation or list of each LIABILITY. The total of all amounts OWED.

LIABILITY The amount owed to another by a business or an individual. Characteristics: 1) represents a transfer of assets or services at a specified or determinable date; 2) the firm or individual has little or no discretion to avoid the transfer; 3) the event causing the obligation has already occurred. Liabilities are often divided into classes: short-term that are due to be paid in less than one year, and long-term that are due to be paid over a period of more than one year.

In accounting, liabilities are listed on the right hand side of a balance sheet statement showing the debts of the business owed to others. As opposed to things owned (ASSETS) or EQUITY by the owner.

In law and insurance, the legal responsibility for an act; the obligation to make good any loss or damage that occurs in a given situation.

LIABILITY CLAIM A request by an insurance POLICY HOLDER for reimbursement from the INSURER following a loss; an INSURANCE CLAIM. See INSURANCE CLAIM.

LIABILITY INSURANCE Financial protection from a loss resulting from the legal responsibility for an act; the obligation to make good any loss or damage that occurs in a given situation; financial compensation for such a loss.

LICENSE A certificate issued under law by a governmental body authorizing an individual or company to do a specific thing; the document for such authorization.

Between two businesses, a contractual agreement whereby one business provides a product, technology or knowledge for a fee to another company.

In international trade, a contractual agreement between a foreign government and a company whereby the company provides a product, technology or knowledge for a fee paid by the foreign government.

LICENSEE   The person or business who holds a valid LICENSE; the one to whom a license is issued. The person or business that holds proprietary rights to a product, technology or knowledge authorized by the owner.

LICENSING   A business practice involving a contractual agreement between two companies whereby one business provides a product, technology or knowledge in exchange for a fee from the other company.

The process of issuing a LICENSE by a government body.

LIEN   A creditor's claim against property; a loan with COLLATERAL property as security for assurance of repayment. When the loan is repaid, the lien is removed. If the money is not repaid, the creditor can seize the collateral property to satisfy the lien. Most often, a lien is placed on real estate for wages or materials expended by contractors and were not paid.

LIENEE   Same as borrower. See BORROWER; LIEN.

LIENOR   Same as creditor; lender. See CREDITOR; LENDER; LIEN.

LIEN WAIVER   A document signed by a contractor or supplier giving up the right to attach the property by a LIEN.

LIFE CYCLE   The term applied to the entire period from business start-up to closeout. The term can similarly be applied to a single product or industry. Also referred to as womb to tomb.

LIFO   See LAST-IN, FIRST-OUT.

LIMITED   See LIMITED COMPANY; abbreviated Ltd.

LIMITED COMPANY   A form of business most common in Britain, comparable to incorporation in the United States wherein the liability of each shareholder is restricted to the amount of the actual investment in the business. Limited company is abbreviated Ltd.

LIMITED LIABILITY COMPANY (LLC)   A type of CORPORATION that is owned by a limited number of shareholders in a small business. Although laws differ among the states, characteristics usually include: a board of directors is not required, transfer of shares is restricted and shares are usually evidenced only by notation on the register instead of certificates.

LIMITED PARTNER   An investor in a LIMITED PARTNERSHIP who has limited liability, is not involved in the day-to-day operation and usually cannot lose more than his or her capital contribution (share of the ownership). See LIMITED PARTNERSHIP.

LIMITED PARTNERSHIP   An organization consisting of a GENERAL PARTNER and one or more LIMITED PARTNERS. The general partner may have little or no investment, organizes the partnership, manages the day-to-day operation, controls the operation and collects a management fee, income and capital gains. The limited partner(s) bear the largest share of the invested capital and receive income, capital gains and tax benefits. The limited partner(s) cannot participate in control of the business. See PARTNERSHIP.

LIMITED POWER OF ATTORNEY   A POWER OF ATTORNEY that bestows specific powers of the signer to another person.

LINE   The primary or most important product of a company, as the main line of products. In larger businesses, people employed in the primary function of the business, as opposed to STAFF.

LINE OF CREDIT   A moral commitment by a bank to make loans to a particular borrower (usually a company). The borrower is allowed to borrow at any time up to a specified limit. A line of credit is not a legal commitment, yet the maximum amount, the fee, the interest rate and time period are specified. As opposed to a contractual LOAN commitment. Also called BANK LINE.

LIQUID   An abundance of cash or cash equivalents; easily converted to cash or cash equivalents. See LIQUIDITY.

LIQUID ASSET   All cash and any security easily convertible into cash. On a balance sheet, liquid assets are the CURRENT ASSETS, including marketable securities and accounts receivable. As opposed to ILLIQUID assets.

LIQUIDATE   To remove a debt by repaying it. To convert into cash. In a case such as bankruptcy, it may be necessary to sell material assets to obtain cash to pay the amount due.

LIQUIDITY   The amount of cash and cash equivalents in a business compared to the amount of debt; a term that describes the SOLVENCY of a business—its ability to repay debts with available cash. Also the ability to sell assets of a business that can produce cash or cash equivalents, often with significant loss of true value. Listed stocks and bonds are more LIQUID than real estate because sale for cash is more easily obtained. Having a good amount of liquidity produces a good credit rating and allows a business to take advantage of market opportunities. One test of liquidity measures the immediate debt paying ability; i.e., the ability to pay CURRENT LIABILITIES with QUICK ASSETS called the QUICK RATIO. If current assets cannot be converted into cash to meet current liabilities, the business is said to be ILLIQUID. See LIQUID.

LISTED SECURITY   Any security (stock or bond) that is actively traded on one of the regulated market exchanges. The most popular stock exchange is the New York Stock Exchange. A stock traded there would be a listed security.

LLC   See LIMITED LIABILITY COMPANY.

LOAN   Money owed to another person or business, such as a bank. In business, a transaction wherein the owner of a property allows another party to use the property. The user customarily promises to return the property after a specified period. Use can be free or conditional on payment of money or barter. See also DEBT.

LOAN AGREEMENT   A document that states limitations and authorized actions as long as money is owed to (usually) a bank. A loan agreement may place restrictions on the owner's salary, dividends, amount of other debt, working capital limits, sales, the number of additional personnel or other factors.

LOAN APPLICATION   A form to be completed by a potential borrower. When the form has been completed with all the information about the potential borrower it is submitted to a financial institution for consideration of a loan.

LOAN COMMITMENT   A written document issued by a lender who agrees to make a loan while the entire loan package is being completed.

LOAN CORRESPONDENT   One who negotiates loans for lenders. The correspondent often services the loan and acts as the collection agent for the lender.

LOAN GUARANTEE   A pledge by a second person with substantial personal wealth to repay a loan by the first person if the first person fails to repay.

LOAN PACKAGE   A loan application; the collection of documents, information and data used by a bank for consideration in making a loan. The data include information submitted by the potential borrower plus data from other sources substantiating the credibility of the borrower.

LOAN PAYMENT   To disburse an incremental amount of money for the partial satisfaction of a debt, usually according to a schedule.

LOAN REPAYMENT   Total satisfaction of a debt; payment in full. In business, the property loaned is most often MONEY. In a money loan, the BORROWER (user of the property) promises to repay the money to the LENDER (owner of the property) under specified conditions, i.e., for a specified period of time or at intervals over a period of time and with INTEREST. The documentation of the promise is called a PROMISSORY NOTE when the property is money.

LOAN SUBMISSION   A loan application that is delivered to a lender with all the information and documents necessary for consideration by the lender.

LOAN-TO-VALUE RATIO   In mortgage financing, the amount of loan a lender will make as a percentage of the appraised (market) value.

LOCAL   In general, the area immediately surrounding the topic of discussion.

In government, any body lower than a state, such as a city, county, community, village or town. As opposed to FEDERAL or STATE government.

In business, a business that is small and usually only has a few locations in a confined geographical area.

LOCAL AREA NETWORK (LAN)   Interconnections of telephone and computer equipment within an office to increase communication speed.

LOCAL DEVELOPMENT CORPORATION   An organization of companies and local governments, within a confined geographical area, that is designed to improve the economy of the area, and that usually provides financing capabilities to member businesses.

LOCATION ANALYSIS   A study of the various business environments to determine the best site for establishment of a business.

LOCATION-LOCATION-LOCATION   A commonly used phrase that emphasizes the importance of the location (site) of a business; the site is the most important environment that attracts customers to a business or could discourage them.

LOCK BOX   An efficient CASH MANAGEMENT system whereby the customer mails payment to a post office box, the bank picks up the payments and deposits them to the firm's account and informs the firm of the deposits made, thus reducing COLLECTION FLOAT. Often a lock box arrangement can be set up in a distant city to collect immediately interest on payments. Surplus funds are later transferred to the firm's home bank.

Also, any post office box where mail is stored until collected.

LOCK BOX SYSTEM   See LOCK BOX.

LOCKED IN   Any situation, usually favorable to the proponent, that is assured of occurrence; guaranteed.

LOGO   A specific design representation for a product or a company; an insignia.

LONG-RANGE   A term used in business planning for a period of time greater than three years. Setting goals and identifying objectives for a long-range period; to provide the basis for actions in the SHORT RANGE.

LONG-RANGE PLAN   A BUSINESS PLAN covering a period greater than three years, such as a ten-year business plan. See BUSINESS PLAN.

LONG-TERM   In business, the definition of long-term is different for different uses. As examples: For assets and loans on a balance sheet, long-term is one year or more; securities owned more than one year (sometimes six months) are defined as a LONG-TERM CAPITAL GAIN for taxing purposes; three years or more is long-term in planning; and a long-term bond has a maturity of ten years or more.

Bankers usually define long-term as ten years or more; INTERMEDIATE-TERM is more than one year but less than ten years; and SHORT-TERM is one year or less. See SHORT-TERM; INTERMEDIATE-TERM.

LONG-TERM ASSETS   Things owned by a business (ASSETS) with an expected life of a year or more. See FIXED ASSETS.

LONG-TERM CAPITAL GAIN   A CAPITAL GAIN resulting from holding an asset for a period greater than one year. See CAPITAL GAIN.

LONG-TERM CONTRACT   A CONTRACT to perform work for another that represents work over an extended period of time.

LONG-TERM DEBT   A liability due in a year or more, such as a mortgage, note or bond, as shown on a balance sheet. Interest and partial principal may be repaid in periodic payments, such as a mortgage. Or interest may be paid periodically over the term of the loan, as a bond, with the principal amount paid at maturity.

LONG-TERM FINANCING   Money borrowed for a period of more than one year; borrowed money (a loan) that is repayable over a period of more than one year is classified as long-term liabilities on a balance sheet. Also, all equity in a business is long-term financing.

LONG-TERM GAIN   See LONG-TERM CAPITAL GAIN.

LONG-TERM LIABILITIES   See LONG-TERM DEBT.

LONG-TERM LOAN   See LONG-TERM DEBT.

LONG-TERM LOSS   Property sold for less than the acquisition price after being held for a period of one year or more.

LOOPHOLE   Areas of the tax code or a contract not specifically clear allowing interpretation by either party to that party's advantage.

LOSS   In an accounting situation, a negative value resulting when expenses are deducted from income of a business as shown on an INCOME STATEMENT. In an investment transaction, the amount by which the ending CAPITAL is smaller than the beginning CAPITAL (invested amount), a loss of CAPITAL. The opposite of a PROFIT.

In insurance, the amount reimbursed (before any deductible) by an insurer resulting from a financial risk covered (indemnified) under an INSURANCE POLICY, such as damage, injury or death.

LOSS LEADER   Any article that a store sells cheaply or below cost in order to attract customers.

LOT   A quantity economical to produce or to purchase; a parcel of land suitable for improvement by construction of a building.

LOWBALL; LOWBALLING   Setting the early price in an arrangement at a low amount to secure business with the intent later to raise the price.

LOWER OF COST OR MARKET   A conservative accounting convention whereby valuation is at the lowest amount, i.e., not over-valued.

Ltd.; LTD   See LIMITED.

M

MACROECONOMICS   The study of an overall economy as a whole entity, such as a national economy. To understand the behavior and interrelationship of major segments, such as industries or markets. Contrasted with MICROECONOMICS.

MAILING LIST   A record of customers or prospects, with complete addresses and telephone numbers, used for advertising solicitations or any other purpose.

MAIL ORDER   A method of retailing whereby goods are ordered by mail or telephone then delivered by the postal service or private delivery service.

MAINTENANCE   The care and work necessary to keep something in the usual operating condition for productive use; general repair and upkeep.

MAJORITY   As related to small business, the one who holds more than 50 percent of a transaction, as a majority stockholder or a majority interest in a real estate deal. The opposite of a MINORITY.
   The age at which a person is no longer a minor and is thus able to enter into contracts freely. The age of majority in most states for contract purposes is 18.
   In a vote, more than half of those voting or more than half of those present and authorized to vote.

MAKE-OR-BUY DECISION   The evaluation of whether a part should be produced by your company or purchased from another company. Factors to consider include production cost, reliability, quality, dependability and available capacity.

157

MAKER   The person (BORROWER) who executes a promissory note and thus becomes liable for payment to the PAYEE. See DRAWER.

MANAGE   To control the business operations; to conduct affairs in a business; to have charge of the business.

MANAGEMENT   The group of people in a business who MANAGE the business; people who make decisions and supervise operations for the owner of a business.

MANAGEMENT ACCOUNTING   The subfield of accounting that develops financial data for management analysis and decisions.

MANAGEMENT BY OBJECTIVE (MBO)   An art of management and technique whereby the actions of analysis, direction and control are focused on the end result.

MANAGEMENT TOOL   Any equipment, procedure or technique that enhances the efficiency with which the business operates.

MANAGER   A person who exercises the art of management; a person who directs or controls the work of other workers or a particular operation within the business.

MANAGING PARTNER   See GENERAL PARTNER.

MANIFEST   See BILL OF LADING.

MANUFACTURE   To produce goods from raw materials or other ingredients by the application of labor.

MANUFACTURER   A producer of goods from raw materials or other ingredients by the application of labor. See PRODUCER.

MANUFACTURING   The industry associated with producing new GOODS and MERCHANDISE. The process of producing products.

MANUFACTURING COSTS   The labor and material expenses incurred during the production of goods.

MANUFACTURING TECHNOLOGY CENTER A not-for-profit shop, office or laboratory that promotes the transfer of technical knowledge to small businesses to enhance productivity and competitiveness. Manufacturing Technology Centers are a program of the U.S. National Institute of Standards and Technology.

MARGIN   In finance, the difference between selling price and some level of cost. Most often in small business, margin refers to sales less cost of goods sold expressed in dollars, called GROSS PROFIT, GROSS MARGIN or gross profit margin.

In economics, the difference between one value and another value.

In bank financing, the difference between the current market value of collateral and the loan amount.

In purchasing shares of stock, the amount of money that must be deposited in an account at a stock brokerage for the purchase of shares of stock, with the remainder being borrowed from the broker. The stock becomes the collateral for the borrowed money. Sometimes expressed as the percent of the total amount that must be paid by the purchaser.

MARGINAL   Close to a limit; on the border between profitable and unprofitable, as in a marginal business.

An economist's term for a change in an economic factor as compared with the economic factor itself. Thus, marginal describes the relationship of the change to the economic factor.

MARGINAL COST   The increase or decrease in the total costs of a business due to a greater or fewer number of units produced.

MARGIN OF PROFIT   See PROFIT MARGIN.

MARKDOWN   A reduction from the original selling price; a downward adjustment in the value of securities. See MARKUP.

MARKET   As a noun, a public place where products or services are bought and sold. The aggregate of potential buyers; the equivalent of DEMAND. Short for MARKET VALUE. As a verb, to sell.

MARKETABILITY   The speed and ease with which a product or service could be bought or sold. In the sale of a business asset, marketability is interchangeable with LIQUIDITY, but liquidity implies preservation of original value.

MARKETABLE   A product or service easily bought or sold, such as assets that are easily converted into cash.

MARKETABLE SECURITY   An investment that is easily converted into cash, such as stocks or bonds.

MARKET ACCESS   The opportunity for a company to sell its products in a specific MARKET, considering competitiveness, regulations and trade restrictions.

MARKET ANALYSIS   Research aimed at predicting or anticipating the salability and profitability of a product or service, based on technical data about the product and the potential market. A study to define a company's market. A forecast of market direction with a view toward sharing or exploiting new trends.

MARKET APPROACH   The general description of a company's assessment and direction in a market.

MARKET CAPITALIZATION   The value of a corporation as determined by the market price of its issued and outstanding common stock.

MARKETING   Moving goods and services from the provider to the consumer. This involves advertising, publicity, promotion, pricing, sale and distribution of the goods and services. Also included is MARKET ANALYSIS to define the market.

MARKETING MIX   A selection of products by a single company to offer several options from which the customer can choose. The advantage to the business is that more customers will likely consider one of the options as opposed to purchasing from another company.

MARKET NICHE   See NICHE.

MARKETPLACE   A location where business is conducted. Same as MARKET, used as a noun. Marketplace also refers to all existing and potential customers.

MARKETING PLAN   That portion of a BUSINESS PLAN dealing with the marketing of the product or service; or similarly, a self-contained plan.

MARKET POSITION   The relationship of a single product or an entire company to others in a specific market; your product/company sales compared to the sales of another; your product/company sales expressed as a percent of the total sales in the market. With the knowledge of your product's or company's current market position, a strategy can be devised to improve your company's market position. Descriptive terms are often applied to the market position, such as leader, challenger or follower.

MARKET POTENTIAL   The amount of sales that could be drawn from the total amount of customers.

MARKET PRICE   In business, the current prevailing value at which products or services are traded between buyers and sellers. See SUPPLY and DEMAND.

In the securities market, the last reported price at which a security was sold; or in OVER THE COUNTER MARKETS, the combined current BID and ASKED prices.

MARKET RESEARCH   Exploration of the size, characteristics and potential salability of a product or service; determining what people want and need. Often market research is accomplished before developing the new product or service to determine the viability of the investment needed for development. Market research is an early step in MARKETING the product or service.

MARKET SEGMENT   That portion of the entire market that is the target of sales potential for a company.

MARKET SHARE   The percentage of industry sales that are sold by a single company or are attributable to an individual product.

MARKET SIZE   The total dollar amount of the potential sales to all customers in a given market.

MARKET STRATEGY   The overall long-range vision or scheme of masterminding the future course or direction of the marketing plan. Selection of the product mix and customer profile for maximum profit potential. Four elements (the 4 "Ps") are often cited as important to effective market strategy, i.e., product, price, promotion and place (distribution).

MARKET VALUE   The price at which buyers and sellers trade similar items in the open marketplace.

In accounting, the valuing of inventory at the current market price; or with the more conservative accounting principle, the "lower of acquisition cost or current market price."

MARK OF ORIGIN   The prominently displayed physical nomenclature on a product that identifies the location where the product was manufactured, such as "Made in U.S.A."

MARKUP   An amount by which the retail selling price of a product is greater than the purchased price or the cost of the services rendered, such as in retailing or wholesaling. Also called initial markup. Many times markup refers to the percent (rather than the amount) that the selling price is greater than the purchased price, such as a markup of 40 percent.

MATERIAL; MATERIALS   Goods purchased for remanufacture into another product by the application of labor. Often material is used in the plural, as materials.

MATURITY   The time at which a note or bond becomes due or payable.

MATURITY DATE   The date on which an amount is due and payable; the date on which the principal amount of a debt instrument is due and payable; the date an installment loan must be paid in full. In FACTORING, the average due date of factored receivables at the time cash is remitted to the seller.

MATURITY FACTORING   A method of financing accounts receivable (FACTORING) whereby the FACTOR performs the entire credit and collection function. The factor remits cash to the seller each month based on the average due date of the receivables. The factor's commission is 0.75 percent to 2 percent depending on the bad debt risk and the handling costs. See FACTORING.

MBO   See MANAGEMENT BY OBJECTIVE.

MECHANIC'S LIEN   A claim against real property made by contractors, suppliers or workers on the property if they are not paid for the work done in construction or repair.

MEDIA   Newspapers, magazines, radio and television used as a means to reach customers by advertising.

MEDIA BUYER   The employee who buys time on radio, television or space in a newspaper or magazine to promote or advertise something.

MEDIA KIT   A collection of data prepared by an advertising agency or media and used as a sales tool to encourage companies to advertise in their medium.

MEETING   A gathering of several persons for the purpose of discussing a particular subject.

MERCANTILE   Dealing with merchants and trade. Commercial as opposed to personal.

MERCANTILE AGENCY   A firm that supplies businesses with credit ratings on other businesses that are or might become customers. Usually industry or geographically specific, they sometimes collect past due accounts or provide trade collection statistics. The largest such firm is DUN & BRADSTREET.

MERCHANDISE   In business, physical things bought and sold; GOODS; commodities; wares; products. Also, to buy, sell or trade as well as to advertise, promote or organize the sale.

MERCHANDISING   The in-store presentation of goods so the goods will be attractive, convenient and visible to shoppers; sometimes used synonymously with the concept of marketing the goods.

MERCHANT   The person or company that sells goods for a profit; a storekeeper; a shopkeeper; a trader. Most often refers to the retail level but also applies to wholesale.

MERCHANT'S LICENSE   A certificate issued by a local government authorizing the sale of products by a merchant.

MERGER   The uniting or combining of two or more interests into one, such as combining two companies into one company.

MEZZANINE LEVEL   In VENTURE CAPITAL language, the stage of a company's development just prior to GOING PUBLIC. VENTURE CAPITALISTS entering at this point have a lower risk than previous stages. See VENTURE CAPITAL.

MICROCOMPUTER   See PERSONAL COMPUTER.

MICROECONOMICS   The study of the individual segments of an economy, such as industries, markets or businesses, to understand the behavior of the economy as a whole. Contrasted with MACROECONOMICS.

MICROLOAN; MICROLOAN PROGRAM   An SBA sponsored program for encouraging lenders to make small loans to small businesses. Loans from a few hundred dollars up to about $50,000 are considered microloans.

MIDDLEMAN   A term for an intermediary business person that is becoming outdated and replaced by MIDDLEPERSON. See MIDDLEPERSON.

MIDDLEPERSON   An intermediary business person or trader who buys commodities from a producer and resells them to a retailer; a go-between.

MINIMUM BALANCE   The least amount of money that can be left on deposit with a bank, without incurring a service charge.

MINIMUM WAGE   The lowest hourly employee payment permitted by law.

MINOR   Of lesser importance; a trivial matter.

Also, a person who has not reached the age of majority (usually considered 18 years of age).

MINORITIES   Plural of MINORITY.

MINORITY   As related to small business, the one who holds less than 50 percent of a transaction, as a minority stockholder or a minority interest in a real estate deal. The opposite of a MAJORITY.

Related to social culture as defined by the Department of Labor, a minority is a group of people who have been socially or economically disadvantaged because of race, creed, color or ethnic background. Minorities include Blacks, Asians, Native Americans and Hispanics, but not women.

MINORITY BUSINESS   As defined by the U.S. Small Business Administration, a business in which majority ownership is held by those who are classified as members of minority groups, such as Blacks, Asian Americans and Native Americans.

MINORITY STOCKHOLDER   Any shareholder or group of shareholders that, in aggregate, own less than half the shares in a corporation.

MINUTE   A division of time equal to one-sixtieth of an hour.

MINUTE BOOK   The compilation of the MINUTES of company meetings.

MINUTES   A record of the chronological proceedings of meetings of the Board of Directors, the Executive Committee or other business group.

MISCELLANEOUS EXPENSES   A catchall location for EXPENSES that cannot be specifically categorized on an INCOME STATEMENT.

MISC. EXPENSES   See MISCELLANEOUS EXPENSES.

MODEM   A device that converts the digital signals of a computer into voice-frequency signals to permit transmission of the information by telephone lines; short for MOdulation/DEModulation.

MODIFIED CASH BASIS   An accounting method whereby income is recognized when cash is received and expense items are recognized when cash is paid for them, except for long-term assets that are accounted on an ACCRUAL BASIS. Most small and start-up businesses use the MODIFIED CASH BASIS accounting method. For alternative methods, see CASH BASIS; ACCRUAL BASIS.

MOM AND POP BUSINESS   Generally a small business (most often retail) operated by a husband and wife.

MONEY   In general, the standard medium of exchange as established by a government (i.e., United States) and the standard of value for describing the worth of other things. The media include: coins; paper money and any substance used as money, such as bank notes, checks or money orders.

In business, any definite or indefinite sum of money.

MONEY PUT DOWN   See DOWN PAYMENT.

MONOPOLY   Control of production and distribution of a product or service by one company (or several companies acting in concert) and characterized by lack of competition. Outlawed by the ANTITRUST LAWS. See also CARTEL; OLIGOPOLY; PERFECT COMPETITION.

MONOPSONY   Dominance of a market by one buyer or group of buyers acting together. Less prevalent than a MONOPOLY.

MONTH   A time period equal to one-twelfth of a year; 30 days.

MONTHLY   Occurring each month; occurring 12 times each year.

MONTHLY CLOSING   The accounting term for preparation of the financial statement for a month, meaning that no further entries may be made in accounts for that month and the books are closed to additional transactions.

MONTHLY REPORT   A document prepared each month that records events that have occurred during the previous month.

MORTGAGE   A debt instrument by which the borrower (MORT-GAGOR) gives the lender (MORTGAGEE) a lien on property as security for the repayment of a loan; most commonly used for real property (real estate). For personal property, the lien is called a SECURITY AGREEMENT, formerly called a chattel mortgage.

MORTGAGEE   The person who holds a MORTGAGE as security for a debt; the one who lends money in a MORTGAGE contract.

MORTGAGE OWNED   A mortgage held; a debt owed to the holder.

MORTGAGE PAYABLE   The amount of a MORTGAGE that remains to be paid as shown on a BALANCE SHEET.

MORTGAGOR   The person who gives a MORTGAGE as security for a debt (LOAN); the one who borrows money in a MORT-GAGE contact.

MULTILATERAL   A compact in which three or more parties participate, such as an understanding, agreement or contract.

MULTIMEDIA   Electronic products that use various media (text, graphics, animation and audio) to deliver information. Often these media are also interactive, allowing the user to pick and choose from a variety of information options.

MUNICIPAL ORDINANCE   See ORDINANCES.

MURPHY'S LAW   "Whatever may go wrong, will go wrong."

N

NAFTA See NORTH AMERICAN FREE TRADE AGREEMENT.

NAME, FICTITIOUS See FICTITIOUS NAME.

NAME, RESERVATION OF The exclusive right to the use of a trade name, fictitious name or a corporate name. Reservation is made by filing the proper application with a state authority and paying the appropriate fee.

NASD The National Association of Securities Dealers, a trade group for regulating investments in small company stocks.

NASDAQ The National Association of Securities Dealers Automated Quotation system, a stock market system for buying and selling small-company stocks.

NATIONAL BUSINESS INCUBATOR ASSOCIATION (NBIA) A not-for-profit organization that promotes the establishment and successful operation of INCUBATORS as an avenue to assist start-up entrepreneurs, especially in new technology. A business that starts in an incubator has a measurably better chance of survival.

NATIONAL FEDERATION OF INDEPENDENT BUSINESS (NFIB) The nation's largest advocacy organization for small and independent businesses.

NATIONAL LABOR RELATIONS BOARD (NLRB) A federal government agency that administers laws concerning labor relations.

NBIA See NATIONAL BUSINESS INCUBATOR ASSOCIATION.

NEGATIVE CASH FLOW   See CASH FLOW.

NEGOTIABLE   In banking, a financial document that can be easily converted into cash, such as a check or promissory note when properly endorsed or properly delivered.

In business, something that can be sold or transferred to another party in exchange for money or settlement of an obligation.

A matter of mutual concern between one or more parties that can be resolved to the satisfaction of all parties.

NEGOTIABLE INSTRUMENT   An unconditional order or promise to pay an amount of money on demand, easily transferable from one person to another, such as a check, draft, promissory note or stock certificate. Must meet the UNIFORM COMMERCIAL CODE.

NEGOTIABLE PAPER   Common expression for NEGOTIABLE INSTRUMENT.

NEGOTIATE   To confer, bargain or discuss a business item with the intent of reaching an agreement. Or to discuss with a view to settle or conclude a business transaction.

In banking, to transfer, assign or sell, such as NEGOTIABLE PAPER.

NEGOTIATION   Conferring, discussing or bargaining to reach an agreement.

NET   The opposite of GROSS. See the definition for the precise business term in question. See also GROSS.

In business in a general sense, the term means what is left over after deducting other amounts, i.e., net income or net assets.

NET ASSETS   The difference between a company's total assets and its total liabilities. Another way of saying OWNER'S EQUITY or NET WORTH, since the subtraction results in a value of assets equal to the net worth.

NET CURRENT ASSETS   CURRENT ASSETS less CURRENT LIABILITIES; another name for WORKING CAPITAL. See WORKING CAPITAL.

NET EARNINGS   See NET INCOME.

NET FIXED ASSETS   On a BALANCE SHEET, the cost of assets minus the depreciation expense incurred to date.

NET INCOME (OR LOSS)   On an INCOME STATEMENT the sum remaining after all EXPENSES have been deducted from INCOME; called NET INCOME, NET EARNINGS or NET PROFIT. When the value is positive it is called NET PROFIT. When the value is negative it is called NET LOSS.

For a business, total SALES less COST OF GOODS SOLD and less OVERHEAD and other expenses. Net income is usually specified whether income taxes have been deducted (NET INCOME BEFORE TAXES) or provisions made for payment of income taxes (NET INCOME AFTER TAXES). Net income after taxes is the amount earned by the owners of the business; in the vernacular, the BOTTOM LINE.

For an individual, gross income less expenses incurred to produce the income. Usually, expenses incurred for the production of income are deductible for tax purposes.

NET INCOME AFTER TAXES   See NET INCOME.

NET INCOME BEFORE TAXES   See NET INCOME.

NET LEASE   A commercial lease in which the lessee pays the rent for occupancy plus maintenance and operating expenses, such as taxes, insurance, utilities and repairs. The rent paid is "NET" to the lessor, such as all profit.

NET LOSS   Net income that has a negative value. See NET INCOME (or LOSS).

NET MARGIN   Net profit before taxes expressed as a percent of net sales. See PROFIT MARGIN.

NET OPERATING INCOME   The balance remaining after deduction of cost of goods sold and overhead expenses from gross income but before debt service.

NET PRESENT VALUE (NPV)   In evaluating an investment, such as a capital expenditure, all cash outflows and all cash inflows are calculated using a DISCOUNT RATE to give the worth (the PRESENT VALUE) of making the investment at a given point in time, such as today. Also, the value today of all future income from a project minus the amount of the investment. See PRESENT VALUE; INTERNAL RATE OF RETURN.

NET PROFIT   Net income that has a positive value. Opposite of NET LOSS. See NET INCOME.

NET PROFIT AFTER TAXES   Same as NET INCOME AFTER TAXES when the value is positive. See NET INCOME.

NET PROFIT BEFORE TAXES   Same as NET INCOME BEFORE TAXES when the value is positive. See NET INCOME.

NET PROFIT ON SALES   A measure of efficiency of a company; divide net income before taxes by gross sales and express as a percent. When compared with prior periods, net profit on sales can reveal trends of management efficiency. See NET INCOME.

NET SALES   An accounting term consisting of GROSS SALES less returns, allowances, freight out and cash discounts allowed.

NETWORKING   Regular communication among businesses or individuals to exchange information for the benefit and growth of the entire group; the sharing of information.

NET WORKING CAPITAL   More precise wording for WORKING CAPITAL to differentiate from GROSS WORKING CAPITAL. See WORKING CAPITAL.

NET WORTH   The amount owned by the owners; the amount by which assets exceed liabilities. The book value of the investments plus retained earnings. Also called EQUITY; OWNER'S EQUITY. For a corporation, net worth is known as STOCKHOLDERS' EQUITY. For a partnership, the value of the total of all the shares of all the partners.

For a proprietorship, net worth is known as OWNER'S EQUITY.

For an individual, net worth is also called PERSONAL NET WORTH, the total value of all possessions (assets), such as cash, checking account balance, stocks, bonds, house, car and personal property minus all debts such as a mortgage, loans and revolving credit accounts.

NET YIELD The portion of gross yield that remains after all costs, such as loan servicing and reserves, are deducted.

NEW ISSUE A stock or bond offered to the public for the first time.

NFIB See NATIONAL FEDERATION OF INDEPENDENT BUSINESS.

NICHE An individual specialization in business. The area of the market where a company or product is particularly strong. This specialization often results in super high quality by the specialist company and elimination of competition because of the uniqueness.

NLRB See National Labor Relations Board.

NOMINAL INTEREST RATE The rate of interest that is stated in a note or contract and may differ from the true or effective interest rate. See EFFECTIVE INTEREST RATE, INTEREST.

NO MINIMUM BALANCE A bank account that can have a zero amount of money on deposit and no service charge will be assessed.

NONCOMPETITION CLAUSE A provision in a contract or lease prohibiting a person or business from operating or controlling a similar business. Often, when a business is sold, the prior owner must agree to a NONCOMPETITION CLAUSE to prevent competition with the new owner.

NON-NOTIFICATION BASIS FACTORING See FACTORING.

NONPERFORMING ASSETS Loans in arrears.

NONPRICE COMPETITION Competition among products, services or companies for sales by means other than the basis of price, such as advertising, superior product quality and perception of benefit to the customer.

NONPROFIT   An association or corporation that is exempted from paying corporate income taxes because it engages in charitable, cultural, educational or socially desirable programs for the public good. Contributions by the public or by businesses are also tax deductible. Also called NOT-FOR-PROFIT.

NONRECOURSE LOAN   A LOAN in which the borrower may have pledged collateral, but the borrower is not held personally liable. The lender of a nonrecourse loan generally feels confident that the property used as collateral will be adequate security for the loan.

NONRECURRING   One time; not repeating. In accounting, often used as a substitute for nonrecurring expenses that are not expected to occur again, such as start-up expenses and large fixed-asset purchases.

NON-SUFFICIENT FUNDS (NSF)   See INSUFFICIENT FUNDS.

NORMAL VALUE   The usual price. See FAIR MARKET VALUE.

NORTH AMERICAN FREE TRADE AGREEMENT (NAFTA)   An agreement among the countries of North America to promote more free trade among themselves.

NOTARY   Short for NOTARY PUBLIC.

NOTARY PUBLIC   A state registered public officer who administers oaths; attests and certifies documents by signature and seal, giving authenticity; takes depositions and affidavits. In the absence of a seal, the notarization is void.

NOTE   A business loan, usually short term; a written promise to pay, stating the amount, the interest rate, the time, the method of payment and the obligation to repay. A note is evidence of a DEBT. A note may be secured or unsecured. Also called PROMISSORY NOTE.

NOTE PAYABLE   A NOTE by a person or business that is due and owing; an obligation or lien that must be repaid and is due.

NOTE RECEIVABLE   An amount loaned to another that is owed and payable to the holder of the NOTE.

NOTES TO FINANCIAL STATEMENTS   A section of an AN-NUAL REPORT that presents clarifying information concerning the financial statements.

NOT-FOR-PROFIT   See NONPROFIT.

NOTICE OF DEFAULT   A legal document, issued by a lender, that advises a borrower that an amount due has not been repaid as promised.

NOTIFICATION BASIS FACTORING   See FACTORING.

NPV   See NET PRESENT VALUE.

NSF   An abbreviation for NON-SUFFICIENT FUNDS. See IN-SUFFICIENT FUNDS.

NULL AND VOID   Having no legal force or effect.

O

OBJECTIVES   The intended results or the intended outcomes. Those GOALS to be achieved or striven for.

OBLIGATION   A debt, note or lien payable; anything that is owed to others; a binding contract; a promise to pay; indebted.

OBSOLESCENCE   A product that is no longer usable due to replacement by newer or better products, accompanied by a decline in value.

OCEAN BILL OF LADING   A contract for goods to be exported that is issued to a transportation company (a SHIPPER), listing the goods shipped, acknowledging their receipt and promising delivery to the person or business named.

OCCUPANCY PERMIT   An authorization issued by the appropriate government body to establish a property as suitable for business use and meeting certain health and safety standards.

OCCURRENCE; OCCURRENCE FORM   In insurance, a method for determining whether or not insurance coverage is available for a specific claim. A claim is paid if the event occurred during the policy period regardless when the business submits the claim. See also CLAIMS MADE FORM.

OEM   Original Equipment Manufacturer; as opposed to an AFTERMARKET supplier.

OFF-BALANCE SHEET FINANCING   Debt-like resources that, by their nature, do not show on the balance sheet, i.e., a long-term noncancellable operating lease.

OFF-BUDGET   DISCRETIONARY FUNDS; money that is permitted to be spent without specific budget allocation in advance.

OFFER   A public or private notice to sell; a manifestation of the intent to enter into an agreement. A promise initiated by one party (a PROPOSAL) to act or perform in a specified manner provided the other party acts in the manner requested after a contract is consummated under the conditions requested. An offer demonstrates willingness by the party who wishes to perform the work to enter into a contract with the party who wants the work done; an offer to sell. See BID; PROPOSAL.

OFFER AND ACCEPTANCE   The two components of a valid contract; a meeting of the minds; an agreement to transact business. See OFFER; ACCEPTANCE.

OFFICE   An enclosed place within a building used primarily for the conduct of business, particularly administrative and clerical work. As opposed to a factory.
  The job of an officer; see OFFICER. Also, the job of an elected official, such as election to the office of mayor.

OFFICER   A top-level executive of a company; one who is invited to attend meetings of the board of directors.

OFFICE SUPPLY STORE   A retail business whose entire operation is offering business forms, materials, stock and equipment for sale to other businesses.

OFFSHORE   A business outside the United States that is owned by United States citizens or corporations. Often such businesses have been located outside of the United States to benefit from low labor costs or to avoid U.S. taxes or regulations.

OFFSHORE FINANCING   Raising money from outside the borders of the U.S.

OIL THE SQUEAKING WHEEL A popular description of management, suggesting that it responds to the loudest voice of the moment rather than following a carefully planned set of objectives.

OJT An acronym for On-the-Job Training; an informal method of learning job skills.

OLD ACCOUNTS ACCOUNTS on which activity has not occurred for a considerable period of time. Most often, customer credit accounts that are uncollectible or approaching the point of not being collectible.

OLIGOPOLY A market situation in which a small number of sellers control the market supply of a product or service, and therefore the seller is able to control the market price. A market situation not like PERFECT COMPETITION or like a MONOPOLY. See also OLIGOPSONY.

OLIGOPSONY A market situation in which a few large buyers control the purchasing power for a product or service, and therefore the buyers are able to drive down the market price. See also OLIGOPOLY.

ONE-WRITE SYSTEM A standardized bookkeeping method wherein only one entry is made to record each transaction. As opposed to DOUBLE-ENTRY bookkeeping.

ON HAND Those things that are on the business premises; those that are in the possession of the business, such as cash on deposit in a bank.

ON-LINE A communication channel that is readily accessible for retrieval of information, such as a telephone line connection to a main frame computer on which data are stored for downloading to a personal computer.

ON OR BEFORE A phrase in a contract referring to the time for performance of a specified act, such as payment of money or completion of a project.

OPEN   The status of an order to buy, sell or transact (an open order) that has not been executed or completed. To establish (open) an account or (open) a line of credit. A loan that has an unpaid (open) balance.

OPEN ACCOUNT   An account with another business; a commercial account. Open account means regular trading and transactions with the other business on credit wherein payment is made at a later date. As opposed to CHARGE ACCOUNT for a person. See ACCOUNT. Also, refers to accounts with other businesses on which money is owed and now due, and to initiate action to begin doing business using an account at that business.

OPEN AN ACCOUNT   To establish a relationship with another business involving trust and cooperative financial transaction of business, such as to set up a bank checking account or to set up a credit account with another business either as a buyer or as a seller. See also ACCOUNT; OPEN ACCOUNT.

OPEN ORDER   An ORDER for goods or services that has not been filled by the supplier or canceled by the purchaser.

OPEN SHOP   A location or company where union membership is not a requirement for employment even if a union is present.

OPERATING BUDGET   An itemized statement of income, expenses, debt service and cash flow during a future period; a projection of the profitability of a business. See BUDGET.

OPERATING COSTS   Same as OPERATING EXPENSES.

OPERATING EXPENSES   The cost of doing business over a period of time. On an INCOME STATEMENT, the expenses which must be met no matter what level of sales has occurred, i.e., rent, utilities, maintenance, administrative and clerical. Operating expenses are fixed expenses and overhead expenses, as opposed to cost of goods sold and other variable expenses. See OVERHEAD; OVERHEAD EXPENSES; INDIRECT COSTS.

OPERATING RATIO   Any of several relationships among expenses arising from business activities, usually expressed as a percent and used for comparative purposes.

OPERATING STATEMENT   Same as INCOME STATEMENT; PROFIT & LOSS STATEMENT. See INCOME STATEMENT.

OPERATIONAL HEALTH AND SAFETY ADMINISTRATION (OSHA)   A federal government agency responsible for promulgating and enforcing occupational safety and health standards and regulations.

OPPORTUNITY COST   The present value of the income that could be earned from using an asset in its best alternative use rather than its current use. Also, the amount of income that is lost by the current use of an asset compared to another or better use of the asset.

ORDER   In business, a request to buy, sell, deliver, or receive goods or services that commits the issuer of the order to the terms specified. Also, direction to an employee to perform certain tasks in the conduct of business.

In banking, a payee's request to the maker, as on a check, "Pay to the order of_____."

In law, a direction from a court of jurisdiction or a regulation.

ORDINANCES   The rules, regulations and codes enacted into LAW by local governing bodies. See LAW.

ORDINARY AND NECESSARY BUSINESS EXPENSE   An expense incurred through the normal course of business, such as rent, supplies and utilities, as opposed to expenses for a specific project or a new venture. Under federal income tax law, ordinary and necessary business expenses may be deducted in the year incurred rather than capitalized and spread over several years.

ORGANIZATION   In a business start-up, the job of accomplishing the collective tasks needed to get the business into full operation in the intended manner. These include business planning, business structuring, financing, marketing, finding suppliers and selecting people for the various jobs.

In business management, the collective relationship of all supervisors and subordinates that defines the authority and responsibility chain of command. See ORGANIZATION CHART.

ORGANIZATIONAL EXPENSES   The cost incurred for incorporation of a corporation or syndication of a partnership prior to operation as a business entity. These expenses may include legal fees, the cost of raising money, accounting fees, design, research and patenting. Also called START-UP COSTS.

ORGANIZATION CHART   A pictorial display of the relationship of supervisors and subordinates; headed by the chief officer or owner.

ORGANIZE   In general, to arrange in an orderly way or to bring into being; establish.

In a business start-up, to perform all the preliminary tasks and functions so that the business can begin operation in the intended manner.

Relating to business management, to arrange a hierarchy of the chain of command from the owner(s) down to the workers. See ORGANIZATION; ORGANIZATION CHART.

In relation to labor unions, the activities undertaken to formulate and begin a labor union.

OSHA   See OPERATIONAL HEALTH AND SAFETY ADMINISTRATION.

OTC   See OVER-THE-COUNTER.

OUTLAY   To spend, usually for a large purchase such as a fixed asset. See EXPENDITURE.

OUTSIDE DIRECTORS   Members of a BOARD OF DIRECTORS who are elected from the business community at large. See BOARD OF DIRECTORS.

OUTSIDE MANAGEMENT   A management consultant or other experienced nonmember of the firm who is invited in to make analyses of operations and recommendations for improvement.

OUTSOURCE   To purchase; procure. Most often outsource is used when a product or service task has previously been accomplished within the company (an inside source) but is now being purchased or is being considered for purchase from another company (an outside source).

OUTSTANDING   In accounting, the amount of unpaid debts and obligations. A document, such as a check or draft, that has not been presented for payment. Also called OUTSTANDING BALANCE.

Concerning shares of stock authorized by a corporation, see ISSUED AND OUTSTANDING.

Any action that is authorized but all activities concerning the action are not yet complete.

OUTSTANDING BALANCE   An amount of a loan that remains to be paid; a note on which there is still a liability.

OUTSTANDING CHECK   A check or draft that was written but has not been presented to the bank for payment.

OVERADVANCE   A method of financing by a FACTOR who makes loans in anticipation of sales. As an example, cash is advanced by the factor to a firm to permit inventory build-up prior to peak selling periods. The security for the loan is the anticipated accounts receivable. See FACTORING.

OVERAGE   A quantity received in excess of the amount ordered; an amount of money received in excess of the amount due; an amount produced that exceeds the selling order amount.

In finance, an expenditure in excess of the amount budgeted.

In retail store leases, an amount of rent payable in excess of the base amount. That is, a percent of the store selling volume in excess of a base sales volume.

OVERHEAD   In a business, the expenses and costs that are not directly associated with the production or sale of goods and services. The normal costs of being in business, such as office, rent, utilities, insurance, advertising, accounting and legal expenses. As opposed to the COST OF GOODS SOLD that directly relate to the products or services for sale. Also called INDIRECT COSTS; BURDEN, OVERHEAD COST, OPERATING EXPENSES.

OVERHEAD COST   See OVERHEAD.

OVER-THE-COUNTER (OTC)   A security that is not listed or traded on an organized stock exchange. Over-the-counter stocks are traditionally those of smaller and emerging companies. Trading is often accomplished through NASDAQ.

OVERTIME   Work by an employee done after the regular work time. Usually more than eight hours per day or 40 hours per week.

OVERTIME HOURS   The number of hours worked by an employee after the regular work period.

OWN   Belonging, relating or peculiar to oneself. To hold title to a property or be in control of a sole proprietorship.

OWNER   The person who owns property or a business entity. In business, the owner is usually the person in control of a sole proprietorship or the person who owns more than 50% of a corporation or a partnership. In property, the one who holds title.

OWNER/MANAGER   One who operates his or her own business.

OWNER'S EQUITY   See EQUITY, NET WORTH.

OWNERSHIP   The provision by which a person or business holds legal title to property or is in control of a sole proprietorship.

P

PAID-IN CAPITAL   Same as CAPITAL INVESTMENT, but excluding more precise components as defined in CAPITAL SURPLUS.

PAID IN FULL   Receipt of the entire amount that was on an invoice; total payment for the work completed; a loan or debt that has no outstanding balance.

PAID-IN-SURPLUS   See CAPITAL SURPLUS.

PAID INVOICE   A bill showing goods and services sold by a seller on which is marked "paid," showing evidence by the seller that the buyer has remitted the total amount due at the time of purchase or in advance of purchase.

P & L   See PROFIT & LOSS STATEMENT.

PAPER   A business term that describes forms of money other than cash, such as mortgage, note, stock, bond or consumer loan. These other forms are often held as security for a collateralized loan.
   In general, the sheets of material that are used for transmitting printed material.

PAPER PROFIT   The illusion that a profit may exist by performing calculations without evidence that the transactions occurred or proof that the profit, in fact, does exist.

PAPERWORK   The recordkeeping chores of maintaining a business. Paperwork is literally the work associated with documenting business activities on paper for later recall.

PAR   The nominal or face value of a security such as a stock or bond as stated in equivalent dollars. For COMMON STOCK or PREFERRED STOCK, the par value is stated in the ARTICLES OF INCORPORATION. In a NEW ISSUE of stock, the sale is at par, and the proceeds of the sale are recorded as EQUITY in the books of the corporation.

PARENT COMPANY   A firm that owns or controls another company, as a subsidiary, through the ownership of voting stock. The company that owns a subsidiary is the parent company.

PARKINSON'S LAW   "Work expands to fill the time available for its completion."

PARTNER   A person participating in a PARTNERSHIP.

PARTNERSHIP   The Uniform Partnership Act that is in force in most states defines a partnership as "an association of two or more persons who carry on a business for profit as co-owners." A partnership can hold title to real property in the name of the partnership, holding by tenancy in partnership. One tax advantage of this form of ownership is that the partnership itself does not pay taxes. However, the partnership must file a partnership information return (Form 1065) showing how much income the partnership distributes to each partner (Schedule K-1). Then each partner is responsible for paying his or her own tax. See also GENERAL PARTNERSHIP; LIMITED PARTNERSHIP; JOINT VENTURE.

PARTNERSHIP AGREEMENT   The document that defines the conditions and limitations of the PARTNERS in a PARTNERSHIP business.

PARTNERSHIP INFORMATIONAL RETURN   See PARTNERSHIP RETURN.

PARTNERSHIP RETURN   The informational federal government document (FORM 1165) used to show the income (or loss) of a partnership. See PARTNERSHIP.

PARTNERSHIP TAX   Partnerships are not taxed as such, therefore, no partnership tax is due. Yet the term partnership tax is sometimes used to refer to the income tax due by an individual, attributed to a proportionate share of partnership income (reported to the individual on federal FORM K-1) that causes an individual income tax as a result of participation in a partnership. See INFORMATIONAL RETURN.

PAR VALUE See PAR.

PASS See PROCUREMENT AUTOMATED SOURCE SYSTEM.

PASSIVE INVESTOR A person who provides equity (an investor) for a business but does not participate in the active operation of the business; the opposite of an active owner/manager.

In taxing, an IRS classification of income such as real estate in which investors often are not participants in the management of the business.

PAST DUE Later than agreed; not on time; untimely. Past due usually refers to a payment that has not been made on time.

PAST DUE ACCOUNT An account that has a payment that was not received by the scheduled date.

PATENT In business, a privilege (certificate) issued by the federal government (or foreign country) that grants exclusive rights (monopoly) to production, sale and profit from the invention of a product for a specific period of time and the right to prevent others from copying the invention. The legal document authorizing exclusive property rights to the inventor of a product or process.

PAY To give money in exchange for a product or service received; to discharge a debt, obligation or expense by giving money in exchange; wages or salary.

PAYABLE; PAYABLES An amount to be paid. Payables are a list of amounts currently due to be paid. See ACCOUNTS PAYABLE.

PAYBACK PERIOD The length of time required before the original cash investment is recovered.

PAYEE   The person to whom a debt instrument, such as a check or promissory note, is made payable; the receiver. See MAKER.

PAYMENT   An amount paid; something that is paid.

PAYMENT AND PERFORMANCE BOND   A bond by a surety that provides the protection of both a PERFORMANCE BOND and a PAYMENT BOND.

PAYMENT BOND   A surety bond by which a contractor assures an owner that all labor and material will be fully paid and that no mechanic's liens will be filed. The bond also assures suppliers and subcontractors they will be paid by the prime contractor.

PAYMENT FLOAT   The period of time between incurring a debt (obtaining credit on a purchase) and disbursement of the money to repay the debt. For a business, it is prudent to extend this period to the maximum without incurring an interest charge. Both internal and external factors affect the float period. Internal factors (which are controllable by the firm) include the speed with which the firm makes payments on vendor invoices. External factors include the grace period, speed of collection by the vendor, as well as the processing time for checks to clear the bank. See FLOAT.

PAYMENT IN FULL   Repayment of the entire amount owed; satisfaction of a financial obligation.

PAYMENT ON DEMAND   An order to comply with an obligation. Often, a contract will include a "payment on demand" clause, which means the debtor must pay the balance when asked, even if the terms of the contract agreement have been met.

PAYOFF   The payment in full of an existing loan. Often payoff means paid in full before the due date.
   A bribe, a gratuity or a gift.

PAYROLL   The list of employees in a company, i.e., the employees who are paid by the company. When a person is employed by a company, that person may say he or she is on the payroll.

PAYROLL JOURNAL   The accounting document that records the wages, salaries, hours worked and deductions for each employee.

PAYROLL RECORD   Complete information concerning wages and salaries paid.

PAYROLL TAX   A TAX paid from wages or salaries by WITH-HOLDING.

PC   See PERSONAL COMPUTER.

P.C.   See PROFESSIONAL CORPORATION.

P/E   See PRICE/EARNINGS RATIO.

PENSION   A payment made to a former employee or to his family after fulfillment of conditions of service with the company, such as age or years of service; payment to an employee after the employee has retired. See RETIREMENT.

PENSION PLAN   The document of a company that describes the requirements, obligations and benefits of the pension program offered by the company.

PERCENTAGE OF COMPLETION METHOD   A procedure for computing partial payments on a large contract wherein identifiable portions of the work may be satisfactorily completed, invoiced and paid before the entire project is completed and paid in full.

PERCENT PROFIT   Percent profit can have several definitions depending on the context used, but most commonly refers to RETURN ON SALES. See RETURN ON SALES; RETURN ON INVESTED CAPITAL.

PER DIEM   An amount paid for each day, or part of a day, usually for travel expenses such as meals and lodging.

PERFECT COMPETITION   A market condition where no buyer or seller has the economic power to alter the market price of a good or service; characterized by a large number of buyers, a large number of sellers, all selling similar products or services, an equal awareness of prices and volume, an absence of discrimination in buying or selling, total mobility of productive resources and complete freedom of entry into the market. As opposed to MONOPOLY; OLIGOPOLY. Also called PURE COMPETITION.

PERFORMANCE BOND   A type of insurance, purchased by a business that will ensure accomplishment of the work for a customer in accordance with the contract. The bond usually provides that if the contractor fails to complete the contract, the surety itself can complete the contract. The insurance company providing performance bonds is called a surety company or simply a SURETY.

PERK   A privilege or benefit, often monetary or property, given to a person by a business, usually to the owners or executives.

PERMIT   An authorization to perform a task, most often by a governmental entity, i.e., a construction permit. See BUILDING PERMIT.

PERSON   A human being; an individual. As opposed to a business, company or firm such as a proprietorship.

PERSONAL   Relating to a particular person; private.

PERSONAL ACCOUNT   An ACCOUNT that is for the transaction of business with a person, as opposed to a COMMERCIAL ACCOUNT for the transaction of business with another company.

PERSONAL CHECK   A CHECK prepared by a person that is used as a substitute for money. See CHECK.

PERSONAL COMPUTER   An electronic device with a keyboard, computing capacity, screen and printer, used by an individual in an office environment to perform work.

PERSONAL EXPENSES   The amounts paid by a person for maintaining the accustomed standard of living for the immediate family.

PERSONAL FINANCIAL STATEMENT A BALANCE SHEET and an INCOME STATEMENT for a person identifying assets, liabilities, net worth, income and expenses. Used to substantiate the person's financial solvency, often part of a loan application for a start-up business. See Self-Help Guide C.

PERSONAL FUNDS Cash and other assets that can be identified separately from the business funds. Often used in context of a START-UP business to identify money contributed by the person, as opposed to other investors.

PERSONAL INCOME TAX Tax paid to a government (federal, state or local) as a percentage of the amount of wages earned and other income.

PERSONAL INJURY INSURANCE Coverage by an insurance company for a physical harm to an individual person.

PERSONAL LIABILITY The obligation of a person to satisfy a business debt to the extent of one's personal assets. Shareholders in a corporation are usually protected against personal liability for the debts of the corporation, unless personal assets have been pledged as security. Avoiding personal liability is one of the advantages of the corporation as a form of legal structure for a small business.

PERSONAL LOAN A LOAN made to a person, as opposed to a commercial loan made to a business. See also COMMERCIAL LOAN.

PERSONAL NET WORTH See NET WORTH.

PERSONAL PROPERTY Things (PROPERTY) that are tangible, but movable; as opposed to REAL PROPERTY, which is tangible but not movable. In accounting, personal property is an asset on a balance sheet like equipment, machinery, automobiles, furniture and office supplies. See also PROPERTY; REAL PROPERTY.

PERSONAL PROPERTY TAX By law, a payment made to a government (usually state or local) and calculated as a percent of the worth of the personal property asset.

PERSONAL SECURITY   A promise by one person to pay the debt of another person; to COSIGN.

PERSONAL USE   Expenditure of money or use of property by a person for private (not business) gain. Differentiation from BUSINESS USE is important because the uses are taxed differently.

PERSONNEL   The people resources of a business. Sometimes, the staff function that is responsible for the people interests in a business.

PETTY CASH   Amounts of money (paper money and coins) kept on the business premises for payment of small incidental expenses.

PETTY CASH FUND   The cash money kept on the business premises for small expenditures.

PETTY CASH VOUCHER   A document for obtaining money from the PETTY CASH FUND and a record of disbursements made from the fund.

PIERCE THE CORPORATE VEIL   Legal jargon applied to the exposure of corporate owners under some conditions whereby creditors can attach personal assets to recover corporate debts. This may occur when the affairs of the corporation are conducted as if no corporation existed. In particular, stockholders can be held liable for corporate acts, such as crime, fraud or to defeat public convenience.

PIGGYBACK   A method of shipping whereby truck trailers are loaded on board a train car for transportation rather than by over-the-road hauling.

PIGGYBACK ARRANGEMENT   A method of distribution whereby a company is able to use the already established distribution channel of another company. This method is particularly effective when the two companies are selling complementary products.

PLAINTIFF   The person who commences a lawsuit; the complainant.

PLAN A scheme or method (formulated beforehand) for making, doing, accomplishing or arranging something for a business, such as a project, product or schedule; a method of proceeding; a written document describing what and how something will be accomplished for a business.

PLANNING The making of a PLAN for the business; a method for doing, accomplishing or arranging business; having in mind a project or purpose for a business.

PLANS The documents that describe "how" something is to be accomplished; a design; a drawing. Examples include: business plan, engineering plan and marketing plan.

PLANS AND SPECIFICATIONS The documents that completely describe the physical and functional definition of a product or service to be performed; what and how the job or project is to be done.

PLANT An asset consisting of land, buildings, machinery, natural resources and furniture used for the manufacture of goods; a FACTORY. In a limited sense, plant is used for only the land and buildings or for description of all fixed assets.

PLEDGE The transfer or delivery of property to a lender to be held as security for repayment of a debt. A legal promise that the property title can be transferred to the lender if the debt is not repaid.

PLP See PREFERRED LENDER PROGRAM.

POINTS In lending, a generic term for interest rate percentage or fraction thereof, depending on usage.

POLICY Short for an INSURANCE POLICY. See INSURANCE POLICY. Wise, prudent or visionary guidance from the very top level of an organization, setting the general direction, as opposed to a law or rule that has distinct limits; a plan or course of action to be pursued by the business.

POLICYHOLDER The INSURED.

POOL   In business finance, a concept of gathering monies from several sources for a single use; to pool the money.

See more specific uses of the term pool used in various aspects of business, such as: INDUSTRY POOL; INSURANCE POOL; INVESTMENT POOL.

PORTFOLIO INVESTMENT   An investment of capital by an individual or another company that has no interest in management or operational participation in the business. The investment is made in order to obtain a financial reward, rather than to gain management control.

POSITIVE CASH FLOW   See CASH FLOW.

POST   In accounting, to transfer financial data from an original document to an account in the books of account, usually in chronological order. Also to transfer from the JOURNAL to the LEDGER ACCOUNTS.

Also, to display a document or product in public view.

POSTDATED CHECK   A check that has on its face a date later than the date of signing and is therefore not negotiable until the later date arrives. A bank will not make payment on a check until the date has passed.

POWER OF ATTORNEY   A written document that authorizes one person to act for another person who has signed the document. The document must be witnessed by a NOTARY PUBLIC or other public official. The power may bestow total authority, as a FULL POWER OF ATTORNEY, or may be restricted to specific actions, as a LIMITED POWER OF ATTORNEY, or may transcend the death of the signer, as a DURABLE POWER OF ATTORNEY.

PPI   See PRODUCER PRICE INDEX.

PR   See PUBLIC RELATIONS.

PREEMPTIVE RIGHT   The opportunity given to existing shareholders to purchase shares of a NEW ISSUE before it is offered to the public.

PREFERRED LENDER   A bank approved by the U.S. Small Business Administration for making GUARANTEED LOANS under the PREFERRED LENDER PROGRAM (PLP).

PREFERRED LENDER PROGRAM (PLP)   A U.S. Small Business Administration program whereby banks are pre-approved to make U.S. Government GUARANTEED LOANS before submittal of the applications to the U.S. Small Business Administration for approval. However, the SBA reserves the right to disapprove the application, whereby the loan then becomes a commercial loan by the bank, usually without advising the borrower. Also see CERTI-FIED LENDER PROGRAM (CLP).

PREFERRED STOCK   Shares of stock that identify ownership in a corporation but generally without voting rights. Preferred stock has prior claim on dividends, earnings and assets before common stock's claim. The dividend paid on preferred stock is usually a pre-determined amount, similar to interest. See STOCK.

PRELIMINARY COST   Expenses incurred in conjunction with, but prior to, actual commencement of a main project. Examples include legal investigations, insurance and financing commitments.

PREMIUM   The up-front consideration necessary to secure a loan, lease or contract.
   In insurance, the amount paid for insurance coverage. UN-EARNED PREMIUM is that portion of premium already paid that must be returned to the insured upon cancellation of the policy.

PREPAID   A remittance before the due date; paid in advance of the due date. See PREPAY.

PREPAID EXPENSES   An entry shown on a BALANCE SHEET that accounts for an amount of money that could be recovered by cancellation of the payment made.

PREPAID INTEREST   An amount of interest expense paid before it is due. For taxing purposes, usually interest must be deducted over the life of the loan; interest cannot be deducted as a tax avoidance expense.

PREPAY   To pay in advance; to pay before the due date.

PREPAYMENT PENALTY   An extra charge required if a loan is paid in full before the due date. Sometimes a penalty may apply to a partial payment made before the due date for the partial payment.

PREPAYMENT PRIVILEGE   A provision in a NOTE that permits payment of money toward the principal before that amount is due, including pay-off of the entire principal balance due.

PRESENT VALUE   The value today of a future payment, reduced by the interest that could be earned at an appropriate COMPOUND INTEREST RATE. That is, the present worth is equal to the future worth (FUTURE VALUE) less the amount of interest that could have been earned. Also applies to a stream of future payments with the interest amount calculated for each payment. See also FUTURE VALUE; INTERNAL RATE OF RETURN; DISCOUNTED CASH FLOW; TIME VALUE OF MONEY; INWOOD TABLE.

PRESENT VALUE ANALYSIS   See DISCOUNTED CASH FLOW.

PRESENT VALUE OF ONE DOLLAR   See the TIME VALUE OF MONEY.

PRESIDENT   The top level EXECUTIVE in a company; usually, in a small company, all day-to-day operations are directed by the president. The corporate position reporting to the BOARD OF DIRECTORS.

PREVAILING RATE   A general term that describes the average interest rate existing in the current market for similar debt instruments.

PREVAILING WAGE   The generally accepted amount being paid for a particular skill of worker. Sometimes a wage rate guaranteed by law. Also called prevailing wage rate.

PRICE   The amount of money being charged for a product or service; the amount asked or paid.

PRICE CHANGE   Lowering or raising a price from its former value, to deal with competitive market pressures to gain an advantageous market position.

PRICE CUTTING   Lowering the price of products or services because of competitive forces in the marketplace.

PRICE DISCRIMINATION   Selling the same good or service at different prices to different buyers, usually an unlawful practice.

PRICE/EARNINGS RATIO (P/E)   The market price of a share of common stock divided by the EARNINGS PER SHARE.

PRICE ELASTICITY   In economics, the extent to which a change in price will cause a change in demand. When prices are inelastic, consumers will continue to buy the same amount regardless of an increase or decrease in prices. On the other hand, when prices are elastic, rising prices will cause a drop in demand; conversely, lowering prices will cause increased demand.

PRICE FIXING   An illegal practice wherein individual companies agree to set prices at a given level, usually higher than a competitive market would sustain. See ANTITRUST.

PRICE LEADER   The company that usually is first to announce price increases in an industry.

PRICING   The act of determining the amount of money to charge for products and services.

PRICING STRATEGY   The theory and practice of evaluating market potential to establish the optimum price of goods and services that results in the greatest profit.

PRIMARY COMMODITIES   Raw materials; commodities in the unprocessed state, such as iron ore and grain.

PRIME   See PRIME RATE. Also short for PRIME CONTRACTOR.

PRIME CONTRACTOR   The CONTRACTOR totally responsible for a project for a customer. Often a prime contractor will employ the services of subcontractors who perform specific portions of the work.

PRIME RATE   The interest rate at which banks will lend to their most creditworthy customers. The prime rate is the standard across the banking industry since less creditworthy customers receive a rate that is tied to prime; usually a higher rate.

PRINCIPAL   In general, the owner of a privately held business or the major party, buyer or seller in a transaction.

In finance, the basic amount invested in a security, exclusive of earnings or interest. A deposit on which interest is either earned or owed. The face amount of a debt instrument. The balance of an obligation, separate from interest.

PRIVATE CORPORATION   See CLOSED CORPORATION.

PRIVATELY HELD CORPORATION   See CLOSED CORPORATION.

PRO BONO   Work, usually by professionals such as lawyers and accountants, which is performed free or at a reduced rate for the public good.

PROCUREMENT   The act of purchasing or of buying.

PROCUREMENT ASSISTANCE   A kind of contract from a government, offering special contract opportunities to qualifying businesses. There are two types of particular interest to small businesses: 1) small business set-aside, whereby the law requires contracts to be awarded to small businesses; and 2) contracts specifically for small and minority-owned businesses, called the SBA 8(a) PROGRAM.

PROCUREMENT AUTOMATED SOURCE SYSTEM (PASS)   A computerized listing of small businesses compiled by the SBA, used as a resource for federal procurement centers and prime contractors.

PRODUCER   A manufacturer; a person or company that works to produce goods (new products) from raw materials and articles purchased from others. As opposed to WHOLESALER, RETAILER or CONSUMER.

PRODUCER PRICE INDEX (PPI)   A measure of change in wholesale prices; revised monthly by the U.S. Bureau of Labor Statistics. Prices are calculated as products move from manufacturing through the distribution stage, before reaching the consumer. The equivalent for consumer goods is the CONSUMER PRICE INDEX.

PRODUCT   Physical things that are bought and sold by businesses; GOODS. Often the physical object resulting from manufacturing operations. Something produced for sale by human effort as raw material is transformed into a more useful form of physical object. A physical thing available for sale; as opposed to sale of SERVICE. See GOODS; MERCHANDISE.

PRODUCT BRAND MANAGEMENT   The development and implementation of a market strategy for a particular product with a BRAND NAME.

PRODUCT DEVELOPMENT   The act of performing research or creative effort to introduce a new product to the marketplace. Devising something new that performs better or costs less than existing products; inventing for practical use.

PRODUCT FACTORS   Important characteristics that influence demand for a product, whether the products are goods or services.

PRODUCTION   The creation of economic value, particularly goods and services for sale to others; to manufacture a product.

PRODUCTION RATE   The number of units manufactured in a given period of time or the time required to produce a single article.

PRODUCTIVITY   A measure of efficiency that relates output to input in a way that provides data for evaluating areas for improvement.

PRODUCT LIABILITY   The responsibility of a manufacturer to a purchaser for reimbursement of loss resulting from using or employing the product.

PRODUCT LIFE CYCLE   The time a product is in existence from start-up to close out, often divided into its constituent phases such as start-up, development, growth, maturity, decline and close out.

PRODUCT MIX   The array of products offered for sale by a company where each product fills a specific customer need.

PRODUCT-ORIENTED BUSINESS   A company whose primary function is to sell GOODS and MERCHANDISE to customers; as opposed to a SERVICE-ORIENTED BUSINESS.

PRODUCTS   The plural of PRODUCT; goods; merchandise.

PRODUCT STANDARDS   Specifications by the manufacturing company or regulations by a government that require minimum levels of quality, health, safety, performance or other characteristics of a product or service.

PROFESSION   An occupation, as a business, requiring advanced education and training principally involving high standards of intellectual skills, such as accounting, law and engineering. Also, a body of persons in any such occupation.

PROFESSIONAL   A person who earns a living in an occupation involving high standards of intellectual knowledge, after the person has successfully completed the required education and training. Practicing a profession. See PROFESSION.

PROFESSIONAL CORPORATION (P.C.)   A legal identification (FICTITIOUS NAME) of a company engaged in providing PROFESSIONAL services, in areas like the law and accounting. Usually abbreviated P.C. following a person's name.

PROFESSIONAL ORGANIZATION   A group of professional business people and companies that join together to promote their common interests. See PROFESSION.

PROFIT In a financial situation, a positive sum after expenses are deducted from income of a business as shown on an income statement; the monetary gain obtained from the use of CAPITAL in a transaction; the proceeds from property or investment; the opposite of a LOSS. See EARNINGS.

PROFITABLE; PROFITABILITY A profit was earned; the ability to earn a profit. See PROFIT.

PROFIT AND LOSS STATEMENT (P&L) The accounting document that displays whether the business has made a profit or has sustained a loss during the accounting period. Most often called an INCOME STATEMENT. See INCOME STATEMENT.

PROFIT MARGIN The relation of various levels of profit to net sales, most often as a percent of sales.
GROSS MARGIN: From gross sales, subtract returns and allowances to arrive at net sales; from net sales, subtract cost of goods sold to arrive at gross profit. Divide gross profit by net sales and express as a percent to obtain gross margin.
NET MARGIN: From gross profit, deduct operating expenses (overhead) to determine net profit before taxes. Divide net profit before taxes by net sales and express as a percent to obtain net margin.
Both gross margin and net margin, when compared with prior periods and with industry statistics, provide a measure of operating efficiency, pricing policy and ability to compete successfully with other companies in the field.

PROFIT OBJECTIVE The amount of earnings (profit) expected from a product or service; the desired profit.

PROFIT PATTERN The trend in an ability to earn; the unique characteristics that produce earnings in a particular situation.

PROFIT POTENTIAL The likelihood that a venture will earn a profit, as opposed to a loss.

PROFIT SHARING; PROFIT-SHARING PLAN An agreement between a company and one or more employees wherein a portion of the company profits are paid proportionately to the employees.

PRO FORMA   A projection of what may result in the future from actions in the present.

In accounting, a BALANCE SHEET or INCOME STATEMENT for a future time, where amounts are based on assumptions of future hypothetical events. As opposed to a balance sheet or an income statement, which summarizes financial transactions that have already occurred. Most often an accountant may simply refer to "pro forma," meaning a PRO FORMA BALANCE SHEET. PROJECTED INCOME STATEMENT is used more often than pro forma income statement. Pro forma is derived from the Latin, meaning "in the form of" a balance sheet or income statement.

PRO FORMA BALANCE SHEET   See PRO FORMA. See also Self-Help Guide F.

PRO FORMA INCOME STATEMENT   Same as PROJECTED INCOME STATEMENT; See Self-Help Guide H. See also PRO FORMA.

PROGRESS BILLING   An invoice to receive a PROGRESS PAYMENT.

PROGRESS PAYMENT   Payments of money for partial completion of portions of a project. PROGRESS BILLING is made, as provided in the contract, for work that has been satisfactorily completed. Progress payments are remitted for the completed work.

PROJECTED INCOME STATEMENT   An approximation of INCOME, EXPENDITURES and PROFIT for a period of time in the future. See Self-Help Guide H for a detailed explanation of the preparation of a projected income statement. See also PRO FORMA.

PROJECTION   A FORECAST; an approximation of future events. Usually a projection is made by extrapolating known information into the future period, considering events that could affect the outcome.

PROMISSORY NOTE   A written promise to repay a specified sum of money either on demand or at a fixed date in the future. Often called simply a NOTE.

PROMOTION   That phase of marketing that highly praises a product or service, often by indirect means. To further the popularity, knowledge or awareness of the product or service.

In personnel matters, to elevate the responsibility and rate of pay of a person in an organization. For example, a person may be promoted to the position of supervisor.

PROMPT PAY   A practice requiring payment within a given period; interest is due on the amount owed, particularly applicable to payment by governments.

PROPERTY   Things to which certain ownership rights or interests are attached; including to possess, to use, to encumber, to transfer and to exclude. Property is either real or personal. See REAL PROPERTY, PERSONAL PROPERTY.

PROPERTY TAX   Taxes required to be paid to a government body as a result of owning property. Most often refers to taxes paid on real estate property.

PROPOSAL   A document prepared by a bidder to perform work at a price and by a time, usually specifying how the work will be done. See also BID; QUOTE.

PROPRIETARY   An idea, document or product which is owned by a company or person, usually protected by secrecy.

PROPRIETOR   The sole owner of a business. See PROPRIETORSHIP.

PROPRIETORSHIP   Ownership of a business or entity. Often used interchangeably with sole or individual proprietorship. As opposed to other business forms such as corporation or partnership. Proprietorship is frequently used in start-up businesses because it is easy to organize and flexible to operate. Sole proprietors are considered self-employed and are eligible for KEOGH accounts for their retirement funds. For tax reporting, use Form 1040, Schedule C. See also SOLE PROPRIETORSHIP.

PROVISION   A clause or condition in a contract.

PROXY   In business, a person authorized to vote on behalf of a stockholder of a corporation; a written POWER OF ATTORNEY given by stockholders, authorizing a specific vote. In general, a proxy is the authorization by a person to act or speak for another.

PUBLIC ACCOUNTANT   An ACCOUNTANT who performs services for the general body of people and businesses, as opposed to an accountant who is employed by another business.

PUBLICATION #334   A document published by the federal government entitled TAX GUIDE FOR SMALL BUSINESSES that contains useful information needed by small businesses about business-related taxes.

PUBLICATION #583   A document published by the federal government titled INFORMATION FOR BUSINESS TAXPAYERS that contains helpful information for preparing a federal tax return for the U.S. government.

PUBLICITY   News about a business that is free and appears in any of the public media, as contrasted with advertising.

PUBLIC OFFERING   The sale, by a company or a large shareholder, of company shares of stock to the public. See INITIAL PUBLIC OFFERING.

PUBLIC RELATIONS (PR)   The act of promoting a specific image for the business.

PUBLIC STOCK OFFERING   The sale of shares of stock in a corporation to the public as a means of raising equity funds. Thereby, more owners of the corporation are acquired and the original owners' share is reduced (diluted). Such a corporation is considered to be a publicly-held corporation, and ownership is transferred through sale and purchase of the stock on the open market to anyone who wants to buy from a person who wants to sell the stock or by means of a stock exchange.

PURCHASE   To obtain goods or services in exchange for money; to procure; to buy; to acquire products or services not available within the business.

PURCHASE ORDER   A written authorization prepared by a buyer for the acquisition of goods or services at a specified price. Once accepted by the seller, the purchase order becomes a legally binding purchase CONTRACT. A purchase order describes the features or characteristics of a product or service important to its purchase.

PURCHASING AGENT   A BUYER for a large company; the employee of a company who purchases goods or services for the company.

PURE COMPETITION   See PERFECT COMPETITION.

PV   See PRESENT VALUE.

Q

QA   See QUALITY ASSURANCE.

QC   See QUALITY CONTROL.

QUALIFICATION   In lending, the process by which a lender reviews a prospective borrower's credit and payment capacity prior to a decision on making a loan.

In general, a characteristic of a person or business that determines the ability to perform a contract or task.

QUALITY   The goodness or badness of a result; the degree of excellence a thing possesses. Quality without an adjective most often means quality better than normal, as contrasted with normal quality.

QUALITY ASSURANCE   That function within a business that reviews the product or service after completion for a determination of the degree of excellence that was accomplished. Follow-up for improvement of deficiencies and correction of the system that produced the errors should produce better quality products in the future.

QUALITY CONTROL   The process of assuring that products or services are made to consistently high standards. Inspection of goods at points in the manufacturing process to measure and report the excellence of manufacture in accordance with the specifications.

QUALITY OF RECEIVABLES   An approximation of those accounts (amounts due for sales made on credit) that can be collected and those that cannot be collected.

QUALITY SUPPORT   Those people in a company with the job of measuring and reporting the degree of excellence of products or services.

QUARTERLY   Occurring once each quarter or three-month period; four times each year.

QUARTERLY REPORT   A document prepared after each three-month period.

QUICK ASSET RATIO   See QUICK RATIO.

QUICK ASSETS   Cash and cash equivalents; things of value that can be sold for cash within one year, not necessarily all CURRENT ASSETS.

QUICK RATIO; QUICK ASSET RATIO   Cash, liquid cash equivalents and accounts receivable (CURRENT ASSETS less INVENTORY) divided by CURRENT LIABILITIES (immediate debts due); a measure of the liquidity of a business. It helps to answer the question, "If sales stopped, could the business meet current obligations with assets that are readily convertible into cash to pay the obligations?" A quick ratio of 1:1 or better is usually satisfactory. Also called ACID TEST RATIO; CURRENT RATIO.

QUORUM   The minimum legal number of people required to be in attendance before a meeting can officially take place or business can be transacted.

QUOTA   Quantity restrictions placed on business transactions, usually by a government body, often on import of foreign goods.
    Also, the number of minorities that must be hired to secure a government contract.

QUOTATION   See QUOTE.

QUOTE   To specify a price for which a company will perform a given amount of work. See also BID; PROPOSAL.

R

R&D   See RESEARCH AND DEVELOPMENT.

RAIDER   An individual or corporate investor who buys into a company with the intent of taking control and installing new management.

RAIN CHECK   A document that is given to a customer by a business for later purchase of merchandise. Sometimes, a business may become temporarily out of stock for an item that has been offered at a discount price. The rain check permits the customer to obtain the discount price during purchase of the item at a later time.

RANK AND FILE   Usually refers to the general overall aggregate of all the ordinary workers in the company. The term originates from the military including those of rank and those who follow.

RATE OF PAY   The usual amount of money that is paid to an employee for a given period worked or for a given amount of output produced regardless of the time taken; expressed in dollars for the period or amount of output.

RATE OF RETURN   The PROFIT or EARNINGS received from an INVESTMENT expressed as a percent. Many other definitions are used for specific applications: RETURN ON EQUITY, RETURN ON INVESTED CAPITAL; YIELD; CURRENT YIELD; YIELD TO MATURITY; DIVIDEND YIELD; INTERNAL RATE OF RETURN.

RATIO   A relationship of one thing to another expressed in numbers, often used in business as a percentage or a multiple.

RATIO ANALYSIS   Comparison of similar items on the basis of percentages rather than in dollars. This method can reveal trends, identify eccentricities and evaluate risks.

RAW MATERIAL   The earliest phase of materials supplied, such as those mined, grown, harvested or distilled. Also refers to the combination of all materials or things needed to produce a given product.

REAL ESTATE   The common term for land, buildings and improvements. In accounting and legal senses, the term REAL PROPERTY is used. See REAL PROPERTY.

REAL ESTATE TAX   By law, a payment made to a government (usually state or local) and calculated as a percentage of the worth of the real property asset (REAL ESTATE) and based on the assessed value as determined by a government assessor.

REAL PROPERTY   Things (PROPERTY) that are tangible but not movable; as opposed to PERSONAL PROPERTY that are tangible but also movable.

In accounting, real property refers to land buildings, structures, fixtures and attached improvements. See also PROPERTY; PERSONAL PROPERTY.

REBATE   A refund or return of a stipulated charge as an enticement to consummate the deal. Often a coupon to stimulate sales.

RECAPITALIZE; RECAPITALIZATION   Alteration of a corporation's FINANCIAL STRUCTURE by exchanging one type of capital for another type of capital. BANKRUPTCY is a reason for recapitalization to relieve the debt load and avoid insolvency. A healthy company may recapitalize to improve a tax situation, improve credit rating and finance equity expansion in defense against corporate raiders.

RECEIPT   A document that acknowledges payment received.

In finance and accounting, the time when money is available for use by the company or the time when a document or product has arrived at the place of business. The piece of paper evidencing the exchange.

RECEIPT BOOK   The original entry accounting document for recording money received.

RECEIPTS   The sum of moneys received during a period.

RECEIVABLE; RECEIVABLES   Anything that is expected to arrive at the business. Particularly in finance and accounting, it is a short form of ACCOUNTS RECEIVABLE.

RECEIVABLES AGING   See ACCOUNTS RECEIVABLE AGING.

RECEIVER   An independent party appointed by a court to receive, preserve and manage a business that is involved in litigation, such as bankruptcy, pending final disposition of the matter before the courts.

RECEIVING   The department or part of a business charged with the material control of all products delivered to the business from suppliers. Also, the act of accepting these products.

RECESSION   A downturn in economic activity; a time generally lacking in prosperity and lacking in growth of business activity. Recession can be global, national, regional, local or even individual, but usually is defined by economists on a national level as two or more successive quarters showing a decline in the GROSS DOMESTIC PRODUCT.

RECONCILE   To perform comparative analyses of two or more accounting sheets to verify accuracy. One of the most common reconciliations in a small business is a comparison of the BANK STATEMENT of checks paid with your own record to provide assurance of the amount of cash in your account at the bank.

RECORD   To put in writing; to store information for retrieval at a later date. Any physical thing that contains information as evidence of something that occurred previously. Records are not limited to paper records.

RECORDKEEPING   The process of maintaining written documentation of events. Recordkeeping encompasses all types of information that must be retained for future reference, whereas BOOKKEEPING specifically means financial records.

RECORD RETENTION   The period of time for which the documents of a company should be saved in the company's files for future proof of transactions by the company. The length of time to save a particular document varies by the type and value of the document.

RECORDS   The total aggregate volume of documents; all the paperwork and other information about a particular subject.

RECOURSE LOAN   A debt instrument wherein the lender can legally require repayment of a loan from personal funds if the collateral is not sufficient to repay the note. As opposed to a NON-RECOURSE LOAN where the lender can only obtain compensation from the collateral or funds of the business.

REDEMPTION AGREEMENT   A type of BUY-SELL AGREEMENT whereby a corporation buys the stock of a shareholder if the conditions of the buy-sell agreement occur.

RED INK   Losses in the form of unprofitable operations, debts or an excess of liabilities over assets.

RED LINE   An action by a company, bank or other entity to cease financial transactions with another entity.

RED TAPE   A common name applied to procrastination and confusing language that invariably occur in any large organization, particularly in governments through laws and regulations. The lack of clarity and excessive paperwork cause delays in activities.

REFINANCE   To negotiate a change in an existing loan or replace an existing loan with a new loan, most often with conditions more favorable to the borrower, such as revising the payment schedule to reduce monthly payments, modify interest charges, extend the maturity date, increase the amount of debt and retire an existing debt by issuing new securities to reduce the cash flow.

REFINANCE A LOAN   See REFINANCE.

REGISTER   A formal record of important information, often kept by an official appointed to do so; a book in which this informatoin is kept; an entry in such a record. Also, a machine (cash register) used to record retail sales.

REGISTRAR   The agent, usually a bank or trust company, responsible for keeping track of shares of stock and bonds.

REGISTRATION   The formal recording in a REGISTER.

REGULAR HOURS   The normal times a business is in operation and open for customers.
   Also, the normal work schedule of an individual employee or the number of hours worked during this period. As opposed to OVERTIME HOURS.

REGULATION   A rule of LAW; laws and POLICIES enacted by a government to control actions of citizens and businesses. In the United States' system of government, laws are enacted to protect citizens against injury. These are promulgated as regulations. Many laws and regulations benefit the small-business person.

REINSURANCE   Sharing the RISK among two or more insurance companies. Part of the primary insurance company's risk is assumed by back-up companies. Thereby, reinsurance allows an individual company to take on clients whose coverage needs are greater than the individual insurance company's capacity alone.

REINSURER   An insurance company that assumes part of the risk in exchange for part of the premium, as back-up, to a primary insurer. See REINSURANCE; INSURANCE POOL.

REMANUFACTURE   Rebuilding used equipment using some new parts so that the rebuilt equipment is as functional as new equipment but at less cost. Often remanufactured products are sold to a different customer from the original user. Not the same as repair or reconditioning.

REMIT   To pay for goods or services purchased.

REMITTANCE　The payment for goods or services purchased.

REMITTANCE ADVICE　The document that records payment for goods or services purchased.

REMITTANCE OF PROFIT　The act of transferring profits earned in a foreign country back to one's home country.

RENT　Money paid by a user (LESSEE) to an owner (LESSOR) of property for use of the property under the terms of a LEASE. Often used interchangeably as a verb with lease; see LEASE.

RENTAL AGREEMENT　A LEASE; the contract defining the conditions by which one person uses the property of another.

RENTER　One who RENTS property of another. Same as LESSEE.

REP　A manufacturer's representative; a firm that sells the products of one or more producers on a commission basis.

REPAIRS　Restore real or personal property to the original or operating condition; minor alterations are made to maintain use of the item rather than purchase a replacement. Repairs do not extend the life of the property or improve the property.

REPAYMENT RISK　The chance that a borrower will not repay a loan when due. See RISK.

REPAY　To provide money (a payment) as prescribed by a loan agreement.

REPLACEMENT VALUE　The amount of expenditure (the cost) necessary to repurchase a similar item. Often used in insurance, allowing purchase of new items for existing items that may be lost due to a covered event.

REPOSSESS　To take back an asset by a lender from a buyer who has failed to make payments when due.

REPURCHASE AGREEMENT　A clause in a CONTRACT or an AGREEMENT that states the conditions under which the original seller may recover title to (repurchase) the item that was sold, i.e., frequently a death but also after a specific event or an elapsed time.

REQUEST FOR PROPOSAL (RFP)   A request by a buyer for a PROPOSAL (BID) from a seller to perform work or provide a service; an announcement of the desire to engage in contract work. The buyer furnishes complete plans and specifications for the desired work; the seller often provides further definition and states a price to perform the work specified. Usually, a request for proposal involves work or service where the provider must perform some amount of design or definition toward the end result in the process of accomplishing the work. See also PROPOSAL; INVITATION TO BID; REQUEST FOR QUOTATION.

REQUEST FOR QUOTATION (RFQ)   A request by a buyer for a QUOTE from a seller to perform work or provide a service. Usually, a request for quotation is for a specific article or task of known characteristics, description and quality. See also QUOTATION; INVITATION TO BID; REQUEST FOR PROPOSAL.

REQUISITION   A document internal to the business for obtaining products, supplies and materials. Also, the act of obtaining these items.

RESEARCH AND DEVELOPMENT (R&D)   That activity associated with the conception, invention, design, development, production and testing of new and improved products or services.

RESERVE   Money set aside in the business books for a specific purpose such as purchase of equipment or real estate.

RESERVE FOR BAD DEBTS   An item listed on a BALANCE SHEET as a subtraction that anticipates some of the ACCOUNTS RECEIVABLE may not be collectible.

RESOURCES   In business, the individual elements that are important to performing the business. Resources can be classified in four major categories; land, labor capital and management. Collectively, these elements, when combined, are the total strength of the business.

RÉSUMÉ   A document that describes personal, education, work experience, skill level and other facts about a person.

RETAIL   The sale of goods or services singly or in small quantities directly to the consumer, or relating thereto. As opposed to WHOLESALE.

RETAILER   A business that deals in retail trade. See RETAIL.

RETAIL PRICE   The amount charged (price) when selling to the general public. As opposed to WHOLESALE PRICE or FACTORY PRICE.

RETAINAGE   A portion or percentage of payments due (PROGRESS PAYMENTS) for work completed on a contract that is held back until the entire job is completed satisfactorily.

RETAINED EARNINGS   NET PROFITS (EARNINGS) kept in the company that accumulates as additional EQUITY in the business after DIVIDENDS are paid to stockholders. Also called EARNED SURPLUS; UNDISTRIBUTED EARNINGS. Retained earnings are distinguished from CONTRIBUTED CAPITAL.

RETAINER   A fee paid in advance to assure services are available when needed, mostly used by professionals such as lawyers, accountants and consultants.

RETIREMENT   Repayment of a debt or obligation.
     Remove from further service, such as permanent withdrawal of an employee from the workforce; cancellation of a stock or bond; scrapping a fixed asset at the end of its useful life.

RETIREMENT PLAN   Prepaid savings (insurance) provisions accumulated during the working lifetime in preparation for old age.

RETURN   The PROFIT from an investment or profit in relation to another business variable, usually expressed as a percentage rate. See also RATE OF RETURN; RETURN ON EQUITY; RETURN ON INVESTED CAPITAL; RETURN ON SALES.

The physical return or exchange of merchandise for CREDIT or REFUND.

The form used to report TAXES to a governmental agency; a TAX RETURN.

RETURN ON ASSETS (R.O.A.) A measure of the efficiency of a business calculated as a percentage; a measure of the percent of profit for each dollar invested in the assets by dividing PROFIT by TOTAL ASSETS. When compared for periods before an expansion of capacity, it is helpful in understanding the increased profit obtained from the expansion.

RETURN ON CAPITAL Expressed as a percent, cash distribution from the sale of a FIXED ASSET; distribution of cash resulting from DEPRECIATION of tax savings; or any other cash distribution unrelated to RETAINED EARNINGS.

RETURN ON EQUITY See RETURN ON INVESTED CAPITAL.

RETURN ON INVESTED CAPITAL; RETURN ON INVESTMENT (R.O.I.) A measure of profitability of the ownership of a business expressed as a percentage. This measure is most important to the owner, because it can be compared with other investments. It is calculated by dividing NET PROFIT for the period by TOTAL EQUITY (NET WORTH) at the beginning of an accounting period. Comparison of the current period with other periods reveals trends; comparison with industry composites reveals the profitability of your company compared to competitors. Return on investment (invested capital) is similar to interest on savings.

RETURN ON SALES A measure of profitability expressed as a percent of SALES; the usual definition of PERCENT PROFIT. The calculation is NET INCOME BEFORE TAXES divided by NET SALES written as a percent. It is a measure of financial efficiency when compared to prior periods or with other companies in the same kind of business, and it varies widely by industry.

RETURNS The plural of RETURN. See RETURN.

REVENUE Same as INCOME; SALES. See INCOME.

REVOLVING LINE OF CREDIT   An amount of credit that is readily available to a company from a bank for immediate borrowing as the need arises at a specified interest rate. The company can borrow and repay without credit application for each transaction.

RFP   See REQUEST FOR PROPOSAL.

RFQ   See REQUEST FOR QUOTE.

RIDER   An amendment to an insurance policy. The rider becomes an integral part of the policy and changes the protection.

RISK   The chance (jeopardy) that a financial deal may fail as opposed to achieve the desired gain. The measurable probability of losing value. As a minimum, not gaining value; as a maximum, losing the total invested amount. There are many types of risk and many factors affecting risk.

To the small businessperson, the RISK OF PRINCIPAL is the greatest risk faced. Risk of principal is the chance invested capital will be lost or as a minimum, decrease in value. A small business lender faces REPAYMENT RISK, the chance that the borrower will not repay the loan as promised.

RISK CAPITAL   See VENTURE CAPITAL.

RISK OF LOSS   The danger attributed to the possibility a hazardous event will occur causing financial drain; the measurable probability such an event will occur. Insurance may be available to minimize the loss. See RISK.

RISK OF PRINCIPAL   The chance that invested capital will be lost. See RISK.

R.O.A.   An abbreviation for RETURN ON ASSETS.

ROADMAP TO SUCCESS   A business plan; the guidelines that identify potential impediments so they can be overcome to achieve profitability.

ROBERT MORRIS & ASSOC. GUIDE   A compilation of average business financial profiles categorized by industry.

R.O.I.   An abbreviation for RETURN ON INVESTED CAPITAL.

ROYALTY   Payment of an agreed amount of money for the right to use a given property, e.g., a patent or copyrighted material.

RULE OF 72   A calculation of the approximate number of years required to double an investment at an interest rate. For example, an interest rate compounded at nine percent would double in eight years ($^{72}/_9 = 8$).

RULE OF 78s   A method of computing a refund of unearned finance charges on contracts wherein the refund is proportional to the monthly unpaid balance at the time of the refund. Under this rule, on a 12-month contract, the lender would retain $^{12}/_{78}$ of the total finance charge the first month, where 12 is for the first month of twelve and 78 is the sum of all the months (12+11...2+1). At the end of the second month, the lender would have retained $^{23}/_{78}$ of the finance charge, where 23 is the sum of 12+11 for the first and second month.

RULE OF THUMB   Unwritten but accepted operating practices that are considered to be average; practical, generally accepted average values for business statistics.

RUNNING A BUSINESS   Same as conducting or operating a business.

S

SALARIED EMPLOYEE   An employee who is paid a SALARY. Distinguished from an employee who is paid for each hour of service (an HOURLY EMPLOYEE).

SALARY   A fixed payment to an employee at regular intervals for service; especially professional service. Distinct from an HOURLY WAGE, salary is usually paid weekly, semi-monthly or monthly.

SALE   In general, any exchange of goods or services for money. In retail sales jargon, a discount.

In finance, income received in exchange for goods or services recorded in the accounting books for a given period, either on a cash (as received) or on an accrual basis (as earned).

SALE-LEASEBACK   A financing technique whereby an owner of an asset sells the asset to another party and immediately leases the asset from the other party under agreement. This technique would free up capital that was invested in the asset and also allow write-off of the lease expenditures as an operating expense.

SALES   The sum of more than one sale.

In accounting, often used interchangeably with income or revenue. See also GROSS SALES; NET SALES.

In retail, often refers to products offered for sale at less than the originally stated price.

SALES CONTRACT   A written agreement between a seller and a buyer to exchange a product or service for money.

SALES CYCLE   The period of time when most sales are made and the period of time when least sales are made. As an example, retail merchandise sales are high just prior to Christmas and lower in the early part of each year. Or lawn mowers sell best in Spring and early Summer.

SALES FINANCE COMPANY   See ACCEPTANCE COMPANY.

SALES FORECAST   The expected revenues (sales) that can be achieved for a period in the future. The projection is developed by estimating the number of units that will be sold at an average sale price per unit.

SALES INVOICE   See INVOICE.

SALES KIT   An assortment of information, literature and samples of products and services available for sale. The information is organized in a manner that facilitates familiarity by new sales-people so they can quickly begin making sales.

SALESMANSHIP   The art of persuading and convincing people to buy what is offered for sale.

SALESPERSON   Any person employed by a business who makes contact with potential customers, attempting to get them to buy the products or services available for sale.

SALES PROMOTION   The function of the selling process that encourages the movement of merchandise or services from a business to customers or clients. Often involves subtle gimmicks that persuade the customer or client to buy.

SALES TAX   A fee that is payable to a state government and is collected by retailers as a percent of sales made. The retailer acts as an agent for the state Department of Revenue.

SALES TAX-EXEMPT NUMBER   An identification number assigned to not-for-profit corporations allowing them to buy goods without paying sales taxes. A retail business that usually collects sales tax must record this number for a sale made to a not-for-profit organization to verify to the state's sales tax revenue office that the sale should not have included collection of a sales tax.

SALES TAX IDENTIFICATION NUMBER; SALES TAX I.D. NUMBER The number assigned by a state Department of Revenue to a corporation or a partnership and used for sales tax recordkeeping. The retailer acts as an agent for the state by collecting and remitting the required amount.

SALES VOLUME The total amount of revenue (sales) received during a given period (or expected to be received). Sometimes, refers to the quantity of goods sold.

SALES VOLUME RATE Same as TOTAL ASSETS TURNOVER.

S&L The abbreviation for SAVINGS AND LOAN ASSOCIATION.

SATISFACTION The payment of a debt or obligation, especially a judgment; the time when a buyer fully pays a debt and title is transferred from seller to buyer; the completion of all work on a contract.

SAVINGS AND LOAN ASSOCIATION (S&L) A depository financial institution, federally or state chartered, principally to promote thrift and home ownership. S&Ls are the most active participants in the real estate mortgage market with long maturities. Depositors earn interest on deposits, often at higher rates than can be obtained from a commercial bank. Usually, S&Ls do not engage in accounts with small businesses.

SBA The United States Small Business Administration. See SMALL BUSINESS ADMINISTRATION.

SBA 8(a) PROGRAM A U.S. Small Business Administration program that is intended to help small businesses that are owned and controlled by socially and economically disadvantaged individuals so they can compete on an equal basis in the mainstream of the American economy. SBA is authorized to promote contracts with these firms for needed government supplies, products and services. Some amount of government procurement is set aside for contracting to SBA 8(a) companies.

SBA 503 LOAN   Long-term fixed asset financing for use in expansion or modernization. Loan requirements: at least 10% equity and a loan up to 90 percent by a federal financing company that includes an SBA guarantee. Similar to SBA 504 LOAN.

SBA 504 LOAN   Long-term fixed asset financing for use in expansion or modernization. Loan requirements: at least 10% equity and a loan up to 90% by a private Certified Development Company backed by an SBA guarantee. Similar to SBA 503 LOAN.

SBA LOAN GUARANTEE   A promise by the U.S. Small Business Administration to reimburse a bank for money lost due to failure by a borrower to repay. Only selected banks are eligible for the program.

SBA 7(j) PROGRAM   A U.S. Small Business Administration program that provides management and technical aid to eligible small businesses in areas of high unemployment. The aid includes services such as bookkeeping, accounting, production, engineering and marketing. Eligible firms and individuals include those socially and/or economically disadvantaged, ones located in high unemployment areas and SBA 8(a) PROGRAM companies.

SBDC   See SMALL BUSINESS DEVELOPMENT CENTER.

SBI   See SMALL BUSINESS INSTITUTE.

SBIC   See SMALL BUSINESS INVESTMENT COMPANY.

SBIR   See SMALL BUSINESS INNOVATION RESEARCH.

SCHEDULE C   The supplementary tax form, as a part of federal income tax Form 1040, used for reporting gains or losses from a sole proprietorship.

SCOPE OF WORK   A description of work that is to be performed; the document that completely describes the tasks necessary for performing a service; a definition of the services to be performed; what and how the service job is to be done.

SCORE; S.C.O.R.E. See SERVICE CORPS OF RETIRED EXECU-
TIVES.

S-CORP. See S-CORPORATION.

S-CORPORATION A corporation that is taxed as a PARTNER-
SHIP by the INTERNAL REVENUE CODE, provided it has 25 or
fewer shareholders and meets certain other requirements. Thus a
small corporation can distribute income directly to shareholders,
avoiding the corporate income tax but enjoying the advantages of
the corporate form. An S-Corporation avoids the double taxation
of corporate ownership. Also known as SUBCHAPTER S-COR-
PORATION; TAX-OPTION CORPORATION; SMALL BUSINESS
CORPORATION. See also CORPORATION.

SDB See SMALL DISADVANTAGED BUSINESS.

SEASONAL Describing a business that has prosperous times
and unprosperous times related to the seasons of the year. Also,
seasonal is sometimes used interchangeably with *cyclical* even
though not directly related to seasons of the year.

SEASONALLY ADJUSTED An amount that has been computed
to account for a SEASONAL VARIATION, so that this amount can
be evaluated on an equivalent basis with amounts in other periods. If all other factors are equal, seasonally adjusted values would
be the same for each period.

SEASONAL VARIATION Regular pattern of economic activity
associated with custom or weather over the course of a year.

SEC See SECURITIES AND EXCHANGE COMMISSION.

SECONDARY FINANCING Other collateral provided by a borrower to obtain a loan.

SECONDARY LIABILITY Agreement by a corporate shareholder
to be financially responsible for a corporate debt if the corporation fails to repay.

SECONDARY MARKET The resale of products or debt securities
to another party; the ability to resell such items to other customers.

SECOND MORTGAGE   A loan secured by real estate that is junior (subordinate) to a FIRST MORTGAGE; a mortgage that is recorded after a first mortgage; a second loan on real estate. In case of default, the first mortgage holder would be paid before payment to a second mortgage holder. See FIRST MORTGAGE.

SECOND ROUND   An intermediate stage of VENTURE CAPITAL financing. See VENTURE CAPITAL.

SECOND STAGE   See SECOND ROUND.

SECRETARY   An EXECUTIVE officer of a company having the responsibility for keeping the records of the company in proper order; takes the minutes of meetings, keeps records of the shareholders, etc.

A clerical job involving routine paperwork, correspondence, typing, files, dictation and other work.

A person in charge of a government department; such as Secretary of State.

SECURED   A debt obligation that is guaranteed by a pledge of assets or other COLLATERAL. If the debt is not repaid, the holder of the note may take title to the asset that was used as collateral.

SECURED DEBT; SECURED LOAN   A loan that is backed by collateral. See SECURED.

SECURITIES   The total group of documents that promise to pay money, earnings or dividends in exchange for investment risks taken by ownership or lending money. See SECURITY.

SECURITIES AND EXCHANGE COMMISSION   A federal government body that regulates the securities industry.

SECURITY   A document evidencing COLLATERAL for money loaned. Also, an instrument that promises to pay money, earnings or dividends by participation in or ownership of a corporation, trust or other property, such as STOCK or BOND. Securities are usually negotiable and therefore are regulated by both state and federal law. To prevent fraud, illegal acts and unsubstantial schemes, transactions in which promoters go to the public for risk capital are monitored. PERSONAL SECURITY is the guarantee by one person to repay another person's debt.

SECURITY AGREEMENT A document that creates a lien upon personal property (chattels), filed on a FINANCING STATE-MENT (Form UCC-1) in accordance with the Uniform Commercial Code.

SEED CAPITAL See SEED MONEY.

SEED CAPITALIST A VENTURE CAPITALIST who invests in an early stage of a new company or new product.

SEED FINANCING See SEED MONEY.

SEED MONEY Initial contributions of financing for START-UP businesses. Seed money provides the basis for additional capitalization to accommodate growth. See also MEZZANINE LEVEL; SECOND ROUND; VENTURE CAPITAL.

SEEK A MARKET To look for a buyer (if you are a seller). Or to look for a seller (if you are a buyer).

SEIZE To take legal possession of, such as to take ownership of property. Also to assign ownership of; to put in legal possession of a particular thing.

SEIZE COLLATERAL; SEIZE THE COLLATERAL By a lender, to take legal ownership of property that has been offered by the borrower as security for a loan after the due date for repayment.

SELF-EMPLOYED Working for oneself.

SELF-EMPLOYMENT TAX The tax paid by a sole proprietor for old age and survivor benefits.

SELF-INSURANCE Having the financial capacity to withstand a financial loss and recover without the backup of another party, such as an insurance company.

SELL To exchange goods or services for money or to offer for sale regularly.

SELLER'S MARKET   A market situation characterized by demand that exceeds supply. Higher prices are often found because of the limited amount of competition and the limited quantity of products or services available for sale. Thereby, sellers can raise prices; buyers are willing to pay the premium price.

SELLING EXPENSE   The cost of acquiring customers, enticing them to buy, delivery of the product or service and collection of the amount paid.

SEMIANNUAL   Occurring twice a year; BIANNUAL.

SEMI-VARIABLE COST   A cost that has both a fixed and a variable component; a cost that is not truly a FIXED COST but is also not truly a VARIABLE COST. See FIXED COST; VARIABLE COST.

SENIOR DEBT; SENIOR LOAN   The loan that would be paid first in a liquidation situation. See SUBORDINATE.

SERVICE   In business, the employment of human effort to tasks such as repair, maintenance and transportation, where the result is other than a physical PRODUCT, GOODS or MERCHANDISE.

   In lending, the procedures, paperwork and effort associated with collection of amounts owed; the cost of this work.

SERVICEABILITY   The ability of a product to perform the designed functions. Also, the ease of repairing a product.

SERVICE BUSINESS   A retail business that engages in labor tasks for the benefit of others for a fee; performs a SERVICE.

SERVICE CHARGE   A fee required to be paid for the handling of an account, usually for unusual or costly procedures; a cost (charge) for service rendered.

SERVICE CORPS OF RETIRED EXECUTIVES (SCORE)   A national not-for-profit organization of retired former small business owners, professionals and managers who provide free counseling to small businesses under the sponsorship of the U.S. SMALL BUSINESS ADMINISTRATION.

SERVICE LIFE   See ECONOMIC LIFE; USEFUL LIFE.

SERVICE-ORIENTED BUSINESS   A company whose primary function is to perform labor tasks for customers; as opposed to a PRODUCT-ORIENTED BUSINESS.

SETTLEMENT   The act of finalizing all factors affecting a transaction, such as credits, charges, costs and fees; to complete a transaction; to conclude a transaction.

7(j); SEVEN J   See SBA 7(j) PROGRAM.

SHAKEOUT   A situation that occurs when a market cannot support all the sellers, forcing some to drop out of that market. The strong sellers survive and the weak sellers cease to sell (shakeout).

SHARE   In business, a unit of equity ownership in a corporation and sometimes a limited partnership. This ownership is represented by a STOCK CERTIFICATE issued by the corporation in the name of the person owning the share. Two types are used: COMMON STOCK and PREFERRED STOCK. PAR VALUE represents the equivalent dollar amount equal to one share's value. See STOCK; COMMON STOCK.

SHAREHOLDER   A person or organization that owns one or more shares of stock in a corporation; ownership is confirmed by being issued a STOCK CERTIFICATE. Shareholders' rights are defined in the ARTICLES OF INCORPORATION and the BYLAWS. Also called STOCKHOLDER.

SHAREHOLDER'S EQUITY   The collective ownership in a corporation represented by total ASSETS minus total LIABILITIES. Also called NET WORTH, EQUITY, stockholder's equity.

SHARE OF STOCK   See SHARE.

SHARE THE RISK   A situation where more than one person or company participates, each assuming part of the risk of loss. Usually, the assumption of loss risk is proportional to the proportion of invested capital.

SHELTER   See TAX SHELTER.

SHIPPING   The transportation of products from one location to another, usually from buyer to seller. Also means the cost of the transportation expense or the department of the company responsible for this function.

SHIPPING CHARGES   The cost of the transportation expense for delivery of products from seller to buyer.

SHOPLIFTER   A person who steals from a retail store.

SHOPLIFTING   Theft by SHOPLIFTERs.

SHORT-RANGE   A term used in business planning for a period of time that is one year or less; sometimes including less detailed planning for a second year in the future. Monthly and quarterly assessment of progress is used for management control. As opposed to LONG-RANGE which is three or more years.

SHORT-RANGE PLAN   A BUSINESS PLAN covering a period of one or two years.

SHORT-TERM   In business situations, short-term usually means one year or less. On a balance sheet, assets held less than one year are called CURRENT ASSETS; loans or trade credit due in one year are called CURRENT LIABILITIES.

In investing, securities, stocks and bonds held for one year or less are short-term and are taxed as short-term capital gains. However, sometimes securities held six months or less are defined as short-term capital gain for taxing purposes. Short-term in planning is one year, although sometimes extends to three years. See INTERMEDIATE-TERM; LONG-TERM.

SHORT-TERM BORROWING   See SHORT-TERM DEBT.

SHORT-TERM CAPITAL GAIN   A CAPITAL GAIN resulting from holding an asset for a period less than one year. See CAPITAL GAIN.

SHORT-TERM DEBT   All debt obligations (loans, trade credit, etc.) coming due within one year; shown on a balance sheet as CURRENT LIABILITIES. See also CURRENT LIABILITIES.

SHORT-TERM LOAN   See SHORT-TERM DEBT.

SHRINKAGE   In retail, the difference between book INVENTORY, as kept in the books of account, and an actual physical count of the merchandise, often the result of employee theft, SHOPLIFTING or spoilage.

SIC CODE   See STANDARD INDUSTRIAL CLASSIFICATION.

SIGHT DRAFT   SEE DRAFT.

SIGNATURE   A person's name written by himself or herself; also a representation of this in a mark, stamp, type, print or deputy's handwriting.

SIGNATURE GUARANTEE   Verification by a bank official that the signature is that of the person writing his or her name.

SIGNS   Printed display boards frequently used to indicate the availability of products or services that are being offered for sale. Signs are of all shapes and sizes, from store window signs to large billboards along major traffic routes.

SILENT PARTNER   An investor in the business who is not active in its daily operation.

SIMPLE INTEREST   The amount of money received from an investment for a period (usually a year); the investment amount times the SIMPLE INTEREST RATE equals the simple interest received. The money is paid in cash or by check and usually is not added to the invested amount, as opposed to COMPOUND INTEREST. See INTEREST; COMPOUND INTEREST.

SIMPLE INTEREST RATE   The annual percentage value used in calculation of SIMPLE INTEREST. Calculated as the additional amount of money received divided by the initial investment amount and expressed as a percent. As opposed to COMPOUND INTEREST RATE.

SINKING FUND   A type of savings scheme by a company; a separate account into which entries (deposits) are made regularly that will be used later for a specific purpose, i.e., to purchase equipment. This method is used because it is sometimes difficult to have the necessary cash available for large purchases.

SITE   A location set aside for a particular use; a plot of ground where the business is situated, or will be located.

SITE RATING   An evaluation and scoring of various business locations to determine the desired location.

SITE SELECTION   The process of evaluating locations for the business and choosing the best alternative.

SKIMMING   An illegal practice wherein an owner may steal a portion of the revenues before they appear on the books. A retailer, for instance, could use cash illegally for purchases without recording either the sale or the purchase.

SKIP ACCOUNT   A PERSONAL ACCOUNT wherein the buyer owing money cannot be found to collect the payment or repossess the goods.

SKU   See STOCKKEEPING UNIT.

S.L. DEPRECIATION; S.L. METHOD   See STRAIGHT-LINE DEPRECIATION.

SMALL BUSINESS   A small business is one that is independently owned and operated, is not dominant in its field and is limited by employment or sale amounts. Yet SMALL BUSINESS, as defined by the U.S. Small Business Administration, has many size definitions depending on the industry, purpose and usage, varying from 100 to 500 employees or from $0.5 to $17.0 million in sales. A most common definition: less than 500 employees. The SBA publishes precise definitions in each category; further, the SBA does not qualify some businesses for loans even though they are small, such as the media, gambling, speculation, real property investment, real property sales, and recreation or amusement enterprises not open to the public. By the SBA definition, 99 percent of all businesses are small.

SMALL BUSINESS ADMINISTRATION (SBA)   A federal government agency created to administer the federal government's program for the preservation, development and encouragement of small business concerns. The SBA is supervised by an administrator appointed by the President. Among other things, the SBA is authorized to make loans to small businesses to finance all aspects of the operation. Most often, the SBA guarantees the loan of a private lender. But the SBA may make loans directly to an individual business where warranted.

SMALL BUSINESS DEVELOPMENT CENTER (SBDC) University campus-based centers that provide counseling, professional analysis, advice and training to small businesses at no cost to the small business. Sponsored by the U.S. Small Business Administration, the service is provided by university faculty, private consultants, business and industry specialists.

SMALL BUSINESS INCUBATOR See INCUBATOR.

SMALL BUSINESS INNOVATION RESEARCH (SBIR) A U.S. Small Business Administration program that requires other agencies of the federal government to set aside research or R&D contracts to be awarded competitively to small businesses. Product or process awards can be made in three phases:

PHASE I: To evaluate scientific and technical merit and feasibility of an idea. Awards can be up to $50,000 and for a period of performance up to six months.

PHASE II: A follow-on award to expand on the successful results of PHASE I and further pursue development. Awards can be made up to $500,000 and a period of performance up to two years.

PHASE III: The commercialization of the results of PHASE II funded entirely with private funds, i.e., no government funding is permitted in PHASE III.

SMALL BUSINESS INSTITUTE (SBI) A service sponsored by the U.S. Small Business Administration that provides confidential and professional management guidance by a college to small businesses at no cost to the small business. The service is performed by University Schools of Business by graduate students and seniors under the guidance of a faculty advisor.

SMALL BUSINESS INVESTMENT COMPANY (SBIC) A federally-funded, private venture capital company that is licensed by the SBA and that usually provides capital for expansion of newer firms producing high-tech products or services.

SMALL BUSINESS WEEK An annual event of one week duration sponsored by the U.S. Small Business Administration to honor small businesses. A national event is held in Washington, D.C.; various other cities conduct their own celebrations.

SMALL-CAPS Small companies; companies with a small amount of capital.

SMALL DISADVANTAGED BUSINESS (SDB) A business, as defined by the U.S. SMALL BUSINESS ADMINISTRATION, that is small and also is owned more than 51 percent by a person who has a disability or is economically depressed due to race, color or sex.

SMART CARD A plastic wallet-sized card containing an imbedded integrated computer chip for storing information and for performing calculations.

SOCIAL SECURITY A federal government program covered by the FEDERAL INSURANCE CONTRIBUTIONS ACT (FICA) wherein mandatory contributions are made by employees and their employers for old age and survivor financial assistance.

SOCIAL SECURITY ADMINISTRATION An agency of the federal government that administers the laws governing the mandatory federal retirement compensation program; enforcer of the FEDERAL INSURANCE CONTRIBUTIONS ACT (FICA).

SOCIAL SECURITY NUMBER The identification number issued for recordkeeping purposes by the Social Security Administration to all citizens of the United States.

SOFT CURRENCY Money (CURRENCY) from a country that is not economically and politically stable, or in which there is not widespread confidence in the exchange rate. The governments of such countries set an unrealistically high exchange rate, and the exchange rate is not backed by gold. As contrasted with HARD CURRENCY.

SOFT DOLLARS Payment of a loan or a promise of payment with money that will be received in the future. Soft dollars are considered as money that is not yet in hand but hopefully will be in hand in the future. As opposed to cash or cash equivalent which is in hand. Contrasts with HARD DOLLARS.

SOFT MARKET A market situation characterized by supply that exceeds demand. Lower prices are often found in order to attract customers. Also called BUYER'S MARKET.

SOFT MONEY See SOFT CURRENCY.

SOFTWARE Computer programs; coded instructions to tell the HARDWARE what to do.

SOLE PROPRIETORSHIP A form of business ownership in which one person owns the entire business, earns all profits and assumes all losses. As contrasted with corporate or partnership businesses. Taxes for a sole proprietorship are reported on IRS Form 1040, Schedule C. See also PROPRIETORSHIP.

SOLVENCY A state of good financial condition that allows debts and obligations to be repaid when due. As opposed to INSOL-VENCY.

SOP Short for Standard Operating Procedure; basic methods and processes by which business is conducted; used for both a formal and an informal reference.

SOURCES AND APPLICATION OF FUNDS STATEMENT See SOURCES AND USES OF FUNDS STATEMENT.

SOURCES AND USES OF FUNDS STATEMENT A financial statement similar to a CASH FLOW STATEMENT that shows: 1) summarized transactions that increase WORKING CAPITAL and 2) summarized transactions that decrease WORKING CAPITAL. For a small business, a CASH FLOW STATEMENT is more meaningful.

SOURCES OF CAPITAL Businesses and persons who can provide money to start a new business. This money can be in many forms such as EQUITY, CAPITAL, LOAN and VENTURE CAPITAL.

SOURCES OF CASH In an accounting analysis of CASH FLOW, sources of cash are those transactions that produce or increase the amount of money on hand, such as payment of cash for goods, collection of an account receivable, cash sale of a fixed asset, earnings not paid as dividends (retained earnings). See CASH FLOW.

SOURCES OF INCOME   Those types of activities, such as sales or other revenue, that cause an increase in INCOME.

SPECIAL TARIFF   A TARIFF levied on the basis of some physical unit or count, such as pound, bushel, yard, dozen or thousand.

SPECIFICATIONS   See PLANS AND SPECIFICATIONS.

SPECULATION   Use of CAPITAL with the anticipation of financial gain but with a higher than average probability of loss. The term speculation implies that a business risk can be quantified; yet, because of the higher risk of loss than for an INVESTMENT, the gain is expected to be higher. Speculation differs from gambling, which is based on random outcomes.

SPECULATOR   A person who looks for large risk business ventures with a large anticipated return but also stands a great chance of losing the entire investment.

SPIN-OFF   An independent company or a product that was recently part of a larger entity but now is separate.

SPREADSHEET   A ledger sheet for a company's financial information, consisting of rows and columns filled with numerical data; a computer presentation of similar data.

SPREADSHEET PROGRAMS   Accounting and financial planning data prepared using computer applications software

SQUARE FOOT COST   See COST PER SQUARE FOOT.

SQUEAKY WHEEL   A term used to describe a situation or person who is so vocal that management attention is drawn to this situation rather than to the situation that will result in the most beneficial outcome.

SRD   See STANDARD RATES AND DATA.

STAFF   The total group of people employed in a business. In larger businesses, staff refers to specialized functions in the business that are not the main line of the business; staff could be people in administrative or accounting functions of a manufacturing business where the main LINE is perhaps computer production.

STAFFING   The tasks of establishing job requirements, recruiting, selecting and hiring desired persons to be employed in a business.

STANDARD INDUSTRIAL CLASSIFICATION CODE (SIC CODE)
A system for classifying businesses based on product or service. Each business is classified by a four digit SIC code for statistical and marketing purposes. A SIC code directory can be found in a local library.

STANDARD INTERNATIONAL TRADE CLASSIFICATION CODE (SITC CODE)   A system for classifying commodities traded in the international marketplace.

STANDARD OF PRACTICE   The ethical and moral rules by which business is conducted; a code of ethics.

STANDARD OPERATING PROCEDURE   See SOP.

STANDARD PRACTICE   Commonly accepted business relationships, procedures or methods used by most businesses in similar situations.

STANDARD RATES AND DATA (SRD)   The bible of the advertising trade containing information about newspapers, magazines, radio, television and other media.

START-UP   The term applied to a business that is just being formed and beginning operation as a business; a new business venture; an entrepreneurial business.
   In VENTURE CAPITAL parlance, start-up is the earliest stage at which a venture capital investor will provide funds to an enter-

prise. Investments or loans made at this stage are called SEED MONEY.

START-UP CAPITAL   The amount of money invested in a business by the owner or owners at the beginning of operations. Sometimes stated as the amount needed to begin operation. As opposed to an amount BORROWED, as a LOAN.

START-UP CHECKLIST   A comprehensive and practical list of items that must be considered in order to begin a successful small business. See Self-Help Guide M.

START-UP COST   The amount of expenditures needed to begin a new business venture.

START-UP LOAN   A LOAN made to a beginning business.

STATE   A government body, referring to any one of the 50 states within the United States of America. As opposed to FEDERAL or LOCAL government.

STATE INCOME TAX   A tax paid to a state government as a percentage of the profits of the corporation.

STATEMENT   A summary for customers of the transactions that have occurred, usually over a month period, e.g., a bank statement lists all deposits and withdrawals and provides a running balance.
      A short form for saying FINANCIAL STATEMENT.

STATEMENT OF CHANGES IN FINANCIAL CONDITION   A document that presents the sources and uses of funds during a specific period. The sources of funds show the origin of incoming money, whereas uses of funds show the destination of the fund expenditures.

STATEMENT OF FINANCIAL CONDITION   See FINANCIAL STATEMENT.

STATE-OF-THE-ART   The most up-to-date thing in its field; on the leading edge of new technology or new knowledge.

STATE SALES TAX See SALES TAX.

STATES AND SMALL BUSINESS A state-by-state directory listing of state offices, programs and recent state legislation affecting small business.

STATE TAX IDENTIFICATION NUMBER; STATE TAX I.D. NUMBER The number assigned by a state's Department of Revenue to a corporation or a partnership used for recordkeeping purposes. Most states have two such numbers, one for STATE INCOME TAX and one for STATE SALES TAX.

STATISTICS Facts or data of a numerical kind that have been assembled, classified and tabulated to present significant information about a given subject. Also, the science of assembling, classifying, tabulating and analyzing such facts and data.

STATUTE The rules, regulations and codes enacted into LAW by Congress (federal law) or by a state legislature (state law). See LAW.

STATUTE OF LIMITATIONS A proclamation that defines the time period within which a specific legal action may be taken.

STATUTORY The nature of, relating to, established by or authorized by a STATUTE.

STATUTORY TAX RATE The tax rate prescribed by law as the prevailing tax legislation.

STELA See SYSTEM FOR TRACKING EXPORT LICENSE APPLICATIONS.

STOCK The collective term that applies to ownership of a corporation and signified by one or more shares (units), such as owning stock in XYZ corporation. COMMON STOCK is the most junior form of ownership; usually carries voting rights at the annual meeting and entitles the holder to dividends paid from corporate earnings. PREFERRED STOCK generally does not have voting rights but has prior claim on assets and earnings over common stock.

Inventory of accumulated merchandise or goods on hand in a retail or manufacturing business; the amount available for sale.

STOCK CERTIFICATE   The document issued by a corporation, and sometimes a limited partnership, that identifies ownership in the corporation. Stock certificates are engraved intricately on heavy paper to deter forgery. The document identifies the name of the corporation, the name of the owner (stockholder), the class of stock, par value (if any), number of shares contained in the certificate and attendant voting rights.

STOCKHOLDER   A person or organization that owns one or more shares of stock in a corporation; ownership is confirmed by being issued a STOCK CERTIFICATE. See SHAREHOLDER.

STOCKHOLDERS' EQUITY   For a corporation, the amount by which assets exceed liabilities. See EQUITY, NET WORTH.

STOCKKEEPING UNIT (SKU)   A standardized numerical method of identifying merchandise including manufacturer, product, size and color, consisting of identifying bars and spaces on hardware items; a BAR CODE.

STOCK REPURCHASE PLAN   A program whereby a company systematically purchases its own shares of stock on the open market then holds the stock certificates in the company treasury.

STOCK SPLIT   An increase in the number of outstanding shares of stock issued by a corporation to existing shareholders without an increase in the amount of investment in SHAREHOLDERS' EQUITY. The only thing affected is a change in the market value of each share outstanding. Subsequent dividends must be calculated on the new total number of shares outstanding.

STOP LOSS   In insurance, a promise by a reinsurance company that it will cover losses incurred by another insurance company in excess of an agreed amount.

In the stock market, an order to a broker to sell stock owned at a SELL price below the current MARKET PRICE. A stop-loss order will automatically sell the stock if the stock price drops to the sell price.

STOP PAYMENT   Revocation of payment on a check after the check has been transferred to the payee but prior to the check being presented to the issuer's bank for payment.

STORE A retail business that sells directly to consumers and, most often, deals in the sale of products.

STORE MONEY A document issued by a business for money on deposit at the business that permits purchase of goods. Usually, store money is given for a refund rather than cash. Thus the purchaser must return to that store to cash the coupon.

STRAIGHT-LINE DEPRECIATION A method of COST RECOVERY of a FIXED ASSET (DEPRECIATION EXPENSE) whereby an equal amount is charged each period during the useful life of the asset after allowing for a salvage value. This is the oldest and simplest method of depreciation. Also called S.L. DEPRECIATION. See also ACCELERATED DEPRECIATION.

STRATEGIC PLAN; STRATEGIC BUSINESS PLAN A document that describes the use of STRATEGY in planning the course of future business operations.

STRATEGY A term used in business planning that refers to the overall scheme of masterminding the future course or direction. Strategy implies careful selection and application of resources for the most advantageous position, in anticipation of future events.
    Also, a trick or scheme for deceiving the competition.

STRAW MAN A preliminary estimate and presentation of an analysis; a first cut of a document; a preliminary draft.
    Also, a person other than the principal acting in a business situation.

STRIKE The refusal of employees to work for a company (or an entire industry) until the employer agrees to their demand for higher wages or other terms or conditions of employment.

STRIKEBREAKER Workers who are willing to work on jobs currently vacated by workers who are on strike.

STRUCTURE For business definition, see BUSINESS STRUCTURE.

STUB That part of a two-part form retained by the preparer as evidence of the transaction.

SUBCHAPTER S-CORPORATION   See S-CORPORATION.

SUBCONTRACTOR   A business (often in the construction indus-try) that does not work directly for the customer of a project but rather for another GENERAL CONTRACTOR or prime contractor and performs that part of the work in the subcontractor's spe-cialty, i.e., a plumbing subcontractor working for a general con-struction contractor who is building a house for a customer.

SUBORDINATE; SUBORDINATED DEBT; SUBORDINATED LOAN   In a liquidation situation where one loan is paid first (SENIOR LOAN) in preference to a subordinate loan (JUNIOR LOAN) that would be paid with remaining funds.

SUBSCRIPTION   An agreement to buy a new securities issue.
   Also, the paid contract to purchase a series of issues of a trade magazine over a specified period.

SUBSIDIARY   A company wherein more than 50 percent of the voting shares are owned by another company, the parent com-pany. Thus, the subsidiary is owned and controlled by another PARENT company. See PARENT COMPANY; HOLDING COM-PANY; AFFILIATE.

SUBSIDIARY ACCOUNT   In accounting, an ACCOUNT that records all the transactions of a particular type and is not a sum-mary account. When preparing financial statements, all subsid-iary accounts pertaining to a specific subject are summarized into a CONTROL ACCOUNT. See ACCOUNT.

SUBSIDIARY LEDGER   A detailed record of an account that is summarized with other similar accounts into a summary ledger entry, called a CONTROL ACCOUNT.

SUBSIDY   Partial payment by a government to a domestic com-pany for goods or services to enhance competitiveness based on the governmental initiative or to minimize the price advantage of im-ported goods or services. Also called government subsidy.

SUBSTITUTION OF COLLATERAL   A provision in a note that permits the borrower to obtain a release of the original collateral by replacement with other collateral acceptable to the lender. To replace one asset as collateral on a note in exchange for release of an asset which is now listed as collateral. The released asset becomes free and clear of the debt.

SUCCESSION PLANNING A structured means of training family members or junior employees who will carry on business activity and fill vital positions in a company; a process critical in the event of death of the primary owner.

SUCCESS RATIO Of a given total of small businesses that begin operations, the percent that survive and continue in business and make a profit. Opposite of FAILURE RATIO.

SUM-OF-THE-YEARS-DIGITS METHOD A method of ACCELERATED DEPRECIATION that results in higher DEPRECIATION charges and higher tax savings in the early years of a FIXED ASSET's useful life than the STRAIGHT-LINE DEPRECIATION method. Calculation of the depreciation for each year is on an inverted scale in proportion to the total of all the digits for the useful life.

SUPPLIES An accounting term describing incidental materials needed in the conduct of business, such as office supplies.

SUPPLY An economist's term describing the amount of a product or service that can be traded at each price, as opposed to DEMAND.
The amount of materials or provisions available for use; STOCK.

SUPPLY AND DEMAND The economic theory of market value wherein price is determined by the interaction of opposing seller and buyer forces; namely, the equilibrium price at which sellers are willing to sell a product at the same price a buyer is willing to pay for the product. See DEMAND; SUPPLY.

SUPPLY CURVE A graphic representation of SUPPLY.

SUPPLY SCHEDULE A numerical tabulation of the quantitative relationship between quantity supplied and price.

SURETY A type of insurance company that guarantees execution of an agreement or contract in the form of a PERFORMANCE

BOND; one who becomes a grantor for another. Thus if the bonded contractor fails to fulfill the terms of the contract or agreement, the surety will step in and complete the work.

SURETY BOND   See PERFORMANCE BOND; SURETY.

SURETY COMPANY   A business that issues PERFORMANCE BONDS; a SURETY.

SURPLUS   A quantity or an amount that exceeds what is needed or used; that which is left over.

Also refers to additional capital. See CAPITAL SURPLUS.

SWEAT EQUITY   A popular expression for equity created by the performance of work or labor by the owner. Usually, little or no salary is taken so the retained earnings build up as equity.

SWINDLE SHEET   Common business jargon for an EXPENSE REPORT.

SYNDICATE   A group of two or more people who are united for the purpose of making and operating an investment, such as a business venture. See also PARTNERSHIP.

SYSTEM FOR TRACKING EXPORT LICENSE APPLICATIONS (STELA)   A Department of Commerce on-line computer program that allows users to access information concerning the status of an export license application.

T

TAKE INVENTORY   The process of counting the goods, products, assets or other property on hand. Frequently used in merchandising where all the products for sale are counted to compare with accounting records of what should be on hand.

TAKEOVER   The acquisition of one company by another, sometimes a hostile situation, by a large creditor at the objection of the current owner.

TANGIBLE   Real. A thing that can be seen, touched and evaluated. As opposed to INTANGIBLE. See TANGIBLE ASSET.

TANGIBLE ASSET   Something owned, an asset, that has physical form such as real property, personal property or money equivalents. Examples include land, cash, real estate, machinery, inventory, accounts receivable and securities. Other than physical property, when an asset has a market value that can be readily verified, it can be considered tangible; otherwise the asset is classified as INTANGIBLE. See ASSET; INTANGIBLE ASSET.

TANGIBLE NET WORTH   See NET WORTH.

TARGET MARKET   That segment of the market that is identified as the primary customer. The specific individuals or firms, distinguished by socio-economic, demographic, and/or interest characteristics, that are the most likely potential customers for the goods or services of a business.

TARGET MARKETING   The process of determining the specific niche from a large customer potential. See TARGET MARKET.

TARIFF   A tax on IMPORTED GOODS, most often computed as a percent of the price charged for the good by the foreign supplier; an import tax rate schedule. Same as CUSTOMS DUTY, DUTY.
   In transportation, the amount payable for shipment of goods.

TAX   A payment required to be made to a government body, resulting from legislation.

TAX ADVICE   Guidance by a professional (usually a lawyer or certified public accountant) to a business concerning business decisions to minimize the tax to be paid.

TAX ADVISOR   A person or firm that provides TAX ADVICE.

TAX BASE   The assessed value of the property subject to taxes.

TAX CONSEQUENCES   The tax payments that result from a business decision. Some decisions cause more tax to be paid than others.

TAX CONSIDERATIONS   In business decision-making, evaluation of the effects of taxes that must be paid as a result of a business's decision. One alternative may require payment of less taxes, and, along with other considerations, sway the choice made.

TAX-EXEMPT NUMBER   See SALES TAX-EXEMPT NUMBER.

TAX-FREE   No payment of tax is required. Usually, things that are normally taxed, but under certain circumstances, tax payment is averted or tax payment is made by another party for the benefiting person. For instance, some amount of products can be imported tax-free (duty-free).

TAX-FREE PERKS   Company benefits to an individual or employee on which the person does not pay tax. Care must be exercised to ensure that only legal means of tax-free income is earned by the employee.

TAX GUIDE FOR SMALL BUSINESSES See PUBLICATION #334.

TAX IDENTIFICATION NUMBER; TAX I.D. NUMBER; TAX NUMBER The number assigned by the federal or a state Department of Revenue to a corporation or a partnership used for recordkeeping purposes. Federal and state governments issue these numbers for income taxes reported by corporations and partnerships. The owner of a sole proprietorship utilizes his or her social security number for this purpose. In addition, states issue state sales tax identification numbers to all firms selling directly to the consumer, for the collection of state sales tax.

TAX LIABILITY The amount of tax owed.

TAX LOSS CARRY-BACK; TAX LOSS CARRY-FORWARD An income tax loss in one year may be used to refund previously paid taxes in any/all of the most recent three years past or may be used to reduce taxes due in any/all of the next 15 years.

TAX PENALTY An additional amount of tax required if taxes have not been paid in accordance with the law, such as from late payment or false statements on a tax return.

TAX PLAN An assessment or estimate of taxes due.

TAX PUBLICATIONS Documents describing taxes, items included, items excluded, tax calculations and other tax information. Often printed by a government agency but could be privately published. See PUBLICATION #334; PUBLICATION #583.

TAX RATE The percentage used to calculate the amount of tax due.

TAX REFERENCES Locations, documents, information sources or other material concerning taxes.

TAX REFORM ACT The enactment of a law by a government body, most commonly the U.S. federal government, that affects the amount of taxes to be paid by a business.

TAX RETURN   The document used for preparing income taxes due and submitting the calculations to a government agency.

TAX ROLL   The public record list of persons and businesses required to pay a tax.

TAX SHELTER   A phrase used to describe some business conditions that reduce the amount of tax due. The effect may be avoidance of a tax payment, reduction of a tax rate or delay in a tax payment to a later period.

TELEMARKETING   Advertising, canvassing or selling over the telephone, with one person speaking to another.

TEMPORARY WORKER   A worker that is not a regular employee of the firm and is hired for a short period.

TENANT   A LESSEE, when the property rented is real estate. See LEASE.

TENDER   An unconditional offer by one of the parties to a contract to perform his or her part of the bargain.

10-K   A disclosure document required by public companies that includes a business description, financial statements and other important management transaction information.

TERM   A period of time; the duration over which activities will occur. Examples include: the period of time for execution of the conditions of a contract; length of time over which loan payments must be made; the length of time a term life insurance policy is in force; the duration of time a board member will serve; the duration of a lease period.

Specifying the nature of an agreement; the provisions of a contract, as in the terms of a contract. See TERMS AND CONDITIONS.

TERM DEBT   A DEBT due to be paid over a period of time, as opposed to be paid entirely at one time in one lump sum.

TERM LOAN   See TERM DEBT.

TERMS AND CONDITIONS The provisions of a contract specifying the activities and actions that must be accomplished and
sometimes the methods used in performance of the contract; a
further definition of the scope of a contract; contract limits; contractual agreements.

TERMS OF PAYMENT Those provisions in a financial exchange
that define the means for satisfying the monetary part of the deal;
the dates, amounts, forms and persons who will pay this money.

TEST MARKETING Small sample analytical experimentation of
new products or marketing techniques to determine effectiveness
before full commitment.

THE FED See FEDERAL RESERVE SYSTEM.

3rd PARTY; THIRD PARTY A person or business that is not a
participant in a transaction but may assist in consummating the
transaction or be affected by the transaction. A third party is not
a principal to the transaction, such as a broker.

THIRD-PARTY CHECK A double-endorsed CHECK that involves
three persons or businesses and a BANK. The primary party to
the transaction is the DRAWER (the preparer of the check) against
funds on deposit in the bank; the secondary party is the PAYEE
who endorses the check by signing on the back and passing the
check to a third party who endorses the check prior to cashing it.
Recipients of checks with multiple endorsers are reluctant to accept them unless the identity and signature of each endorser can
be verified.

3-5-10 RULE See ACCELERATED COST RECOVERY SYSTEM.

THRESHOLD COMPANY A business that is progressing beyond
the entrepreneur stage, striving to achieve long-term growth and
prosperity.

TIGHT MONEY MARKET An economic condition in which loans
are difficult to obtain because of limited money supply, yet the
demand for borrowing is high and often associated with high
interest rates.

TIME DRAFT   See DRAFT.

TIME OF INCORPORATION   The date a state CERTIFICATE OF INCORPORATION is issued; or generally reference to that time.

TIME-PRICE DIFFERENTIAL   The difference between the purchase price of something and the higher total price of the same thing if purchased on an installment basis (including finance charges). Under truth-in-lending laws, a lender must disclose the time-price differential as well as all finance charges on an installment contract.

TIME SHEET   A document that records the hours worked by an employee; most often, hand-written by the employee.

TIMES-INTEREST-EARNED RATIO   A measurement of a business's ability to pay its debts; a multiple by which recurring income provides for payment of interest income. If a business can keep current on its interest payments, the business can usually refinance principal and maintain the confidence of creditors.

TIME VALUE   See TIME VALUE OF MONEY.

TIME VALUE OF MONEY   A generalized economic principle whereby inflation, interest rate or earning power cause the worth of a dollar (PRESENT VALUE) today to be greater than the worth of a dollar in the future (FUTURE VALUE). See INTERNAL RATE OF RETURN.

TITLE   The document evidencing ownership of property whether real or personal property.

TOOL   An implement, instrument or utensil used to increase a person's natural ability or capacity to do work. Most often tools are handheld, but the term can also apply to anything used to increase work output, such as a machine tool or a personal computer.

TOOLS OF THE TRADE   The TOOLS, instruments or devices necessary to the accomplishment of a trade, occupation or business.

"Tools of the trade" has been adopted as an idiom, meaning those things needed and used to perform a specific task.

TOTAL ASSETS   The sum of all ASSETS; the sum of both CURRENT ASSETS and FIXED ASSETS.

TOTAL ASSETS TURNOVER   The efficiency with which assets are employed in the production of sales; divide TOTAL SALES for a period (a year) by TOTAL ASSETS to determine the number of times each dollar of assets becomes a dollar of sales during the period. Comparing similar periods and similar industry statistics determines measures of efficiencies by which the assets are employed in the business.

TOTAL COSTS   In accounting, the sum of all EXPENSES (costs), including both FIXED VARIABLE and COSTS for the period.

TOTAL EXPENSES   Same as TOTAL COSTS.

TOTAL INVESTMENT   The sum of all EQUITY in a business; the amount of invested capital. See INVESTMENT.

TOTAL LIABILITIES   On a BALANCE SHEET, the sum of all the amounts owed; the sum of LIABILITIES.

TOTAL RETURN   An expression of RETURN ON INVESTMENT, taking into account all moneys received (PROFITS), including EARNINGS, DIVIDENDS, INTEREST, capital APPRECIATION and TAX CONSIDERATIONS.

TOTAL SALES   See SALES.

TOTAL VOLUME   Usually refers to the total amount of sales in dollars during a period, but also refers to the quantity of output or quantity of sales made. See SALES.

TOTAL WORKFORCE   On a national or regional level, the aggregate number of persons who are capable of and desire to work. The total workforce consists of the persons who are employed (are working) plus those who are unemployed (not working), but desire to work.

TRACK RECORD   Prior financial and operating statistics; the proof of successful operating performance. In making a credit evaluation, the lender looks at the debtor's past history of paying other creditors.

TRADE   Buying or selling of goods and services; to exchange for money; commercial companies that do business with each other.
   To barter; to exchange goods for goods.

TRADE ASSOCIATION   A group of businesses that join together collectively to promote their common interests.

TRADE CREDIT   An open account with suppliers of goods and services. For a business, trade credit is an important external source of working capital by buying now and paying later, although this source can be very expensive when translated into an annual interest rate. Trade credit is shown on a balance sheet as a liability, called ACCOUNTS PAYABLE. Also, a firm's record of payment with suppliers. Consult DUN & BRADSTREET or MERCANTILE AGENCY ratings of credit worthiness of other businesses.

TRADE-IN   A product owned by the customer that is exchanged as part payment or credit toward the purchase of a new, similar product.

TRADEMARK   A distinctive name, symbol, motto or emblem that identifies a product, service or firm. A certificate issued for such identification by the federal government for a specified period of time, granting the right to prevent competitors from using similar marks in selling or advertising. Thereby, the trademark provides legal protection of the name or symbol used in commerce.

TRADE SHOWS   Exhibits of merchandise or services for the benefit of companies in a particular trade, usually held in exhibition halls, hotels or civic centers.

TRAFFIC   The number of customers (vehicles or potential customers) who visit a business location. Those people who can be considered available as customers of the product or service.

TRAFFIC FLOW   The volume of vehicles or customer activity in a given situation or at a given location; the number of potential customers passing a given area during a period of time in which selling is under way.

TRANSACTION   In accounting, any event or condition that must be entered in the books of account for the company because of its effect on the financial condition of the business, such as to buy, sell or trade. More broadly, a business deal or agreement.

TRANSACTION COST   The cost of exchanging one asset for another asset; the cost of buying or selling. Examples include sales commissions, brokerage fees, legal fees and advertising cost.

TRANSFER   To move from one location to another; to relocate. To move cash assets from one account to another.

   In accounting, to record information from one document onto another document.

TRANSFER AGENT   The bank or trust company authorized by a corporation to maintain the official record of each registered shareholder's name, address and number of shares owned.

TRANSFER LIST   The compilation of the trail of stock certificates from one stockholder to succeeding stockholders.

TRANSMITTAL LETTER   A letter that is sent with a document, security or shipment describing the contents and the purpose of the transaction.

TRANSPORTATION   The movement of goods from one location to another, particularly delivery of products to a customer.

TREASURER   An EXECUTIVE officer of a company having the responsibility for keeping the FINANCIAL records of the company in proper order; oversees the accounting functions, prepares the financial statements and other money matters.

TREASURY BILL   A United States government security that is sold to the public for an investment term not to exceed one year.

TREASURY SHARES   See TREASURY STOCK.

TREASURY STOCK   Stock that has been re-acquired by the issuing corporation. Therefore, it is issued but is not outstanding
and can be resold. The company owns its own stock. Treasury
stock has no voting rights and does not pay dividends.

TRIAL BALANCE   An accounting term applied to preliminary,
perhaps incomplete, INCOME STATEMENTS; the process of obtaining a preliminary conclusion on profitability. More specifically,
a list of account titles and their debit and credit balances that is
used to determine whether posted entries are equal and to establish a basis for summary into financial statements. To make a trial
balance is a major step in closing the accounting books for a period.

TRIPLE NET LEASE   The lessee, in addition to rent, assumes
payment for all expenses associated with the operation of a property, including fixed expenses (such as taxes and insurance) and
operating expenses (such as maintenance and repair). Thus, the
lessee pays rent, fixed expenses and operating expenses. Same as
NET LEASE.

TRIPLICATE   One of three identical copies. See IN TRIPLICATE.

TROUBLE-SHOOTING   The process of evaluating a malfunction-
ing product to determine the cause; testing to find the source of
the problem so that corrective action can be implemented.

TRUTH IN ADVERTISING   A law that requires media presenta-
tions to contain a fair representation of the product or service.

TURNAROUND   For a business in trouble, turnaround describes
a business in the process of getting out of trouble. Also, vice versa.

TURNAROUND COMPANY   A company that is now in financial
trouble, one that is headed for financial trouble or one that is just
emerging out of financial trouble and there is optimism that the
company can be operated at a profit. In any of these predica-
ments, the company can be saved (turned around) and made
profitable by changing the methods of operation of the company.

TURNAROUND LOAN Temporary financing to assist a borrower to acquire another business or to buy its own stock.

TURN-KEY The point at which a project or product is ready for use, especially a complicated venture. Thus all of the ingredients and necessary functions are performed in advance of the turnkey point so the project can be operated by someone else immediately upon start-up.

TURN-KEY COSTS Those necessary expenditures that are incurred before a product or project is ready for use.

TURNOVER A measure of the frequency of occurrence of business activity during a period of time. Usually expressed as a ratio obtained when the total amount is divided by the changes that occurred during the period. Examples include turnover of accounts receivable, inventory, employees and capital. Often when the word turnover is used without other adjectives, the reference is to INVENTORY TURNOVER.

TURNOVER RATIO A comparative measure of TURNOVER comprising three commonly accepted relationships, i.e., sales-to-receivables, sales-to-inventory and sales-to-fixed-assets.

TWO-PART FORM A form with carbon paper between the two layers so that two copies are received when one is prepared.

TYPES OF CAPITAL The various forms of money sources (EQUITY) available to a business, such as personal funds, sale of stock, partners, home equity loan, life insurance loan and investors.

U

UCC   See UNIFORM COMMERCIAL CODE.

UNAUDITED   The opposite of AUDITED; information supplied by a business that has not been the subject of an AUDIT by an independent CERTIFIED PUBLIC ACCOUNTANT; preliminary or unproven financial information.

UNDERCAPITALIZATION   Starting a new enterprise without enough money to carry through the start-up phase, a common cause of failure.

UNDISTRIBUTED PROFITS; UNDISTRIBUTED EARNINGS; UNDISTRIBUTED INCOME   Profits not paid to stockholders (but still belonging to them). Undistributed profits are usually reinvested into the company's operation.

UNEARNED PREMIUM   See PREMIUM.

UNEMPLOYED   A person who desires to work but cannot work because no suitable job exists.

UNEMPLOYMENT   A situation concerning a person, wherein the person desires to work but is unable to work because no suitable job exists for that person. In a national or regional sense, the total group of such persons.

UNEMPLOYMENT FIGURE   See UNEMPLOYMENT RATE.

UNEMPLOYMENT INSURANCE   Insurance coverage for payment of moneys to individuals who fit a precise definition of being unemployed.

UNEMPLOYMENT RATE   The numerical value of unemployed persons as a percent of the TOTAL WORKFORCE.

UNEMPLOYMENT TAX   By law, the amount required to be paid to a state or federal government by a company for insurance on persons employed by the company to cover unemployment payments to the person if the person is later LAID OFF.

UNETHICAL   Lacking in moral principles; failing to conform to an accepted code of business behavior.

UNFAIR AND DECEPTIVE PRACTICES   Sales practices that are misleading and tend toward unfair, unethical or immoral business behavior. Although the sales practice may not involve deception, it may still be illegal under the regulations of the Federal Trade Commission if it is unfair to the public.

UNFAIR COMPETITION   Any advantage gained by a supplier in the marketplace through the use of UNFAIR AND DECEPTIVE PRACTICES.

UNIFORM COMMERCIAL CODE (UCC)   A body of law that attempts to codify and make consistent throughout the country all law relating to commercial transactions, such as sales contracts and chattel mortgages as well as personal property transactions, including negotiable securities and commercial paper.

UNION   The combination of two things bonded together; to join together.
   Also, an organized group of workers who perform similar work, as a LABOR UNION.

UNION EMPLOYEE   A worker for a company who is also a member of a LABOR UNION.

UNION SHOP   A company that permits a nonunion employee to be hired provided the employee joins the union within a stated period of time after employment.

UNION WORKER   See UNION EMPLOYEE.

UNISSUED STOCK   That portion of the AUTHORIZED SHARES of stock in a corporation that have not been sold (issued). When unissued stock is sold, as authorized by the Board of Directors, it becomes issued stock. Unissued shares of stock cannot pay dividends and cannot be voted. Unissued stock must not be confused with TREASURY STOCK. See AUTHORIZED SHARES.

UNIT VALUE   The value or price of a single product in a large quantity; the value relating to a unit of measurement, such as dollars per square foot.

UNIVERSAL PRODUCT CODE (UPC)   Identifying bars and spaces on items that determine the manufacturer and the specific product; a BAR CODE.

UNIVERSE   The total from which a sample is taken or a description of all those that could be considered applicable to the situation at hand.

UNLISTED SECURITY   A security that is not actively traded on a recognized and regulated exchange, e.g., NASDAQ. Stock held in a private corporation would be an unlisted security.

UNSECURED   See UNSECURED LOAN.

UNSECURED DEBT   See UNSECURED LOAN.

UNSECURED LOAN   A debt instrument, such as a note, that has no collateral value. The note is backed only by the trust that the debtor will repay, not by any security or collateral.

UPC   See UNIVERSAL PRODUCT CODE; a BAR CODE.

UP-FRONT COST   Those expenses incurred at the beginning of a business (START-UP COST) or in beginning a new project (PRELIMINARY COST). Sometimes referred to as sunk cost.

UPSTREAM   Counter to the direction of goods from the producer toward the consumer; counter to the normal flow of funds, i.e., from the borrower up to the lender. The opposite of DOWNSTREAM.

USEFUL LIFE   That period of time over which an asset is expected to remain economically feasible to the owner; the time an asset is used; the period of time used for depreciation. Also called ECONOMIC LIFE; SERVICE LIFE.

USER   A term that describes people who use computers. Sometimes user describes a person that uses something besides a computer.

USES OF CASH   In an accounting analysis of CASH FLOW, uses of cash are those transactions that reduce the amount of money on hand, such as installment loan payments, payment of salaries, cash purchase of an asset and payment of taxes. See CASH FLOW.

USE TAX   A tax imposed on the purchaser of tangible personal property that is not for resale or consumption in the business, rather the property will be used in the production of income. Use tax is paid in lieu of sales tax for goods that are consumed.

USURY   The act of charging a rate of interest in excess of that permitted by law.

UTILITIES   The basic services needed to function in the modern world, such as water, sewer, gas, electricity and telephone. The utility company providing the service may be privately owned or may be controlled by the local government. But usually the function performed is the only one available and therefore is a monopoly. Small businesses should understand the amount of utility expenses that are required for operation of the business.

UTILITY COSTS   The cost of providing basic UTILITIES services, such as electric, gas, water, sewer and telephone. Often, these items are listed in financial documents simply as utilities.

V

VALUATION   The process of appraising the worth of a product, service or business

VALUE   Worth expressed in money units; the equivalent amount of money that would be exchanged for a product or service; the power of a good or service to command an exchange of money for another good or service.

VALUE-ADDED   The increase in worth of a product due to change in its form or function by manufacturing, packaging or other method; the difference between the amount a company sells a product for and what was paid for materials and labor used to manufacture the product.

VALUE-ADDED TAX   A tax on the difference between the purchase cost and the selling cost, mostly due to labor required to change the form or function of a product plus profit.

VARIABLE COST   A cost that is dependent on quantity of output; a cost that varies in proportion to the quantity produced and is incurred as a direct result of operation of the business. Theoretically, variable costs are zero if there is no production. As opposed to FIXED COST.

VARIABLE EXPENSES   See VARIABLE COST.

VARIABLE INCOME   An income that depends on the amount of products or services delivered (SOLD) during a period. As opposed

261

to FIXED INCOME, which is received on a regular periodic basis and is a constant amount.

VARIANCE ANALYSIS An evaluation of the causes of deviations from a planned outcome. In marketing, a variance results from either a price change or a volume of sales change.

VAT See VALUE ADDED TAX.

VENDOR A supplier of goods or services of a commercial nature; a seller of merchandise. Also a retailer; especially a retailer without an established place of business, such as a sidewalk vendor.

VENTURE See BUSINESS VENTURE.

VENTURE CAPITAL A source of business investment associated with a relatively high-risk opportunity. Sources of financing for small and start-up businesses. Usually, the risk is of a higher order than conventional financial institutions are willing or able to bear. About $1 billion is invested yearly in venture capital. In return for taking the higher investment risk, a VENTURE CAPITALIST is usually rewarded with some combination of equity ownership rights in the business. Stages of risk levels from start-up (highest risk) are SEED MONEY, SECOND ROUND, MEZZANINE LEVEL and INITIAL PUBLIC OFFERING (least risk, but still there is significantly more risk than for conventional lending). Yet venture capital is less risky than ADVENTURE CAPITAL. Also called RISK CAPITAL.

VENTURE CAPITAL FIRM A business operated by a VENTURE CAPITALIST. See also VENTURE CAPITAL.

VENTURE CAPITALIST An individual or firm that invests in relatively high-risk business situations. A venture capitalist seeks to invest in firms with rapidly growing sales and expects substantial profits, often investment in new developments is desired. A venture capitalist provides equity financing as opposed to a loan. Therefore, the venture capitalist is an owner of the business and seeks to exercise control over the business. See VENTURE CAPITAL. See also ADVENTURE CAPITAL, which is a more speculative investment than venture capital.

VESTED INTEREST A present right to a thing; title to property; ownership although perhaps without current possession, such as a renter. Time and effort devoted to a project.

VICE-PRESIDENT The second highest ranking EXECUTIVE officer in a company, reporting to the PRESIDENT. In the absence of the president, the vice-president is in charge of day-to-day company operation.

VOICEMAIL The use of a recording device on the receiving end of a computer telephone transmission that records incoming information. Similar to a letter but computer-generated and transmitted by wire.

VOID To have no legal force or binding effect; an annulment; not enforceable. A void agreement is no contract at all. To void a previously valid contract eliminates the enforceability of the contract.

VOLUME An amount or quantity. Often the expression of the GROSS SALES of the business.

VOLUNTARY BANKRUPTCY A legal proceeding of bankruptcy when a debtor brings a petition to a court by his or her own action. The objective is an orderly and equitable settlement of obligations. See BANKRUPTCY; INVOLUNTARY BANKRUPTCY.

VOLUNTARY TRADE RESTRAINT A quota by an exporting country that limits the quantity of exports.

VOTING RIGHTS Usually, the shares of stock in a corporation that entitle the shareholder to vote on issues of the corporation. Also applies to individual officers who sit at Board of Directors meetings.

VOUCHER A document serving as evidence (proof) that money was received or that payment was made. In some types of businesses, a voucher is issued as evidence that work was completed, permitting payment by a third party, such as a bank.

VOUCHER SYSTEM A method of paying for work completed by the use of VOUCHERS. See VOUCHER.

W

WAGE   Money paid to a person for work done, usually figured on an hourly or piecemeal basis; also a SALARY.

WAIVER   To give up or surrender a right voluntarily, such as to forgive a provision in a contract.

WAREHOUSE   A building used to store merchandise or other materials or equipment.

WARRANTY   A promise that certain facts are true. A promise by a seller covering title, performance and physical condition of a product or service.

WAYBILL   See BILL OF LADING.

WEEK   A period of time equal to seven calendar days; five working days and two weekend days; one-52nd part of a year.

WEEK DAY   The days of the week normally associated with working, i.e., Monday through Friday. As opposed to WEEKEND, Saturday and Sunday.

WEEKEND   The days of the week normally associated with non-working days, Saturday and Sunday. As opposed to WEEK DAY, Monday through Friday.

WHITE COLLAR; WHITE-COLLAR WORKERS   People who work in a "white shirt" office environment; generally people who work in offices. As opposed to BLUE COLLAR workers, people who work in a shop, factory or construction job.

WHOLESALE   The sale of goods or services in large quantities and at lower prices to someone other than consumers. Sales to a retail businesses, jobbers, merchants, manufacturers, industrial firms, commercial, businesses and institutions or relating thereto. Sometimes called middleperson, middleman or distributor. As opposed to RETAIL.

WHOLESALE PRICE   The amount charged (price) for items sold to other companies, usually for resale at retail price. The wholesale price is higher than FACTORY PRICE but less than RETAIL PRICE.

WHOLESALE PRICE INDEX   See PRODUCER PRICE INDEX.

WHOLESALER   A business that deals in wholesale trade. See WHOLESALE.

WIDGET   An hypothetical product name used as an example during explanation of accounting, finance or economic theory. The symbolic American gadget.

WINDOW DRESSING   A ploy used in documents and pictures to make something appear more attractive than it actually is, often used in advertising, selling and marketing. If a distortion of the facts occur, window dressing may be unethical or illegal.

WITHHOLD   To keep back a portion of the total amount until the entire project or product is available to the purchaser; non-disclosure of pertinent facts, amounts or information.

WITHHOLDING   In employee wages, to deduct an amount required by law for payment of taxes or other amounts due.

WOMB-TO-TOMB   See LIFE CYCLE.

WORKERS' COMP.   A commonly used term for WORKERS' COMPENSATION INSURANCE or workers' compensation payments. See WORKER'S COMPENSATION.

WORKERS' COMPENSATION; WORKERS' COMPENSATION INSURANCE Mandatory state and federal insurance programs under WORKERS' COMPENSATION LAWs that pay a salary to employees who may be injured on the job.

WORKERS' COMPENSATION LAW Both the federal and state governments have laws requiring employers to provide medical and lost-wage insurance coverage for their employees who may be injured on the job.

WORKFORCE The aggregate of workers ready and able to perform jobs in a particular field or the total workers available in the region or even in the entire country.

WORKING CAPITAL In accounting, CURRENT ASSETS less CURRENT LIABILITIES equals working capital; also called NET WORKING CAPITAL; NET CURRENT ASSETS. This measure serves as an indication of the amount of readily available funds that can be used in operation of the business. As such, working capital finances day-to-day business operation (called the CASH CONVERSION CYCLE), allowing bills to be paid while awaiting payment of cash for sales.

Internal sources of working capital include RETAINED EARNINGS, allocation of POSITIVE CASH FLOW from sources such as DEPRECIATION or DEFERRED TAXES, and savings achieved through operating efficiencies. External sources of working capital include TRADE CREDIT, SHORT-TERM LOANS, TERM DEBT, EQUITY FINANCING not used for long-term assets.

WORKING CAPITAL RATIO A measure of the volume of sales by a business that is conducted with its amount of WORKING CAPITAL; NET SALES divided by WORKING CAPITAL.

WORKING PAPERS In accounting, the handwritten entries and transactions recorded in accounts; the basis for calculations relating to the accounts.

WORK IN PROCESS In manufacturing or other long-term projects, those partially completed products that are still in the production process; products that have begun production as raw materials but not yet been completed as finished goods.

WORKMAN'S COMP.; WORKMEN'S COMP. A commonly used, but incorrect, term for WORKERS' COMPENSATION INSURANCE.

WORK SHEETS Supporting papers used in the preparation of reports.

WORTH Material value, especially when expressed in terms of money; the quantity or amount of something that can be exchanged for an amount of money; wealth; possessions; riches.

WRITE-DOWN To reduce the value at which an asset is carried on the books to reflect a decline in value.

WRITE-OFF To remove an asset from the accounting books, as an uncollectible debt. Also, a tax deduction.

W-2 See FORM W-2.

X, Y, Z

YEAR END   December 31st of a calendar year; the last day of a FISCAL YEAR. The date when the financial records are CLOSED for the year.

YEARLY   Events that occur at intervals of 365 days, 52 weeks or 12 months. The most common cycle for measuring and comparing financial performance.

YES-MAN   A person who always agrees and apparently does not exert an opinion of his or her own. Particularly, someone who always agrees with the boss or supervisor regardless of personal convictions.

YIELD   In business or investing, the amount of RETURN (PROFIT) expressed as an annual percentage rate of the amount of capital invested; the RATE OF RETURN; the RETURN ON INVESTED CAPITAL. For a loan, the total money earned on a loan—that is, the ANNUAL PERCENTAGE RATE of interest multiplied by the term of the loan and by the principal amount invested.

Other definitions of yield include: the agricultural output in terms of quantity of crops and the amount of revenue received by a government as a result of a tax.

YIELD TO MATURITY   The return on an interest-bearing investment, usually applied to a BOND. Yield to maturity measures the RATE OF RETURN of the bond if held to maturity, considering purchase price, redemption value, time to maturity, coupon yield and the time between interest payments.

YTM   See YIELD TO MATURITY.

ZERO-BALANCE ACCOUNT   A corporate checking account that provides decentralized disbursement control. After checks are written, a deposit is made exactly equaling the amount of the checks written. The account always returns to zero when all checks have cleared the bank.

ZONING   The regulation of structures and uses of property within designated boundaries, usually within local governmental jurisdictions. Generally, the classifications of zones are heavy industry, light industry, commercial, residential and farm.

Marketing and Selling Your Product or Service

Your idea for starting your own business may or may not be "feasible"—in other words, is it practical, workable, achievable or do-able?

Obviously, feasibility is the first thing you must investigate before you invest. If you have not completed the start-up checklist (Self-Help Guide M), do that now, before beginning a marketing analysis! The start-up checklist presents critical decision-making questions for you to answer that will help you determine the feasibility of your business idea.

Researching Your Market

If you are ready to begin analyzing the market potential of your business idea, you should start the investigation by conducting a "market research study."This boils down to studying the market in-depth so that you understand precisely the important "drivers."Drivers are the factors that make for success or cause failure. You must understand the market better than your competition; otherwise, your competition will be more successful than you.

In order to design a strategy for entry into a market with a good chance for success, you need reliable information about the market and its dynamics. What's its size? Who is the competition? What are the requirements for entry? What shifts in customer habits and preferences are prompting adjustments in supply, price, quality and competition? What's the outlook for growth or decline?

271

Low-Budget Research Options

To answer these questions, you can employ a wide range of practical, low-budget research options. You don't need to employ elaborate opinion sampling and similar costly and time consuming techniques usually associated with big business projects. Moreover, many of these opinion and sampling surveys are useless and give wrong signals. The following are some practical, low-budget means for doing your market research:

1. Use "secondary" sources, such as available and published information about industries, performance and product trends pertinent to your business interests. Sources of such information are listed in this self-help guide.

2. Search for a mailing list of addresses of your prospects. Get help from university marketing majors to design and prepare a sample questionnaire.

3. Search for the appropriate trade association and trade magazines covering the industry you plan to enter, and ask for information bearing on entry into the field.

4. Before you start a blind search, make certain you know exactly what business you want to be in. You can't find the answers if you don't ask the right questions. For example, don't say, "I'm in the computer business" if you use a computer to provide data and statements for an accounting service. And if you plan an accounting service, determine if you can narrow the field of service to some target market, such as recordkeeping and statements for independently-owned repair shops. Only with such precisely defined market targets will you be able to find the data that are most appropriate to answering your market research questions.

Sources of Information for Your Research

The best way to start researching the marketing prospects for your kind of business is to seek the help available, free of charge, from your public library's business reference department. Most public libraries have a list of reference materials that contain specific data and information on a great variety of businesses. Here is a partial listing of sources that may be found in your public library:

1. *Small Business Sourcebook,* which is a one-stop reference listing specific kinds of businesses, published by Gale Research.

2. *Successful Business Library,* which is a practical step-by-step guide including worksheets and examples. The loose-leaf bound material is written by qualified professionals such as lawyers, certified public accountants and others.

3. *The Encyclopedia of Associations,* which contains a list of names, addresses and telephone numbers of trade associations that you can contact for trade specific information.

4. *Standard Rates and Data* or trade magazines in your field that contain advertising information.

5. *Key Business Ratios,* published by Dun & Bradstreet.

You should ask your librarian for the publication that lists all the businesses in your area. Most contain a listing of businesses categorized by SIC code, which can be applied to a wide variety of marketing uses.

Governmental agencies also offer population, geographical, demographic, income, spendable income, cultures and other data from their massive data banks. In addition to the Departments of Commerce and Labor, there are other governmental agencies on federal, state and local levels with marketing and sales statistical data. Copy machines are usually available.

In addition, computer, video and audio reference material may be available. The reference librarian can help you locate the kind of information you need. If the amount of information is insufficient for your needs, ask the librarian for listings of other libraries and sources likely to have the specific data. Sometimes, you can request that the library purchase the information.

Your local Chamber of Commerce will be happy to provide local statistical data about your area and other helpful information concerning the local business community.

The U.S. Small Business Administration, Department of Commerce and Department of Labor publish considerable data on the national economy and national business trends. States and local governments often can provide similar data.

A good overview of your business or industry can be obtained by contacting the appropriate trade association and trade magazines. Persons covering the specific industry for the association or magazine are well placed in their respective industries and know what is going on. They also know what special skills and methods are most critical to success. Often, they are personally acquainted with operatives in the field and can discern the winners from the losers. So it is worthwhile to check with them as one significant aspect of your "market research" in your "market plan development."

Obtaining Operating Data

A key to marketing success is to ensure that the business is a profitable business because unprofitable businesses cannot survive. The objective of a business is to earn a profit, not to lose money. So the best way to determine potential earnings for any specific kind of business is to examine the standard operating ratios for that kind of business.

An "operating ratio" is a comparison of two numerical values, expressed as a percentage. In marketing, you should understand the relationship between various expenses and net sales as ratios. Operating ratios can be found in several published services in your public library's business reference department. Specifically, ask to see these publications:

Annual Statement Studies, from Robert Morris & Associates.

Key Business Ratios, from Dun & Bradstreet.

Trade associations are listed in the *Encyclopedia of Associations*, Volume I, Part I.

Trade magazines are listed in the *Standard Rates and Data* service.

To find the *cost of doing business* (for specific trades in the retail, service, wholesale and manufacturing sectors), ask for the appropriate trade association and the appropriate trade magazines covering the field.

The trade association and trade magazines for your specific industry should be contacted to obtain any annual reports covering the cost of doing business that is compiled from members and subscribers on a periodic basis. The experience averages are realistic guides to the potential of your business. But remember, the amounts represent the experience of on-going, established businesses. You, as a newcomer, could experience significantly different values. However, you will have an idea of the norms that exist.

Remember, all these data are averages. This means they reflect the middle of the best and the worst. And you should never be satisfied with the "average." Strive to be the best!

Sources of Supply

Who will be your suppliers? Are there several competitive sources for the goods and materials for your business? Quality, price, dependable delivery, quantity breaks and many other factors will have an affect on your ability to be competitive.

There are directories of manufacturers, wholesalers, importers and other types of suppliers in the reference section of your public library. An elaborate, detailed directory of manufacturers is published in several volumes, entitled *The Thomas Register*. But there are others also. Often, it is an annual practice for each nationally circulated trade magazine to publish an annual directory or a catalog issue of all suppliers in the industry. This special annual issue is also listed in *Standard Rates and Data* service.

Components of a Total Marketing Plan

Marketing, in the broadest meaning of the term, encompasses the total plan to be followed in selling your product or service. Marketing includes pricing, packaging, promotion, advertising and selling as well as market research and the logistics of the enterprise, i.e., the movement of the goods.

Understand the *primacy* of the marketing concept. Marketing focuses the efforts of the owner/manager on prospective new customers (called prospects) as well as retaining existing customers. The important thing about marketing is to satisfy customers needs. All the activity of the business must be aimed at satisfying the needs of the customer and in building benefits, value and confidence in fulfilling that "customer-oriented" mission. The owner/manager must think "customer first."

"Customer first" means that you do not start your planning by concentrating on production, the form of organization or other parts of a business plan. You must start with concern for marketing. Develop an overall strategy and a plan to sell your product or service—profitably. To accomplish this, you must screen prospects, find potential customers and create an incentive that convinces each prospect to buy the things that you offer for sale. If this activity is successful, you will then have customers. Without customers, a company has no sales. And without sales, there will be no company. If you understand and apply "customer first" in your business, you comprehend the *primacy* of the marketing concept.

To make a sale, the owner/manager must create an environment that stimulates a *desire-to-buy* in the mind of the prospect or potential customer.

A *product* can create a desire-to-buy because the prospect can see the product and its usefulness, benefits, quality, price and serviceability. The company can advertise, display and demonstrate. Products can be sold much easier than services.

In marketing a service, unfortunately, there is little on the surface that permits a buyer to differentiate between one company and another. Therefore, the success of a service-oriented company depends upon your ability to communicate superior skills in problem identification and solution. Thus you create a desire by the buyer to select your service over a competitor's service.

Note that "customer" is usually referred to in the singular rather than in the plural, as "customers." This is because your success depends upon satisfying each customer one at a time. When you have satisfied more than one customer, then you will have "customers."

The issue of "customer first" is critical in three marketing areas: *price, quality* and *performance.* You meet the customer's need by doing well in any one area or a combination of the areas; that is, low price, better quality and higher/better performance. If you satisfy a customer's need, that customer will buy from you.

Newly created products or services (such as patented or copyrighted ones) can often capture a high market share at a higher price when they are associated with significantly higher performance. So if your product or service can outperform the competitor, you can often reap a higher profit margin, provided your development costs can be recovered early, before other competing products or services are introduced.

Each big business was started by one person with an idea, the guts to proceed and the marketing savvy to stimulate the customer's need. One person started the small business that grew into a large business. You, also, may be one of these people. Can you picture yourself beside Henry Ford (Ford Motor cars), George Eastman (Kodak cameras), Harvey Firestone (Firestone tires), Thomas Edison (Consolidated Edison electric power), Bill Gates (Microsoft Computer software), Steve Jobs (Apple Computer hardware) and others? Do you remember hula hoops, pet rocks, Pierre Cardin, Chanel #5? If you have a new idea and guts, go for it!

Marketing Plan Fundamentals

The first marketing plan is often too general, too complex or too ambitious. Often, an owner/manager must prepare more than one draft of the marketing plan before he or she is satisfied that the plan describes the intended approach to marketing the product or service.

Who is the marketing plan written for? And why should the plan be written? If you are writing a marketing plan to show to others, the plan probably will not achieve its intended purpose of guiding you as the owner/manager. Having this guidance is vital to your understanding of elements and forces that drive your success or failure. Thus the most important reason for writing a plan is to educate yourself about the market so that you can concentrate your resources in a manner that will achieve the greatest gain with the least amount of effort. To ensure the most value to your understanding of your market:

Make it simple. Find measures that you can count, such as "things" rather than "dollars."

Set goals and objectives. At the same time, remember market conditions are an unpredictable environment. Be as precise as possible. However, you should understand that your projections may not be accurate.

Make it flexible. You need to understand the complex forces which drive the market, the pressures of competition and the probability that business conditions will change.

Start your market research with an evaluation of your perceived customer and what that perceived customer needs. During the evaluation, determine if the perceived customer is "in fact" a potential customer and thus develop a marketing strategy that fulfills the needs of this group of potential customers. How will you win their business? What will they pay for? How much? Following this strategy, you should be able to develop customers, i.e., those who buy from you. The marketing plan as a whole consists of:

1. **Market Research.** Market research is concerned with identifying your prospects and potential customers. This effort should produce quantitative answers to who, where, why, when and how prospects are converted into active buyers. This part of the marketing function will provide you with a clearer profile of your prospects and active customers. Included should be an analysis of competitors and what makes them successful since you must win each new customer by convincing him or her to buy from you rather than from the person the individual now buys from. Determine the size of the potential market and your target share of this market. You must know more about your market and your prospects than your competitors. And the way to learn this information is to conduct market research.

2. **Type of Selling Program**. This relates to identification of the kind of business, such as retail, wholesale, technical or service.

3. **Sales Promotion.** This is the strategy part of the plan. It identifies the innovations to stimulate demand or buyer interest in your particular service or line of products. Often, a gimmick may be used to attract attention or to set your product or service above other competitors'. A gimmick over a long period of time, however, will lose its luster, and fundamental marketing axioms will prevail, that is, the importance of price, quality and performance.

4. **Advertising.** The tactical approach to the market is in the advertising since advertising implements the thrust of the promotion. Its goal is to stimulate interest in or, at least, alert your prospects about your enterprise and its services or products. Advertising is the means by which customers learn about your enterprise and its products, by broadcasting awareness of the specific attributes of the product or service.

5. **Merchandising**. This is the detailed application of methods used to reach customers for the most effective sale of your service or products. Site selection is sometimes one of the most important ingredients in reaching potential customers, and maybe critical to the success of the business.

6. **Pricing Policy.** Profitable pricing is obviously a key element in your success. Determining the price that will give you the best mix of volume and profit is neither a simple nor an easy process.

In pricing a product or service, first you must know your expenses with precision. But you will also have to take into consideration extraneous or "outside" factors in the market. These include competitive prices or traditional prices. Moreover, the starting point for pricing products is different from that for pricing services. Let's look at how these differ:

Pricing a product. Manufacturers, wholesalers and retailers are selling a product that cost them an amount that should be known or can be calculated. The known base cost of the goods is then marked up to a level that is estimated to cover all manufacturing costs and operating expenses so as to provide a profit. Anticipated volume determines the base cost, since larger volumes and faster turnover usually are associated with lower prices. Often, all items do not sell at the originally intended or marked up level, so some part of the inventory must be sold at reduced sales price levels or disposed of in other ways. This markdown lowers the average or realized profit margin. Experience, to a large degree, will help determine what the initial markup should be in order to allow for later markdowns that will produce an average sales price, above costs and expenses, to yield a profit.

Pricing a service. Pricing a service is usually based on one of three considerations: 1) cost, plus a percent above cost; 2) a dollar amount per job; 3) a dollar amount per hour (hourly rate). Each method requires information about the costs and expenses for performing the service. The considerations of cost, expenses and profit are identical to product pricing. However, in place of inventory control and inventory management, a service business must consider the number of productive or billable hours that can be expected as a percentage of the total hours of available business service. Downtime, or unproductive time, must be managed. A reasonable expectancy is to sell or bill about 70 percent (or similar factor) of the total billable hours to ensure operating expenses (overhead) are covered in the flat rate or the hourly rate charged.

7. **Quality**. Quality means *fitness for use* or fitness for the application for which the product or service was designed. Assurance of a consistent quality attracts repeat business. So the quality assurance aspect of marketing is related to customer acceptance and the cost-effectiveness of the product or service.

8. **Inventory Control and Distribution**. This topic relates to the optimum (the best) levels of products to carry and is, therefore, concerned with such management considerations as reorder points, delivery schedules, distributor access and location. The most important aspect of inventory control is its effect on cash flow, and, therefore, it affects the amount of capital required to operate the business. Fast turnover is the goal.

9. **Selling**. Personal contact with prospects and customers is the selling activity. Also selling involves the necessary activity for collecting the money, transferring the title and moving the product from inventory to buyer. In the case of a service business, selling confidence and benefits are just as important as in selling a product or merchandising. But you are selling an intangible, and prospects must be willing to accept the course of action you have established.

10. **Profit Objective**. Every company is profit-motivated and intends to earn a profit. But earning that profit is much more difficult than setting a profit objective. The owner/manager must establish competitive prices and continuously evaluate every element of cost to ensure that all costs are covered sufficiently to have an amount left over—the profit amount.

An Outline of the Marketing Plan

Since organization of information is important to comprehension, the marketing plan should contain information on the following:

1. Product or service
2. Site selection/merchandising

3. Market size and potential

4. Competition

5. Price strategy and pricing

6. Sales strategy/method/volume

7. Advertising and promotion

8. Distribution

9. Profit objectives

Selling Tips

To develop the plan itself and successfully sell your product or service, here are some selling tips:

1. *Listen to your customer; study the customer's needs.* The customer buys to fill his or her needs or wants. The customer does not buy because you wish to sell. If the customer does not recognize the need, you need to "create the idea so the customer sees the need."

2. *List benefits in terms of a customer's needs.*

3. *Be aware of customer's moods and manners, and how they influence buying readiness.*

4. *Ask the right questions.*

5. *Provide assurances that you are filling customer's needs.*

6. *Counter customer resistance or objections.* These may stem from habit, fear, price, competition, misinformation, incomplete information, a personality clash or negative atmosphere.

How to
Write a Business Plan

A business plan is your pathway to profit. You must write the plan yourself. Do not ask an accountant, consultant, an instructor or a student to write the plan for you. They may do a creditable job on the plan, but, they will be making many important decisions that you personally need to make. Use the counseling and advice of these people, but write the plan yourself.

There are two main reasons for preparing a business plan:

1. **The plan assists you**. This is its most important purpose. The knowledge you gain about the business is vital to the success of the business. While preparing the plan, the decisions you make will determine the future course and success of the business. Once you start your business, the plan will be a guide to the conduct of your business and a measure of progress.

2. **The plan is available for you to show to others who may help you with execution of the business activity**. But, this should be a secondary purpose. For instance, you may need the business plan in order to obtain a loan from a bank. Therefore, the plan must be believable. The business plan should convince a potential lender that you are a good financial risk. The plan will show your equity investment and the collateral that will secure the loan. The plan will also demonstrates that you will earn enough money from sales to repay the loan. Unless you can demonstrate to the banker that you are organized and are carrying out your pre-planned activities, you probably will have difficulty obtaining a loan. Listen to the banker rather than complain about not getting the loan. He

may tell you important facts because the banker will probably review more business plans in one week than you will see in a lifetime.

In building your pathway to profit, you need to consider the following questions: What business am I in? What goods or services do I sell? Where is my market? Who will buy? Who is my competition? Why will they buy from me and not my competition? How much money is needed to operate my company? Who will do the work—me or others? How much do I pay others? When should I revise the plan? Where can I go for help? Nobody else can answer such questions for you. As an owner/manager, you must answer them yourself while you draw up your business plan.

Before beginning to write your business plan, answer the questions contained in A Start-Up Checklist for Small Businesses, Self-Help Guide M. The answers to these questions are vital to your self-analysis.

It takes time, energy and patience to draw up a satisfactory business plan. As you proceed, you may find prior assumptions or decisions need revision. Make these changes as you see the need. Condense the size of the plan to a maximum of about 25 pages. Concise statements, tables or charts are much more meaningful than a lot of words that say practically nothing. But bear in mind, anything fundamental or essential that may be left out may create an additional cost of business operation that could drain money when that situation unexpectedly occurs later. If you leave out or ignore key items of expense, your business is headed for disaster. Also, if you are too optimistic in making sales estimates, your business is headed for disaster. Keep in mind that your final goal is to put your plan into action to guide the operation of the business.

Things vs. Dollars

An automobile dealer sells cars. The sales volume in monetary amounts (dollars) is a result of the number of cars (units) sold. The dealer cannot have sales dollars of income without the sale of units. So to estimate sales income, the owner should estimate the number of cars that will be sold at an average sales price. Thus success is first measured by the number of cars sold, not the dollar amount. Remember always to think in terms of *units first,* then in the monetary amounts that result from the number of units.

In preparing your business plan, start by estimating the number of things to be sold then apply average sales prices for these things to determine sales income. Too many people merely estimate dollar amounts without considering quantities. Later, if the sales income is not achieved, without knowing the planned vs. actual units, there is no way to initiate corrective action.

Apply this theory to your business plan. It works with both products and services. Apply this theory not only to all sources of income but also to all types of expenditures. Examples: number of lawns mowed, number of house calls made, number of walk-in people at the service counter, gross number of products ordered, and number of times you will need to consult with your lawyer. Of course, you can collect many small items into larger groups, but you should avoid skipping directly to amounts of money.

Realism

Make realistic estimates! Do not overestimate! Big numbers in the plan may sound good. But they must be substantiated with detail so they are believable. If your estimates are too big, who are you fooling? Yourself! It is your plan. Which will be better for you and your business: to exceed a conservative plan or fail to meet unachievable or "blue sky" fictional targets?

If you have borrowed money, how will you explain to your lender that sales were not as good as your optimistic expectations so his loan cannot be repaid? How will you explain to your lender that you didn't allow for an expenditure, so his loan cannot be repaid? He won't have any sympathy when he initiates involuntary bankruptcy proceedings. Do not overestimate.

Also, be cautious about being too low in your estimates. Low sales goals, may not provide enough challenge for you to achieve the best possible performance.

Marketing

Read the discussion contained in Self-Help Guide A on marketing and selling. Incorporate this important element into your business plan.

What the Lender Looks For

When you start a business, your Personal Financial Statement (PFS) tells how wealthy you are and demonstrates how much investment you can make into the business. Also, the PFS tells your salary history and your standard of living. It is difficult for most people to lower their standard of living. Thus, the business plan must provide a personal income to which you are accustomed.

You must demonstrate that you have managed your personal financial affairs before you add the complexities of managing a business. Your PFS is a major information source for such an evaluation. For more information on the PFS, refer to Self-Help Guide C.

To demonstrate that the business is viable, a potential lender will review the business plan documents that you have prepared. These include the Pro Forma Balance Sheet, the Projected Income Statement and the Cash Flow Projection. These documents will show the lender whether or not you are a good risk for lending his money. See Self-Help Guides E, F, G, H, and I for more information.

A lender is in the money business. The lender is not in the type of business you wish to start. Neither does the lender want to be in the type of business you wish to start. So, what happens if you cannot repay a loan? The lender must protect his financial interest. Usually, he takes control of the collateral and will sell the collateral to recover the amount of money loaned. This action may force you out of business. Otherwise, the lender would be required to take over the business's operation. He does not want to manage the business, neither is he qualified to manage the business. So he resorts to the only legal action available—he seizes the collateral.

The lender does not want to liquidate the collateral or your business. He only takes this action in order to recover the money he loaned to you because you did not meet your obligation.

Business Plan Preparation Assistance

If you need help in writing your business plan, many aids are available. Contact your local university, college or high school business department. Most libraries have plan outlines and a few completed business plans as guides. Contact other similar businesses in your area and your business trade association. Call the U.S. Small Business Administration for help or contact retired former small business owners to counsel you.

Several computer programs are also available that ask the pertinent questions. When you answer these questions, the computer program fills in some of the prose to make an excellent skeleton for you to polish into a final business plan. The answers to many of the questions in the Start-Up Checklist, (Self-Help Guide M) can be used to provide information that will be included in your business plan. Through these and similar sources, you should locate ample guides and examples for your business plan. But you, alone, must do the grunt work. You, alone, must put the words and numbers on paper.

Business Plan Contents

A brief outline is provided below, along with a sample business plan, for you to use in preparation of your own business plan. But, also search for and use a more complete business plan preparation guide. The U.S. Small Business Administration provides several good guides that are available from the SBA, SCORE, SBDC, SBI and Chambers of Commerce. A business plan contains:

1. **Executive Summary**—The introduction should be compelling so that the reader cannot avoid reading the entire plan. A one-page summary of the contents of your business plan would include the most important elements of each plan section. Necessary content includes:
   - The Company—A description of the company and structure.
   - The Industry—Is it an embryonic, growth or mature opportunity?
   - The Product/Service—Is it unique? Why will people buy?
   - The Market—Who will buy? How/where will you reach customers?
   - The Economics—How will this business make a profit?

   The remainder of the plan substantiates the executive summary. The suggested format and content here include all necessary elements and considerations. The total plan should not exceed 25 pages.

2. **Description of the Company**
   - Explain company expertise/experience/background.
   - Nature of business—New start-up, expansion, or purchase of an existing business.
   - Structure—Corporation/partnership/proprietorship. Why?
   - Organization/key personnel—Resumes and investment by each.
   - Location: Where? Why? Advantages?

3. **The Industry**
   - Nature of the industry and types of companies therein.
   - Company sizes, investments required, sales, profitability.
   - Age of industry—Embryonic? Growth? Mature?
   - What sets your business apart from other companies in the industry?

4. **Description of Product or Service**
   - The product or service to be offered.
   - The level of competitiveness of the product.
   - Why will people buy from you rather than others?

5. **Marketing Thrust** (See detailed explanation in Self-Help Guide A)
   - How customers will know about you and your products.
   - How you will attract customers and convince them to buy.
   - Product features advantageous to the customer.
   - What customers' needs you will satisfy to get them to buy.
   - Your market niche.
   - Sales strategy, marketing goals and how they will happen.

6. **Economics and Financial Information**
   - What equity investment you will make.
   - Level of borrowing necessary? How much? From whom?
   - Start-up costs, capital equipment, facilities.
   - Sales forecast—How many, price for each, profit margin?
   - Overhead expenses, fixed vs. variable expenses, unknowns (if you haven't thought of everything and planned for it, the surprise expenditures may drain too much cash).
   - Pro Forma Balance Sheet, Projected Income Statement, Cash Flow Projection, Personal Financial Statement.

For more detailed guidance in preparing your Business Plan, consult *The Business Planning Guide*, David H. Bangs, Jr. (Dover, NH: Upstart Publishing Co., Inc., 1993).

Example Company
Business Plan

Executive Summary

Example Company is a sales/service business that sells and installs commercial telephone systems, fax machines, voice mail, computers and peripherals. Additionally, Example Co. sells service contracts. The business generates revenue primarily by selling commercial phone systems and computers at a 25 to 30 percent gross profit and providing labor at a gross profit of 60 to 80 percent. Example Co. is operated as a sole proprietorship with two regular employees.

The business began in 1981 and was founded by R. A. Zajac. Example Co. currently sells its products/services in a local market. The reasons our customers have told us they purchase our products is because of competitive pricing on quality name brand equipment, good reputation for service and central location in the metropolitan area. Our goal is to capture two percent of this small business market by 1999.

Example Co. sells its products/services to its customers through one sales representative. Example Co. needs two additional sales people to achieve its short-range goals. Its primary short range goal is to increase sales to new customers by making more new customer contacts with cold calls and phone solicitations. In order to achieve the primary short-term goal, Example Co. must spend at least eight hours per week on cold calls by phone or in person, establish contacts with property management companies and set up referral programs whereby existing customers receive a bonus for referring a new customer.

The Business

Example Company sells commercial telephone systems, fax machines, voice mail, computers, peripherals and service contracts. We purchase our equipment and materials from wholesale distributors of communication equipment and wholesalers of computer products.

In general, customers are small- to medium-sized businesses of all types in the metropolitan area. The business is unique in that we offer sales, installation, support, full service, and upgrades on a number of brand name products. The business generates revenue and profit by selling commercial phone systems and computers. In addition, we provide labor and service contracts. Our major costs for bringing our products to market are equipment purchase costs, sales commissions, overhead (rent and utilities), insurance and labor for ongoing customer support.

The customer profile for the business is small- to medium-sized businesses; that is, businesses requiring installation of 2 to 30 phone lines with 2 to 120 telephones.

We currently spend $230 per month on a yellow pages advertisement. This is the same as other businesses our size. We do not spend money on any other type of advertising.

Example Company's office is located at 1101 Manchester Road, which is in West County, three blocks west of Market Blvd. This central location helps facilitate sales calls and reduces our delivery costs. Example Co. currently occupies 600 square feet of office and storage space.

Example Co. is operated as a sole proprietorship and we currently have two subcontractors. The subcontractors require and have obtained technical communications installation experience. In addition, Example Co. offers certification seminars to subcontractors on many of the products we install and maintain.

In order to maintain the lowest possible cost of sales, Example Co. currently purchases from ten distributors of communications equipment. In this manner, competitive price shopping permits equipment purchases to be at the lowest possible cost.

Our competitors generally charge more than our firm for the same service. This is partially due to union wage scales. We are a non-union shop.

We get our information about what products our customers want by talking to existing customers. There seems to be little difference in the demand for standard products. Yet the demand for these products is increasing in size based on the change in population characteristics and the rapid development of computer and communications equipment.

The quality of our human resources is excellent. The subcontractors are experienced and very motivated to achieve the various production and quality assurance objectives we have set. We plan to use a management information system that produces key production, quality assurance and sales objectives to enhance performance. The key production, quality assurance and sales data will be available on a weekly basis. Data are not currently compared to previously established goals for the week, and deviations are not currently the primary focus of the management staff. However, we intend to implement these service-quality indicators.

Customer service policies are as follows:

1. Two-year warranty on all products is double that offered by the competition, which offers one-year warranties.

2. We offer two-hour response time in emergencies as does the competition.

3. The competition offers 24-hour service, whereas we currently do not. The cost associated with offering 24-hour service would be excessive.

The image for attracting customers to Example Company is service that is prompt, dependable, economical, friendly, concerned and caring.

We currently do not offer credit other than net 30 or bank cards. We could offer credit, but we would have to add these costs to the price of the service.

The Market

Our customer base consists of 500 offices including doctors, brokers, retailers and manufacturers. The scope of our market is local. There are 150,000 potential customers in this market area where 50 competitors hold approximately 99 percent of the market. Our goal is to capture two percent of the market within the next four years. Major reasons for believing this goal is possible include low overhead, competitive prices, a broad range of brands and very good reputation for service.

After a careful market analysis we have determined that approximately 70 percent of our customers are men and 30 percent are women. Customers, by percentages, fall in the following age categories: under 16: 0%, 17-21: 5%, 22-30: 15%, 31-40: 20%, 41-50:

25%, 51-60: 25%, 61-70: 10%; and 71+: 0%. The percentage of customers by net income level is: less than $10,000 : 5%, $10,000—20,000 : 5%, $20,000—30,000 : 10%, $30,000—40,000 : 40%, $40,000—50,000 : 35% and $50,000+: 5%. The reasons customers have given for purchasing our products are competitive pricing on quality name equipment, good reputation for service and central location in the metropolitan area.

At Example Co., one of the two subcontractors is a sales representative. We will need four additional sales people to achieve our sales goals. These salespeople will need experience in office communications equipment or computer sales or service. We currently attract 5 percent of our customers from local directories, 30 percent from the Yellow Pages, 2 percent from signs, 10 percent from family and friends, 30 percent from current customers, 3 percent from competitors (cooperative arrangements) and 20 percent from sales calls. The most cost effective of these has been referrals from existing customers.

Our service differs from the competition in that it is less expensive, more personal and more flexible in that we offer more brands of equipment.

Our advertising emphasizes the strong points of service, good reputation, competitive pricing, the handling of all major brands and courteous personnel.

Our advertising should tell customers and prospective customers the following facts about the business and services offered:

- We want to help our customers.
- We offer very competitive pricing.
- We offer prompt, courteous service.
- We are an established business.
- We offer a wide selection of brands.
- We sell new and used equipment.
- We take trade-ins.
- We offer free quotes.

The Competition

Our pricing is below most or all of the competition. About three businesses failed last year. But, about 10 new firms opened in the same year.Major competitors of our firm are:

1. Advance Communications—because they seek the same target market at similar price.

2. Par Communications—same as above.

3. MTC (Metro Telecommunications)—same as above.

4. Southwestern Bell Telecom—they are known, have a good reputation, good penetration, a large sales force, significant resources and close proximity.

Company Organization

The organization chart for Example Company is as follows:

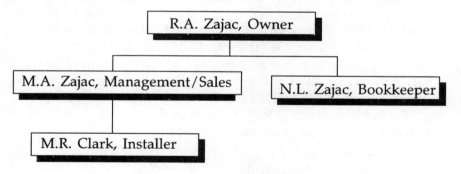

Goals Implementation

The short-term goals for the business are: 1) increase sales to new customers by making more customer contacts with cold calls and phone solicitations, 2) add one or more additional service and installation people and 3) broaden our reputation as a full systems integration company serving computer and phone needs.

In order to achieve the first short-term goal, we must 1) require sales representatives to spend at least eight hours a week on cold calls by phone or in person and 2) establish contacts with property management companies and set up referral programs.

In order to achieve our second short-term goal we must 1) increase new sales and installations and 2) take on more service calls and service contracts.

To achieve our third short-term goal, we must 1) include computer systems integration in all advertising and 2) notify existing customers and referral sources of our systems integration ability.

The long-term goals for our business are: 1) generate annual sales of half a million dollars within five years, 2) hire a sales team of five regular employees and service staff of five regular employees within five years, and 3) acquire our own office and warehouse facility by purchase. The most important thing we must do in order to achieve the long-term goals for our business is increase sales consistently at an average of 35 percent annually.

Financial

Sales have averaged between $80,000 and $120,000 per year for the last four years. Most recently, the sales have been between $80,000 and $95,000 per year with income to the sole proprietor of about $12,000 per year. (See the attached balance sheet for current status.) We recognize that an equity of $12,000 will limit our capacity to increase sales. Therefore, in the next year, we plan to increase equity to $18,000. This will be accomplished by increasing sales and earnings. Along with this, the owner's salary will increase by a lesser amount to build equity.

Future Market Trends

Example Co. faces some potential threats or risks. These threats include the introduction of fiber and digital technology to the small- and medium-sized customer base. We believe we can accommodate this new technology by preparing to provide equipment and service in this advanced communications equipment. Therefore, we plan to train our workforce in fiber optic and digital technology.

EXAMPLE COMPANY
BALANCE SHEET
AS OF DECEMBER 31, 199X

CASH	$2,000	ACCOUNTS PAYABLE	$5,000
ACCOUNTS RECEIVABLE	$3,000	ACCRUED INCOME TAXES	$0
INVENTORY	$8,000		
CURRENT ASSETS	$13,000	CURRENT LIABILITIES	$5,000
TRUCK - FIXED ASSET	$7,000	PROMISSORY NOTE	$3,000
		TOTAL LIABILITIES	$8,000
		OWNER'S EQUITY	$12,000
		TOTAL LIABILITIES &	
TOTAL ASSETS	$20,000	OWNER'S EQUITY	$20,000

Personal Financial Statement

A personal financial statement is your own personal measurement tool for evaluating what you own and its value compared to how much you owe to others. The difference is your net worth—the value of your accumulated wealth. If prepared regularly, you can determine the growth of your net worth from year to year. Thus, by evaluating the areas of rapid growth and the areas of meager growth, you can structure your future personal financial decisions for the greatest financial reward. In addition, a personal financial statement is the document by which others can judge your credit worthiness. Thus, a personal financial statement has three primary purposes:

1. Individual self-analysis of financial progress. In this regard, the personal financial statement reveals the year-by-year growth of your net worth.

2. Inclusion in a business plan for substantiation of your personal financial management ability.

3. Evaluation by a lender to determine your ability to sustain credit and verify your ability to repay a loan.

For these purposes, a personal financial statement is designed to document the important elements of a person's financial status and the persons ability to meet financial obligations. Thus the document is divided into several parts to identify the needed information in a logical and organized fashion. Since many business relationships are entered into by married persons, a personal financial statement must necessarily be prepared by each spouse or jointly to include both people. For completeness, a typical personal financial statement should include the following categories of information. At the end of this Self-Help Guide, a sample personal financial statement is included.

Individual Information

This section of the personal financial statement identifies the person by name, address, phone, etc. When applying for credit, the lender will verify this information as well as the social security number and the person's signature at the end of the form.

Other Party Information

In a marital situation this person would be the spouse. Or when a person does not possess sufficient financial resources (net worth) to obtain credit on his or her own, the person must rely on the good standing of another party to back the loan. The other party would be a co-signer. This means if the borrower does not repay the loan, the other party must repay the loan. Sometimes people underestimate the importance of this other person. Because of love, trust or friendship, this other party is willing to commit his or her own personal wealth from confidence in the individual. If both parties fail to realize the gravity of the commitment, the bond of love, trust or friendship may be strained when the co-signer must repay the loan.

Statement of Financial Condition

The net worth of the person is documented in this section. By listing the things owned (assets) and subtracting the things owed (liabilities), the amount of net worth is determined.

Sources of Income

Personal debts are often repaid from salaries and other personal current income. This section lists these amounts as evidence that a loan can be repaid from the income amounts. However, for a person beginning a business, a salary from another job may not exist. Therefore, the ability to borrow is diminished because there may not be an income from which to repay the business loan. If you plan to quit your present job and live on the income from the business, you must account for the changed personal income.

Personal Income

Perhaps, you now work for somebody else. As an employee, your employer makes payments for things that you yourself must pay when you own your business. Therefore, if you expect to earn a living from the business, your business income must be higher than your current take-home pay. This could raise your equivalent wages by 25 percent to 50 percent. Additions include: paid vacation, paid holidays, social security, health insurance, retirement benefits, unemployment compensation and workers' compensation. So be sure to consider this effect on your personal income when you decide to go into business for yourself.

Contingent Liabilities

Lenders do not like surprises that may prevent them from being repaid. Since contingent liabilities are potential cash drains that would draw money from the loan repayment, they must be disclosed to the lender.

Schedules

In substantiation of the statement of financial condition, several schedules are provided for listing detailed amounts or types of financial information. Thereby, the sum of the individual parts is listed in the statement of financial condition.

Responsibility Statement

The individual who signs a personal financial statement must verify that the information is true and current and relates to the individual's material net worth. Therefore, completion of the statement must be done with deliberate conscientiousness.

Personal Financial Statement

OMB Approval No. 3245-0188

PERSONAL FINANCIAL STATEMENT

U. S. SMALL BUSINESS ADMINISTRATION

As of _____, 19_____

Complete this form for: (1) each proprietor, or (2) each limited partner who owns 20% or more interest and each general partner, or (3, ... stockholder owning 20% or more of voting stock and each corporate officer and director, or (4) any other person or entity providing a guaranty on the loan.

Name	Business Phone ( )
Residence Address	Residence Phone ( )
City, State, & Zip Code	

Business Name of Applicant/Borrower

ASSETS	(Omit Cents)	LIABILITIES	(Omit Cents)
Cash on hands & in Banks . . . . $		Accounts Payable . . . . $	
Savings Accounts . . . . $		Notes Payable to Banks and Others . . . . $	
IRA or Other Retirement Account . . . . . $		(Describe in Section 2)	
Accounts & Notes Receivable . . . . . . $		Installment Account (Auto) . . . . $	
Life Insurance–Cash Surrender Value Only $		Mo. Payments $	
(Complete Section 8)		Installment Account (other) . . . . $	
Stocks and Bonds . . . . $		Mo. Payments $	
(Describe in Section 3)		Loan on Life Insurance . . . . $	
Real Estate . . . . $		Mortgages on Real Estate . . . . $	
(Describe in Section 4)		(Describe in Section 4)	
Automobile–Present Value . . . . $		Unpaid Taxes . . . . $	
Other Personal Property . . . . $		(Describe in Section 6)	
(Describe in Section 5)		Other Liabilities . . . . $	
Other Assets . . . . $		(Describe in Section 7)	
(Describe in Section 5)		Total Liabilities . . . . $	
		Net Worth . . . . $	
Total . . $		Total . . $	

Section 1. Source of Income		Contingent Liabilities	
Salary . . . . $		As Endorser or Co-Maker. . . . . $	
Net Investment Income . . . . $		Legal Claims & Judgments . . . . $	
Real Estate Income . . . . $		Provision for Federal Income Tax . . . . $	
Other Income (Decribe below)* . . . . . $		Other Special Debt . . . . $	

Description of Other Income in Section 1.

*Alimony or child support payments need not be disclosed in "Other Income" unless it is desired to have such payments counted toward total income.

Section 2.   Notes Payable to Bank and Others.   (Use attachments if necessary. Each attachment must be identified as a part of this statement and signed.).

Name and Address of Noteholder(s)	Original Balance	Current Balance	Payment Amount	Frequency (monthly,etc.)	How Secured or Endorsed Type of Collateral

Personal Financial Statement, continued

Section 3.	Stocks and Bonds. (Use attachments if necessary. Each attachment must be identified as a part of this statement and signed).				
Number of Shares	Name of Securities	Cost	Market Value Quotation/Exchange	Date of Quotation/Exchange	Total Value

Section 4.   Real Estate Owned. (List each parcel separately. Use attachments if necessary. Each attachment must be identified as a part of this statement and signed).

	Property A	Property B	Property C
Type of Property			
Name & Address of Title Holder			
Date Purchased			
Original Cost			
Present Market Value			
Name & Address of Mortgage Holder			
Mortgage Account Number			
Mortgage Balance			
Amount of Payment per Month/Year			
Status of Mortgage			

Section 5.   Other Personal Property and Other Assets.   (Describe, and if any is pledged as security, state name and address of lien holder, amount of lien, terms of payment, and if delinquent, describe delinquency).

Section 6.   Unpaid Taxes. (Describe in detail, as to type, to whom payable, when due, amount, and to what property, if any, a tax lien attaches).

Section 7.   Other Liabilities. (Describe in detail).

Section 8.   Life Insurance Held. (Give face amount and cash surrender value of policies – name of insurance company and beneficiaries).

I authorize SBA/Lender to make inquiries as necessary to verify the accuracy of the statements made and to determine my creditworthiness. I certify the above and the statements contained in the attachments are true and accurate as of the stated date(s). These statements are made for the purpose of either obtaining a loan or guaranteeing a loan. I understand FALSE statements may result in forfeiture of benefits and possible prosecution by the U.S. Attorney General (Reference 18 U.S.C. 1001).

Signature:	Date:	Social Security Number:
ignature:	Date:	Social Security Number:

PLEASE NOTE: The estimated average burden hours for the completion of this form is 1.5 hours per response. If you have questions or comments concerning this estimate or any other aspect of this information, please contact Chief, Administrative Branch, U.S. Small Business Administration, Washington, D.C. 20416, and Clearance Office, Paper Reduction Project (3245–0188), Office of Management and Budget, Washington, D.C. 20503.

How to Get a Business Loan

Many people who are just starting a business do not understand the financial implications of a request for a business loan. Your belief that you can make a profit may not be sufficient to convince the lender to make a loan to you. This is especially true if you have not established a prior relationship with the lender.

There are three elements that must exist before a business loan can be made:

1. **Equity**. Equity is investment of your own money into the business. If you are not willing or able to commit some amount of your money, then you will have difficulty getting a loan because you will have nothing to lose if the business fails. Without equity, you would be placing all the business risk on the lender. Your personal financial statement is evidence that you have equity (net worth).

2. **Collateral.** You must have assets that can be used as security for making the loan. These assets must be of sufficient value and salability by the lender so that he or she could sell them to recover the amount owed. The value of the collateral usually exceeds the loan amount in order to account for a quick cash sale and the liquidation cost if the lender must recover his or her money.

3. **Income.** You must be able to prove that the business will earn enough profit to make the loan payments when they are due. A viable business plan should serve as verification of this requirement.

Usually, a lending institution will provide its own application form for you to fill out. Carefully complete the form, since each item is vital to your ability to get a loan. The most effective means of satisfying these requirements is to prepare a personal financial statement and a business plan. For a start-up business, unless your personal financial condition is good, the information you supply may be insufficient for a favorable loan decision.

Analyze the various financial institutions and sources for borrowing money in your area. Determine the best approach for requesting financing from these institutions. Contact them in a methodical manner. You may also locate private lenders or venture capitalists who can provide financing. A venture capitalist, however, will usually require an equity position in the business; this means that the venture capitalist may own more of the business than you. Furthermore, venture capitalists demand significantly high rewards for their investment risks. The U.S. Small Business Administration office in your area may be able to provide guidance in locating financing.

Sources of Financing

The following is a list of possible sources for financing. Often, some of these sources are overlooked. Yet, one of these sources may provide the money needed. There are two general categories of financing: 1) your money invested in the business commonly called equity and 2) money borrowed from a lender.

Equity

This is your investment in the start-up business or the business you are buying. Equity may also include others who invest and share ownership in the business. If you can provide all or most of the money needed, then you will keep entire control without being subjected to the demands of other investors or a lender. You may be surprised to discover that one of the sources listed below may provide the funds needed as your equity in the business.

1. **Personal Funds**: like savings and investments.

2. **Gift**: from a relative or friend directly to you. Then you invest the money in the business. Obtain a letter from them acknowledging the gift.

3. **Loan**: from a relative, friend or business associate directly to you. Then you invest the money in the business. Present a signed note to the person wherein you promise to repay the loan by a stated maturity date. This would be a personal loan rather than a business loan. If you later try to obtain a bank loan, there is a strong possibility the bank will place the personal loan note on standby and subordinate the note to the bank debt.

4. **Life Insurance Policy**: You may borrow against the cash value of a life insurance policy.

5. **Partners or Other Investors**: These individuals would become part owners for their investment.

6. **Sell Stock or Securities**: If you incorporate, you can sell part ownership (shares of stock) to others.

7. **Refinance Your Home**: You may borrow against the equity in your home, but consider this option carefully? If the business fails, you have lost your investment in the business. In addition, you have lost the income you had hoped to get from the business and may also lose your home because you cannot make the loan payment. Consequently, refinancing is not a recommended option.

8. **Personal Property**: You can sell or refinance personal property, such as a car, boat, antiques, jewelry, equipment.

9. **Venture Capital**: Venture capitalists deal mainly in new products or inventions. They will assume a very high risk but in return they demand high compensation for the risk incurred. In most cases, a venture capitalist will want a majority ownership and control of the business because he or she is taking more financial risk than you. Thereby, you will work for the venture capitalist.

Collateral

Collateral is defined as assets that you or the business own that will secure a debt you incur from a lender. You will forfeit this collateral to the lender unless you repay the loan. (This means, you will give ownership of this collateral to the lender.)

Generally, when you purchase an item of real or personal property, the property itself may be used as collateral. In most cases, the value of the collateral must be more than the entire amount of money you want to borrow. This means you may be able to borrow a portion of the value of the collateral, an amount equal to that which the lender can sell the item if you default. Then, if you default, the lender will be forced to take control of the collateral and sell it in order to recover the money which was lent to you. Types of collateral include:

1. **Business Assets**:
   a. Real property (real estate, land, buildings).
   b. Security agreement investments, chattel mortgage on personal property.
   c. Personal property and other property (equipment, vehicles, inventory).
   d. Long term loans receivable.
   e. Accounts receivable.
   f. Contracts for sale.
   g. Intangible assets (patents, copyrights or trademarks).
   h. Assignment of leases.

2. **Personal Assets**:
   a. Borrower's signature (your signature).
   b. Co-signer, co-maker and/or guarantor's signature.
   c. Savings account.
   d. Certificate of deposit.
   e. Investment security (stocks & bonds).
   f. Life insurance policy (cash value).
   g. Security agreement (chattel mortgage on personal property).
   h. Personal property (car, boat, jewelry, furniture).
   i. Real property (real estate, home, vacation home).

Business Income

Borrowed money must be repaid. Therefore, you must be able to demonstrate that your business will generate sufficient income (sales) to pay all the bills plus have enough left over to make payments on the loan. If your business plan is properly prepared and is based on financially solid economic principles, the evidence of your ability to make the loan payments will be easily understood. If not, you will have a difficult time convincing a lender that you are a good risk.

The lender will expect to be paid before you pay yourself a salary. Yet he or she will analyze your needs for personal money, such as food, clothing and shelter. The lender fully understands that if you personally get into a financial bind, it is too easy to pay yourself or to borrow from the business without realizing the disastrous consequences to the operation of the business. Therefore, the lender will be more comfortable making a loan to a person who does not need the income from the business for his personal survival.

Borrowed Money

You must assemble all the information about equity, collateral and business income before you can consider a loan. If you need to obtain a business loan, the lender will usually require your (and other investors') equity to be at least 25 percent to 50 percent of the total money needed. For any loan, you must provide collateral as insurance that you will repay the loan.

1. **Bank Loan.** The first place you should try to get a loan is from the bank where you now do your personal banking. The bank knows you and your credit history. So the bank would most likely be able to make a loan to you. A bank where you do not do your personal banking, is less likely to have the confidence to lend money to you. Your SBA office can provide a list of banks that make loans to small businesses in your area.

2. **Savings and Loan.** A savings and loan is not a bank. S&Ls deal mainly in real estate loans and long maturity loans. A credit union deals mainly in personal financing rather than business financing. Only rarely do these institutions make commercial loans.

3. **Commercial Lenders.** The Yellow Pages of your telephone book (under loans) may contain a list of lenders, other than banks, that may lend money to businesses.

4. **Insurance Companies.** Generally, insurance companies lend to large corporations for real estate, office buildings and plant expansions. But a local insurance company may make a loan to your business.

5. **Trade Credit.** Suppliers of materials, products or services may allow an extended repayment period while you have time to collect from your customer.

6. **Accounts Receivable.** You can get cash for your receivables, but less cash than you would get if you collected the accounts yourself. You, in effect, sell the receivable accounts to the collector, called factoring.

7. **Inventory.** You can borrow money against the inventory you have on hand. The inventory becomes the collateral.

8. **Credit Card.** You could get a cash advance against your personal credit card to provide quick cash for the business. But, the interest rate is very high compared to other forms of credit. Credit cards are expensive forms of credit and should not be considered unless the circumstances demand this means of credit.

9. **If You Are Purchasing an Existing Business.** Ask the seller to carry-back a note. In effect, the seller of the business would be making the loan to you so that you can buy the business from him. Then, while you operate the business, you can pay him back from the profits of the business.

Let's look more closely at this issue of borrowing money. The length of time for a term loan varies:

1. **Short-Term.** Less than one year. Most common for purchase of assets that turn over quickly.

2. **Intermediate-Term.** Up to ten years. Usually for personal property fixed assets.

3. **Long-Term.** Repayment over greater than a ten-year period. Usually for real property fixed assets; real estate.

Loan Request Package

A loan request package contains:

1. **Loan Application Form.** This form is provided by the potential lender.

2. **Business Plan.** Narrative that explains the experience of the applicant, plans for operating the business, industry trends, products, services, long-range objectives, etc.

3. **Personal Financial Statement.** Records of your personal assets, liabilities, net worth, income and expenses.

4. **Business Financial Information.** If the business is a start-up, you need to provide a pro forma balance sheet plus projected income statements and projected cash flow statements. If purchasing an existing business, provide historical financial data on the business, such as a balance sheet and income statement in addition to projected information.

How Much Should You Borrow?

The business plan should identify the amount of borrowed money you will need. If this planning is not thoroughly evaluated, some unexpected expense could later make business operation very difficult. In your planning, have you considered the following "up front" expenses and fees; loan commitment fee, professional fees, insurance, licenses, permits, utility deposits, security deposits, office supplies, material costs and wages before sales are made? Even if you have sales from the first day, these expenses must be paid before net sales income has been received. Thus, these amounts must be paid from the owner investment or borrowed money. And it is for this reason that lenders often require 25 percent to 50 percent owner equity investment before a loan will be considered.

You are not the first borrower who walked into the lender's office asking for money. The lender probably makes more loans in one week than you will ask for in your entire lifetime. Consider how much more lending knowledge he or she must have? Further, a lender probably understands, better than you, about your ability to make a profit. Surely, the lender has seen many dreamers and people with non-salable ideas. Often, your projections may be blue sky, meaning they are not likely to be achieved. Wouldn't you be better off if the lender convinced you not to go into business because you would lose your equity?

Remember, to exceed a conservative estimate of profit is better than to lose money. Ask yourself the question, "Is my request believable?"

Balance Sheet for a Small Business

The balance sheet for a business shows what was owned by the business and what was owed by the business at a point of time in the past. In the *Language of Small Business*, the definition for a balance sheet is:

Balance Sheet

A financial statement of an individual or firm showing assets, liabilities and net worth on a given date, usually the close of a month. One way of looking at a business is the value of things owned (assets) listed beside the debts owed to others (liabilities) along with the amount owed to the owners (net worth or owner's equity). In the accounting equation, assets equal the sum of liabilities plus equity. A Balance Sheet shows the state of affairs at one point in time, whereas, an Income Statement shows results over a period of time.

The important thing about a Balance Sheet is that it must provide a level of detail that is appropriate for the needs of the owners. With a personal computer, a Balance Sheet can easily be produced monthly. But for many businesses, a year-end Balance Sheet may be all that is required.

A Balance Sheet shows financial status at a point of time in the past to summarize what was owned and what was owed at that time. Thus the Balance Sheet records the sum of transactions that have already occurred. On the other hand, for a point of time in the future, a Pro Forma Balance Sheet would describe what is expected to be owned and owed at a future time. The Pro Forma Balance Sheet is described in Self-Help Guide F and is required

311

for a start-up business. However, it is necessary to understand the theory and concepts of a balance sheet before a Pro Forma Balance Sheet can be prepared. So continue with this section to understand balance-sheet theory.

Accounting Equation

Accounting theory defines the mathematical relationship of financial business management by the Accounting Equation. At all points in time, the terms of the Accounting Equation must be in balance, hence the name balance sheet. In equation form, the accounting equation is:

ASSETS	= LIABILITIES	+	EQUITY
owned by the business	= owed to others	+	owed to owners

Thus the equal sign in the accounting equation separates those items listed in the left column of a balance sheet and those items listed in the right column. See the balance sheet for the Example Company. The totals of both columns are the same, i.e. in balance. The balance sheet is prepared for any previous point in time, referred to in the document title by "as of a date." For Example Company, the "as of" date is September 30, 199X.

There are many names for the items that can be found in each of the elements of the accounting equation. The specific nature and type of business often determines the item names. For simplicity, the Example Company shown here includes only basic terms that should be found on the majority of balance sheets for small businesses. To present the facts on a single page, summary account classifications are used to show the financial condition of the company. Obviously, these items are summaries of many individual transaction entries. A typical balance sheet would generally include the following listings:

Assets

The things owned by the business are generally separated into two groups:

1. **Current Assets,** which are cash and those items that can readily be converted into cash within one year.

2. **Fixed Assets,** which are those things that are not expected to be consumed or converted into cash within one year. Often the original purchase price of these assets is shown along with a subtraction for the Accumulated Depreciation that has been charged as an expense in prior periods.

Liabilities

The things that are owed to others are also separated into two groups:

1. **Current Liabilities,** which are any debts or obligations that must be paid within the next year.

2. **Long-Term Liabilities,** which are debts and obligations due one year or more in the future.

Equity

Equity is also called Owner's Equity, and sometimes is referred to as Net Worth, since this is the amount owed by the business to the owners of the business. Although not shown in the Example Company, often Owner's Equity is separated into two or more parts:

1. **Initial Capital Investment,** which is the amount of the original investment made by the owners.

2. **Retained Earnings,** which are profits earned by the company but not paid to the owners as dividends in order to build the equity position.

Balance Sheet Preparation

Normally, a balance sheet would be prepared by a professional CPA, accountant or bookkeeper. The author advises that the small business person employ a professional for preparation of the balance sheet.

Example Company
Balance Sheet as of September 30, 199X

ASSETS		LIABILITIES	
Current Assets:		**Current Liabilities:**	
Cash	$ 2,150	Accounts Payable (a)	$8,077
Accounts Receivable	1,700	Long-Term Debt Now Due	1,440
Merchandise Inventory	3,900		
Supplies	450	Total Current Liabilities:	$9,517
Pre-Paid Expense	320		
		Long-Term Liabilities:	
Total Current Assets:	$ 8,520	Note Payable (b)	$535
		Bank Loan Payable (c)	1,360
Fixed Assets:		Mortgage Payable (d)	9,250
Building	$ 4,500		
Fixtures & Leasehold		**Total Long-Term Liab:**	$11,145
Improvements (e)	13,265		
Equipment	3,115	**Total Liabilities:**	$20,662
Trucks	6,500		
		EQUITY	
Total Fixed Assets:	$27,380	Owner's Equity	$15,238
		Total Liabilities	
Total Assets:	$35,900	**and Equity**	$35,900

Notes to the Example Company financial statement:

(a) Accounts Payable:	Eldredge's Inc.	$3,700
	Lesswig's	4,119
	Paxstone	180
	B&B Refrigeration	78
	Total	$8,077

(b) Dave Hall for electrical work.

(c) Term Loan secured by 1984 Ford and 1989 Chevy.

(d) Mercantile Mortgage Co.

(e) Includes $4,000 in improvements since June.

Preliminary Balance Sheet Analysis

The Example Company balance sheet was deliberately made to show a bad financial condition to illustrate the dangers. Following are some measurements and ratios to be used for evaluation of your balance sheet.

1. **Working Capital.** Working capital is calculated by subtracting current liabilities from current assets, and it evaluates your ability to pay immediate obligations from current moneys available. Cash is only a portion of working capital. In the Example Company, working capital is negative ($8,250 - $9,517 = $-997), a dangerous position for a small business.

    A low (or negative) working capital position is a major danger signal. A firm with a low negative capital situation is said to be illiquid, meaning that it may be impossible to pay debts when due. Interest charges may add to the debts and cause the problem to become worse by making the capital situation more illiquid. Cash must be raised quickly by adding owner's equity, selling fixed assets or incurring a long-term debt to replace short-term debt. Your small business should try to keep twice the amount of current assets as the amount of current liabilities.

    To increase the amount of cash, several measures can be taken, including a) collection of accounts receivable, b) factoring accounts receivable, c) spreading accounts payable over a longer term, d) getting a working capital loan (i.e., a long-term loan to be paid from operating profits), e) selling off inventory and f) selling fixed assets.

2. **Ratio Analysis.** This technique permits comparison of percentages rather than comparisons in dollars. In terms of percentages, making comparisons with prior periods or with financial statements from other companies permits a more meaningful and informative evaluation of your company's financial status. Among the more useful ratios are:

    a. *Current Ratio.* Current ratio measures the liquidity of a company, i.e., its ability to pay current obligations from available moneys. Current ratio is calculated by dividing current assets by current liabilities. For Example Company, divide $8,520 by $9,517. This yields a current ratio of 0.89, which is well below a safe current ratio of 2.0. The Example Company is in an illiquid condition. However, you need to know exactly what is represented by the figures to make a meaningful analysis. Inventory composition, quality of receivables, time of year and position in the sales cycle are all possible factors affecting the current ratio.

A word of caution: The rule of thumb ratios are far from infallible, since the date on which the balance sheet is drawn and the kind of business will affect the ratios produced. Some companies need a current ratio of 2.7 to be considered liquid, whereas others can get by with 1.5 or less.

b. *Acid Test*. Another, more stringent comparison, the acid test (also called quick ratio), determines the ability to pay all current debts from readily available cash. Acid test is calculated by dividing the most liquid current assets (cash, securities and current accounts receivable that are collectible) by current liabilities. Acid test excludes items of current assets such as inventory, supplies and prepaid expenses that cannot be easily sold for cash to pay current amounts owed. For the Example Company, dividing $3,850 by $9,517 produces an acid test ratio of 0.40. A rule-of-thumb ratio should be 1.0.

c. *Debt-to-Equity* . In the Example Company, you may note owner's equity ($15,238) is less than the long-term debt ($20,662). In effect, the creditors "own" the business, and bankers would be reluctant to extend further loans. In many business situations, a debt-to-equity ratio of one-to-one is considered good.

Possible solutions to this type of problem would include? 1) adding equity by the owners, 2) owners taking less salary to build retained earnings and 3) selling a fixed asset that carries a long-term loan. The best solution is to obtain new equity investment by the current owners or by selling part ownership in the business to another equity investor. For instance, a $10,000 sale of stock would add $10,000 to cash, also producing a more acceptable, more positive working capital situation.

3. **Comparison.** Comparison of year-end balance sheets over a period of years will highlight trends and spotlight weak areas. Since Example Company is new, this option is not possible. However, Example Company can compare its business to other,

similar businesses. Typical standards for comparison can be found in publications in your public library.

4. **Comparative Statistics.** For effective ratio analysis, it is valuable to obtain similar ratios from statistical data of other similar businesses. However, these statistical ratios may be difficult to locate. The following sources may yield comparative statistical ratios for you.

   - Trade associations. Trade association information is apt to be very specific for each industry or field. Contact your trade association or check your local library for *Ayer's Directory of Associations*.
   - *Annual Statement Studies*, which your banker or local library will usually have. Robert Morris Associates is a good resource.
   - Dun & Bradstreet's *Key Business Ratios* and *Cost of Doing Business: Partnerships & Proprietorships*. It also publishes a similar publication on public corporations.
   - A friendly competitor who is willing to exchange financial statement information. If the competitor is in a non-competing location, he or she may be willing to share the information.
   - Your banker and accountant can provide help in finding current trade information.
   - Your local library, business school and/or Chamber of Commerce.

Pro Forma
Balance Sheet
for a Small Business

A pro forma balance sheet is a balance sheet made for a point in time (a date) in the future. Therefore, this type of balance sheet forecasts what is expected to be owned and owed at that point in time. In this self-help guide, two specific types of pro forma balance sheets are explained:

1. The start-up company beginning pro forma balance sheet.

2. An existing company pro forma balance sheet that has been derived from projected income statement information for a future point in time.

Before beginning to read this section on a Pro Forma Balance Sheets, please read the discussion of a Balance Sheet in Self-Help Guide E. You need to understand the theory and concepts of preparing a balance sheet before a pro forma balance sheet can be prepared.

This self-help guide includes several Example Co. start-up balance sheets for illustration to help you understand the interim steps in the process of preparing a start-up company pro forma balance sheet. It is not necessary for you to prepare a start-up pro forma balance sheet for each of these steps, but you must prepare one just prior to beginning company operations. This pro forma balance sheet will describe how much owner investment is needed, the fixed assets that must be acquired, the operating current assets and the amount of debt that must be incurred.

319

Start-Up Company
Beginning Pro Forma Balance Sheet

During business start-up, an analysis must be made to determine the amount of investment that will be made by the owners (owner's equity) into the business. When made, these amounts are, therefore, owed back to the contributors. These amounts are shown on the right side of the pro forma balance sheet as equity. At the same time, since the amounts are normally in cash, they become cash assets of the business that are listed on the left side of the pro forma balance sheet. Thus the pro forma balance sheet remains in equality (in balance). The left side shows the amount of cash that is owned by the business and the right side shows the amount that is owed back to the owners. Both totals are the same. In the start-up of Example Company, an investment of $15,000 cash is intended to be made. Immediately after the investment is made, the Example Co. start-up pro forma balance sheet would appear as follows:

ASSETS		LIABILITIES	
Current Assets:		**Current Liabilities:**	
Cash	$15,000	None	
		EQUITY	
		Owner's Equity	$15,000
Total Assets:	$15,000	**Total Liabilities and Equity**	$15,000

You will need to open a checking account at a bank in the name of the company so that the cash invested in the business is segregated from your personal money. After such an investment, the bank account would contain $15,000 on deposit.

Let's take this start-up one step further. Amounts borrowed from others (liabilities) are listed on the right side of the pro forma balance sheet and the cash received (assets) are listed on the left side.

In the situation of Example Co., a loan will be made in order to buy a building and renovate the building to permit operation of the business. The cash received from the loan will be paid immediately to the contractor for the building and the renovation. Thus, the business will own the renovated building (a fixed asset) and the business will owe an amount back to the lender for the amount of the loan (a long-term liability). The lender will not allow Example Co. to borrow the entire amount required to purchase the building and do the renovation. Therefore, Example Co. must pay part of the building and renovation cost from cash in the company cash account (a reduction of the asset cash and an increase of the fixed asset building and renovation as fixtures and leasehold improvements). Both sides of the pro forma balance sheet are still equal. Example Company needs to borrow $10,000 and use $3,000 of its cash to buy and renovate the building: $8,500 for the building and $4,500 for renovation. The downpayment of $3,000 from cash will be required to get the loan. And the loan will be secured by the improved building. After the entries for these planned transactions are made, the pro forma balance sheet would appear as shown below:

ASSETS		LIABILITIES	
Current Assets:		**Current Liabilities:**	
Cash	$12,000	none	
Total Current Assets:	**$12,000**	**Total Current Liabilities:**	**0**
Fixed Assets:		**Long-Term Liabilities:**	
Building	$ 8,500	Mortgage Payable	$10,000
Fixtures & Leasehold			
Improvements	4,500	**Total Long-Term Liab:**	**$10,000**
Total Fixed Assets:	**$13,000**	**Total Liabilities:**	**$10,000**
		EQUITY	
		Owner's Equity	$15,000
		Total Liabilities	
Total Assets:	**$25,000**	**and Equity**	**$25,000**

Often, a company can get a loan for purchasing a specific fixed asset, such as land, building or equipment. The fixed asset can be used as collateral for the loan. But, remember, the amount that can be borrowed for a single piece of collateralized asset is less than the value of the asset. Some amount of company cash must also be used. Although cash is an asset, theoretically the cash will come from the owner's investment (equity) in the business.

The cash contributed (investments and loans) is the total amount of money available to buy equipment or materials to be used during operation of the business. If cash is to be spent to buy equipment, the form of the asset merely changes from a cash asset to a fixed asset (equipment). Example Co., for instance, needs a truck that costs $9,350. So, to purchase the truck, Example Co. will make a downpayment of $1,900 and get a one-year term chattel mortgage loan for the balance ($7,450). Thus the balance sheet for Example Co. would appear as follows, just prior to beginning operations:

ASSETS		LIABILITIES	
Current Assets:		**Current Liabilities:**	
Cash	$10,100	Truck Chattel mortgage	$7,450
Total Current Assets:	$10,100	**Total Current Liabilities:**	$7,450
Fixed Assets:		**Long-Term Liabilities:**	
Building	$8,500	Mortgage Payable	$10,000
Fixtures & Leasehold			
Improvements	4,500		
Truck	9,350	**Total Long-Term Liab:**	$10,000
Total Fixed Assets:	$22,350	**Total Liabilities:**	$10,000
		EQUITY	
		Owner's Equity	$15,000
		Total Liabilities	
Total Assets:	$32,450	**and Equity**	$32,450

On the other hand, if an owner contributed the truck to the business as his or her equity, the money equivalent of the equipment value would be listed on both sides of the balance sheet as owner's equity and as fixed assets. Again, both sides remain equal.

The preparation of this pro forma beginning balance sheet is a normal step in forming a new business and is accomplished during the preparation of the business plan. Prepare your pro forma balance sheet so that it will include all the elements that are required prior to beginning operation of the company. Some amount of cash should always be present in a start-up pro forma balance sheet to pay expenses that arise before sales can replenish the cash account. Surely, money will be needed for goods, other purchases, wages and office supplies.

Start-up company pro forma balance sheets have been prepared for Example Co. as illustrations. You should use these illustrations as format guides. But you should also understand that the individual items listed and the amounts will be different for your start-up company.

The foregoing has described the considerations for preparing a pro forma balance sheet. If it is confusing, you may require an accountant to assist you. When prepared, the start-up company pro forma balance sheet will show the equity, assets and liabilities that will be needed by the start-up company before business operations are begun. Most often, start-up requires expenses such as legal fees, incorporation fee, accounting fees, equipment purchase fees, initial material purchases, wages, supplies, prepaid insurance premium, rent, utilities, downpayments, office and advertising. These expenses cannot be paid without investment of equity capital by the owner of the business. To say this differently, you cannot expect to borrow the entire amount needed.

Existing Company
Pro Forma Balance Sheet

During preparation of a business plan, projected income statements will be made to reflect income, expenses and profit (loss) for each future period of expected operation of the business (see Self-Help Guide H). A projected profit for a period will add an amount to owner's equity, called retained earnings. Since the money is left in the business to build equity in the business, a newly prepared pro forma balance sheet for the date at the end of the period will show higher retained earnings and correspondingly higher cash. In a similar manner, a projected loss will decrease retained earnings and the total owner's equity for a future pro forma balance sheet will be less than the invested amount.

In this manner, a pro forma balance sheet will reflect the expected financial condition of the company at some future point in time, assuming the business operations result in the profit or loss shown on the projected income statement.

Things vs. Dollars

To maintain reality for your pro forma balance sheet, each future dollar amount must represent something physical. If necessary, reread the section on things vs. dollars in Self-Help Guide B to refresh your understanding.

Summary

As you can see, considerable knowledge of accounting is necessary for the preparation of a pro forma balance sheet. Therefore, it is suggested that the start-up business owner utilize the services of a professional to assist with the preparation of the pro forma balance sheet. Yet, the professional accountant cannot perform the entire task without your help and knowledge, because he or she does not know your individual situation, i.e., equity, type of equipment, facility, cost and material needed.

Income Statement for a Small Business

Over a period of time, a business will produce income (make sales) and incur expenses (pay bills). When expenses are subtracted from income, the result is either positive (a profit) or negative (a loss). The summaries of these transactions are displayed on an Income Statement (also called Profit & Loss Statement or Operating Statement).

An Income Statement, as discussed in this self-help guide, is for a period of time in the past and summarizes transactions that have already occurred. That is, an income statement is a summary of the records for sales made and payments made during a prior period. These data are used for analysis of what has occurred and for income tax reporting. The income statement is prepared for the period by adding the amounts from all the sales tickets (income) and subtracting all the payments made to others (expenses).

The next self-help guide, Self-Help Guide H, will discuss the Projected Income Statement, which is for a period of time in the future. This projected income statement is used to anticipate business activity, so as to plan the expected sales and expenses, analyze potential problems and take steps to avoid catastrophic problems from occurring. A projected income statement will be needed by a start-up business. But the concepts of an income statement must be understood before learning about a projected income statement.

Income Statement Equation

During a period of time, the business may have a profit or a loss. These transactions are summarized on an income statement. Profit or loss is calculated as the difference obtained by subtracting expenses from income. The income statement shows the total amount of sales (income) and summaries of all the categories of expenses. This calculation in equation form for the period is as follows:

INCOME	-	EXPENSE	=	PROFIT or LOSS
sales made	-	paid bills	=	a change in EQUITY

Profits or losses affect the amount of ownership in the business. At the end of each period, the equity of the owners is increased by a profit. Or the equity is decreased by a loss. That is, equity plus a profit or equity minus a loss would produce the new equity amount shown on a balance sheet for the date at the end of the later period.

Accounting Equation

To account for operation of the business over a period of time, the accounting equation discussed in Self-Help Guide E must include these two more terms (income and expenses). Thus, in equation form, the complete accounting equation is as follows:

ASSETS = LIABILITIES + EQUITY + [INCOME - EXPENSES]
sales made - paid bills

A profit during a period increases the owner's equity in the business. Similarly, a loss during a period decreases the owner's equity. Thus the balance sheet at the end of the period is different from the balance sheet at the beginning of the period by the amount of profit or loss that occurred during the period.

Income Statement Analysis

At the end of each period, you should analyze the results of your business operations. The income statement is a primary source of information for evaluating the financial performance of your business. However, preparing analysis reports is wasted unless time is taken to evaluate the good and poor effects of your management of the business. The review will not change the facts stated on the reports. But, the review will help you understand what changes to make for more success in the future. You can increase your profit by:

Increasing the Amount of Sales

1. Get more customers at the same average sale amount per customer. Advertise, promote, add new product line, increase territory, change marketing form, etc.

2. Raise the average sale amount per customer. Get larger orders or raise prices.

Decrease the Amount of Expenses

1. Reduce the Cost of Goods Sold. Reduce the cost of materials; improve production labor efficiency; reevaluate production processes; eliminate steps in the process; make more economical and efficient purchases; lower material handling costs; buy in larger quantities; find lower cost substitutes; take advantage of discounts; etc.

2. Reduce Operating Expenses: cheaper rent; more efficient automobile or truck operation; pay off a loan to eliminate interest expense; etc.

Calculate expense amounts as a percentage of sales and apply the various ratios. See the sample income statement format. Compare current period performance with earlier periods. Compare your company's financial statistics with similar companies listed in reference books found in the public library or borrow a copy from your bank. Robert Morris Associates' *Annual Statement Studies* is a good reference comparison.

The Sample Income Statement that follows shows income, expenses and profit. Your accountant will prepare a similar Income Statement for your business. Note the percent ratios for comparison with other periods.

Sample Income Statement Format

		Amounts	Percents
(1)	**Sales:**	$1,000	100%
(2)	**Cost of Goods Sold:**	600	60%
(3)	**Gross Profit:**	400	40%
(4)	**Operating Expenses:**		
	Salaries and Wages	150	
	Payroll Taxes And Benefits	38	
	Rent	80	
	Utilities	40	
	Maintenance	20	
	Office Supplies	5	
	Postage	-	
	Automobile	20	
	Insurance	10	
	Legal and Accounting	5	
	Interest	3	
	Others, Miscellaneous:		
	_____	-	
	_____	-	
	_____	-	
	_____	-	
(5)	**Total Expenses:**	371	37%
(6)	**Profit (Loss) Pre-Tax:**	29	3%
(7)	**Taxes**	6	1%
(8)	**Net Profit (Loss):**	$23	2%

Explanation of Sample:

NOTE: An Income Statement may also be called an Operating Statement; a Profit & Loss Statement; a P&L.

(1) **Sales:** Sales can be shown in any of the following ways:
   a. *Gross Sales*: Equal to the total amount sold at the prices recorded at the time of each sale. Also called Income; Revenue; Gross Income.

b. *Net Sales*: Equal to Gross Sales less returns, allowances, freight costs, discounts and other deductions. Sales commissions are often subtracted from gross sales.

c. *Combination*: The heading of Sales with subtitles showing Gross Sales less Returns, Allowances, Commissions, Freight Out, etc. and then showing the resulting Net Sales.

Note: Although sales taxes may be collected, and your accounting records will include the sales tax amounts, sales taxes are not normally included in the preparation of an Income Statement. In fact, when collected, sales taxes are not part of the business's finances. Your business merely acts as an agent for the state for the collection of sales taxes from the consumer; the sales taxes are owned by the state even though you may have temporary custody of the moneys.

(2) **Cost of Goods Sold**: COGS is equal to the sum of expenditures for materials and labor necessary to produce the products/services that were sold. Usually, COGS is the cost of inventories applied to sales. Also called Cost Of Sales and Direct Costs.

(3) **Gross Profit**: Equal to Sales (1) less Cost Of Goods Sold (2) Sometimes called Gross Margin. This represents the profit on sales before subtraction of Operating Expenses. That is, if no operating expenses were incurred, this would be the profit before income taxes.

(4) **Operating Expenses**: The expenses that must be met no matter what level of sales has occurred, i.e. rent, utilities, maintenance, etc. These costs are not directly associated with the production or sale of goods and services, and they are usually incurred without regard to sales, customers or contracts. The order in which they are stated is not important, but thoroughness is important to ensure all costs are included. Sum trivial amounts together under summary headings. Isolate individual items if the individual total becomes significant, arbitrarily five percent of sales. Also called Overhead, Overhead Cost, Overhead Expenses, Indirect Cost, Indirect Expenses and Burden.

(5) **Total Expenses**: Equals the sum of all the individual Operating Expenses.

(6) **Profit (Loss) Pre-Tax**: Equals Gross Profit (3) minus Total Expenses (5). When the value is positive, your business has made a profit; when the value is negative, your business has sustained a loss. Also, when the value is positive, this is the tax base for calculation of the amount of income tax due.

(7) **Taxes**: Equal to the amount of income taxes due.

(8) **Net Profit (Loss)**: This value represents the success of your business and is equal to Profit (Loss) Pre-Tax (6) minus Taxes (7).

Projected Income Statement for a Start-Up Small Business

A projected income statement is for a period of time in the future and is similar to an income statement that has been made for a period of time in the past. But the projected income statement is an estimate of the amount of income that will be received and of the expenses that must be paid, and assumes whether a profit or loss will result during that future period of time. To understand a projected income statement, it is first necessary to understand an Income Statement (see Self-Help Guide G), and then understand the process of making estimates and projections.

Projection Estimates

Income and expense projections are forecasting and budgeting tools used to estimate income and anticipate expenses. For most small businesses, projections covering one- to five-year periods in the future are adequate. If you are trying to get a loan, three-to five-year projections are adequate for most bankers. In some cases, a longer range projection may be valuable.

You don't need a crystal ball to make your projections. But you must make good judgments about the things that affect your financial condition and your business plan. Failing to plan can be disastrous. Indeed, in financial planning, an inaccurate projection is better than no plan. Remember, the worst plan is to have no plan at all! Yet predictions of future events are never 100 percent accurate.

The projections are made by estimating income (a sales forecast) and anticipating payments that must be made (estimated expenses). While no set of projections will ever be accurate, experience and practice tend to make the projections more precise. Even if your income projections are not accurate, they will provide rough guides to permit measurement of your progress toward your short-term sales goals. Likewise, expense projections become the base for your budgets.

There is nothing sacred about projections. If the projections are wildly inaccurate, modify them with the information you have learned since preparing the original projection. Make them more realistic. But more important, assess areas for improvement in the operation of your business as well as improvement in your forecasting techniques. As a caution, don't fall into the trap of modifying the projection to equal what actually happened. This is a waste of time and accomplishes nothing toward planning for the future.

Over the short period, trends will emerge and may sometimes be extended to identify what to expect in the longer term. Of course, if you find that you have omitted a major expense item or discover a significant shortfall of income, you must make immediate adjustments to your operations. It is more important to change your operations to account for the occurrence. Later you can revise the projection, if desired. In other words, don't revise the plan just so the plan does not differ from what actually occurred. Rather, observe the differences and evaluate them to understand the cause. Then correct the cause of the problem.

Projection Preparation

The reasoning behind income and expense projections is simple. Most expenses are predictable, and income doesn't fluctuate dramatically. So, the future should usually be similar to the past. Yet, unusual circumstances inevitably occur. These unusual circumstances must be anticipated and considered. If you are a start-up business, look for financial statement information and income ratios for a business similar to yours. You can find information in Robert Morris Associates' *Annual Statement Studies*, and trade publications, and from sources such as trade associations and businesses similar to yours.

It is important to be systematic and thorough when you list your expenses. The expense that causes the most serious problems (makes the business illiquid) is almost always one overlooked or seriously misjudged, and therefore not planned for. There are some expenses that cannot be foreseen, and the best way to allow for them is to be conservative in your estimates and to document your assumptions.

Understate expected Sales and Overstate anticipated Expenses. This situation will be most beneficial when actual sales exceed the expected sales, and expenses underrun those anticipated. This is being conservative in your estimates.

When making financial projections, it is always better to exceed a conservative budget than fail to meet an optimistic projection. However, large deviations can also create problems, such as not enough capital to finance a capital expenditure needed for growth. Basing income projections on hopes is hazardous to the health of your business. Hoping for lots of sales and high profits won't make them happen. Be realistic because your budget is an extension of your forecasts.

A projected income statement should be standardized and consistent with your accounting system. The list of items and the time period should be the same. If consistent, a projection can be converted to a budget and used later for comparison of actual expenditures to determine variances. Analysis of the variances will allow a determination of corrective action needed. Detect deviations as soon as possible to correct minor problems before they become major. This will also permit you to seize opportunities while they are still fresh.

Assumptions should be recorded for later reference to help remind you of how the original forecasts were calculated and justified. Footnotes will also aid during a review prior to preparing a later projection for a future period.

Projected and actual income statements should be reviewed regularly, usually monthly, and at least quarterly. Make it a habit. Adjustments are easier when discovered early.

If you are a sole proprietorship, you may use the format for income tax preparation, Form 1040, Schedule C. The basic form is standardized, generally accepted and can be used "as is." However, every business has peculiar accounts that apply. If you have peculiar accounts, add them. You can also use the same format as shown in Self-Help Guide G. Modify subheadings to accommodate your individual business needs.

A conservative sales forecast and a pessimistic statement of expected expenses will result in the least surprises later. Do not "blue sky" your gross sales to make the profit picture look good or you may be sorry later. REMEMBER, it is better to have actual sales exceed the forecast and expenses be less than expected. Don't be surprised by a loss because you did a sales job on yourself.

Things vs. Dollars

Go back to reread the section on Things vs. Dollars in Self-Help Guide B. You must first make estimates of the number of things in order to calculate the dollar amount. Avoid the practice of skipping this vital step.

Sales Forecast

The forecast of expected sales is the basis for your financial planning. Be realistic? Do not use hoped-for sales as a basis for planning expenses. Often, the importance of a carefully-planned sales forecast is not understood during the rush of getting started with the business operation. It is very important to state assumptions for later reflection on how the forecast was made. Write down the assumptions as you make them. Use the methods discussed in Self-Help Guide A for marketing and selling.

A sample method for determining the sales forecast is as follows. In this example, the company is interested in installing hot tubs.

1. Determine the number of potential customers you will reach by advertising. Obtain the circulation volume from the media. In this example, we chose a local suburban newspaper for the advertisement. By calling the circulation department, we learned the number of newspapers that are distributed.

    Suburban Newspaper Circulation: 96,900

2. Guess how many prospects (leads) will be developed from the advertising. That is, perhaps 0.1% of the circulation will become leads. Call or contact every lead as a potential customer.

    Number Of Lead Telephone Calls (0.001 x 96,900):   97
    Repeat telephone calls may require about three calls to each potential customer (i.e., 291 total telephone calls).

3. Estimate the number of genuinely interested potential pur-
    chasers. Follow-up calls should be made regularly to each
    potential customer (97) until you have a clear indication they
    are not interested in buying or they have bought a hot tub
    from your company. The number of people who are interested
    in buying a hot tub may be 10 percent of the genuine leads.
    Estimate the number of sales visits that will be made.

    Number of Sales Visits (0.1 x 97):   10

4. Estimate the number of sales that will be made as a result of
    the sales visits. Perhaps 20 percent of the follow-up visits may
    result in a sale.

    Number of Hot Tub Installations (0.2 x 10):   2

5. Calculate the amount of sales that would be made as a result
    of the advertisement in the suburban newspaper. By observa-
    tion or industry statistics, you may have determined the aver-
    age sale amount for the installation of a hot tub. In this ex-
    ample, a hot tub installation would average $5,000 for each
    sale.

    Sales Estimate in Dollars (2 x $5,000): $10,000

    Note: Estimates (or guesses) were made for each step of the
    sales forecasting process, except for the circulation of the sub-
    urban newspaper (96,900). Perhaps, your internal company
    records were analyzed to determine the average amount of
    sales dollars ($5,000) for installation of each hot tub.

The steps in the above process are important. Do not dwell on
the numbers or amounts in this example since these will vary
widely for each industry, company and type of product or service.
Make your estimates by starting with things that you can count,
such as the advertising media circulation, the number of products
that will be sold or the number of service sales calls that will be
made. In the example above, the sales amount of $10,000 resulted
solely from the sale of two items as a result of advertising in a
newspaper with a circulation of nearly 100,000. We also knew the
average hot tub installation costs about $5,000. You want your
projections to reflect the realities of your business. How can you
do this if you do not understand the reasons and why you expect

your projections to happen? It is most important to remember that the estimated sales resulted from first estimating the number of potential customers that would be reached by the advertising. The estimated sales did not result from a simple statement, "I think I can make $10,000 in sales."

Product Lines

If you have more than one product or service, it may be useful to make your forecast for each product line separately. In our Hot Tub Company, there might be one product line for installation of the hot tub and another product line for service calls.

After arriving at the individual projections for each product line, sometimes it is helpful to average two estimates as a "most likely" sales amount. You could do this by arranging each product line amount in three columns:

1. **Low**: Put down the sales you expect if everything goes wrong— poor weather, loss of market share, new competitive product is introduced, increased competitor activity, etc. Assume sales people will be loutish, lazy or surly.

2. **High**: Assume everything works out the way you hope—all your promotional efforts succeed, the market grows dramatically, competition wanes, and suppliers fill all orders promptly.

3. **Realistic**: Determine a realistic middle-of-the-road between the low and the high, perhaps the average of the high and the low. This approach will usually result in a more accurate sales forecast than a one-time estimate. Surely you have forced yourself into a more logical thought pattern.

Estimating Expenses

You can apply a similar process to the anticipation of expenses. This is particularly true for expenses related to sales. Some expenses are more easily predicted once the sales forecast has been established—for instance, the Cost of Goods Sold and Commissions. The amount of error will be the same. But do not make the mistake of making all expenses a percentage of sales, because Operating Expenses, unlike Cost of Goods Sold, are not proportional to the amount of sales.

Certainly, many Operating Expenses occur whether or not you have sales. For instance, rent, utilities and office salaries must be paid even if you have not made one sale. These expenses can often be projected based on prior period experience. If you are estimating rent, the rent for the next period should not vary greatly from the prior period. For a start-up, once you have chosen the area where you will locate your business, visit it to determine the typical monthly rent you can expect to pay. Follow a similar process for anticipating each Operating Expense.

Compare your projections with similar businesses in your area or with information from Robert Morris & Associates. This comparison will provide realism and objectivity to your Projected Income Statement.

Forecast Time Period

A small business should make a one- to three-year projection for both internal operations planning of the business and presentation to a potential lender. Make the first-year projection by month and the two succeeding years by quarter. Then make a three-year summary on one page. This three-year summary will be very useful in understanding your business plans and explaining your projections to a potential lender.

If you are already in business, or if you are buying an existing business, compare historical income statements from the preceding two or three years. In the absence of audited financial statements, tax returns should be used.

Projected Income Statement

	January	February	March	April	May	June	July
SALES							
Gross sales	$13,855	$13,620	$14,835	$14,735	$14,530	$15,890	$17,4
returns & allowances	$125	$120	$135	$135	$130	$140	$1
Net sales	$13,730	$13,500	$14,700	$14,600	$14,400	$15,750	$17,3
COST OF GOODS SOLD							
Cost of materials	$9,080	$8,750	$9,479	$9,422	$9,323	$10,220	$11,2
Cost of labor	$805	$970	$1,105	$1,090	$1,045	$1,120	$1,2
Total COGS	$9,885	$9,720	$10,584	$10,512	$10,368	$11,340	$12,4
GROSS PROFIT	$3,845	$3,780	$4,116	$4,088	$4,032	$4,410	$4,8
OPERATING EXPENSES							
Salaries	$1,900	$1,900	$1,900	$1,900	$1,900	$1,900	$1,9
Payroll taxes & benefits	$237	$238	$237	$238	$237	$238	$2
Rent	$550	$550	$550	$550	$550	$550	$5
Utilities	$160	$165	$180	$200	$200	$180	$1
Maintenance	$25	$25	$25	$25	$25	$25	$
Office supplies	$25	$25	$25	$25	$25	$25	$
Postage	$15	$15	$15	$15	$20	$35	$
Auto expenses	$150	$150	$150	$150	$150	$150	$1
Insurance	$70	$70	$70	$110	$110	$110	$1
Legal & accounting	$125	$125	$125	$125	$125	$125	$1
Advertising	$450	$450	$450	$450	$450	$450	$4
Licenses & fees	$9	$9	$9	$9	$9	$10	$
Telephone	$85	$85	$85	$85	$85	$85	$
Equipment depreciation	$0	$0	$0	$455	$455	$455	$9
interest	$0	$0	$0	$250	$250	$250	$3
Miscellaneous							
Total Operating Expense	$3,801	$3,807	$3,821	$4,587	$4,591	$4,588	$5,1
NET PROFIT (LOSS) PRE-TAX	$44	($27)	$295	($499)	($559)	($178)	($2

Projected Income Statement

	August	September	October	November	December	Total
SALES						
Gross sales	$20,120	$22,960	$23,665	$23,970	$22,265	$217,910
returns & allowances	$180	$195	$200	$195	$190	$1,910
Net sales	$19,940	$22,765	$23,465	$23,775	$22,075	$216,000
COST OF GOODS SOLD						
Cost of materials	$12,822	$15,345	$15,976	$16,119	$14,913	$142,680
Cost of labor	$1,535	$1,650	$1,715	$1,795	$1,585	$15,640
Total COGS	$14,357	$16,995	$17,691	$17,914	$16,498	$158,320
GROSS PROFIT	$5,583	$5,770	$5,774	$5,861	$5,577	$57,680
OPERATING EXPENSES						
Salaries	$1,900	$1,900	$1,900	$1,900	$1,900	$22,800
Payroll taxes & benefits	$238	$237	$238	$237	$238	$2,850
Rent	$550	$550	$550	$550	$550	$6,600
Utilities	$165	$185	$185	$185	$185	$2,160
Maintenance	$25	$25	$25	$25	$25	$300
Office supplies	$25	$25	$25	$25	$25	$300
Postage	$45	$50	$50	$50	$50	$400
Auto expenses	$150	$150	$150	$150	$150	$1,800
Insurance	$110	$110	$110	$110	$110	$1,200
Legal & accounting	$125	$125	$125	$125	$125	$1,500
Advertising	$450	$450	$450	$450	$450	$5,400
Licenses & fees	$10	$10	$10	$10	$10	$115
Telephone	$85	$85	$85	$85	$85	$1,020
Equipment depreciation	$955	$955	$955	$955	$955	$7,095
interest	$300	$300	$300	$300	$300	$2,550
Miscellaneous						$0
Total Operating Expenses	$5,133	$5,157	$5,158	$5,157	$5,158	$56,090
NET PROFIT (LOSS) - PRE-TAX	$450	$613	$616	$704	$419	$1,590

Preparing
Cash Flow Projections

A regular analysis of cash flow will help avoid many financial problems. Moreover, a cash flow projection can make the difference between success and failure as well as the difference between growth and stagnation. Actually, a cash flow projection is THE MOST IMPORTANT TOOL available to the small business person. If a small business was limited to only one financial statement, the Cash Flow Projection would be the one to choose.

Cash Flow Projection

A prediction (forecast) of future money sources and uses; a cash budget; a cash flow forecast; forecasted receipt of cash and forecasted disbursements of cash. Cash flow is different from income and expenses. A cash flow analysis can be compared to a coin purse. Money must first be put into the purse (source) before money can be taken out (used). A cash flow projection, therefore, would analyze those times in the future when money is expected to be received (source) and those times in the future when money is expected to be disbursed (used).

Cash Flow Analysis

A small business owner should regularly prepare a cash flow analysis because it will show the small business owner:

1. How much cash will be needed.

2. When the cash is needed.

3. Where the cash will come from.

341

CASH FLOW STATEMENT for EXAMPLE CO. as a START-UP BUSINESS

All values in dollars

	BEGINNING TRANSACTIONS	Jan END	Change for Feb	Feb END	Change for Mar	March END	Change for Apr	April END	Change for May	May END	Change for June	June END
CASH RECEIPTS:												
Owner initial investment	$15000											
Additional equity									$5000			
Cash sales							$800		$1450		$600	
Accounts Receivable Collection									$80		$425	
TOTAL CASH RECEIPTS:		$15000		$0		$0		$800		$6530		$1025
CASH DISBURSEMENTS:												
Down payment on building	$3000											
Merchandise purchases	$2550		$2475		$885		$1000		$1550		$1130	
Salaries & wages							$1000		$1000		$1000	
Payroll withholding payment							$250		$250		$250	
Utilities	$200		$100		$100		$100		$100		$100	
Office supplies	$400											
Truck expenses	$45		$60		$45		$75		$50		$45	
Legal & accounting							$175					
Advertising	$60		$60		$75		$50		$40		$80	
Licenses & fees	$150				$60						$60	
Telephone			$75		$75		$75		$75		$75	
Mortgage loan payment			$485		$485		$485		$485		$485	
Truck loan payment			$240		$240		$240		$240		$240	
Incorporation expenses	$850											
TOTAL CASH DISBURSEMENTS:		$7255		$3495		$1965		$2450		$3790		$3465
ENDING CASH ON HAND:		$7745		$4250		$2285		$635		$3375		$935

4. What type of cash to look for—equity, debt, operating profits or sale of fixed assets.

A cash flow projection attempts to budget the cash needs of a business and shows how cash will flow in and out of the business over a period of time. Cash flows into the business from sales for cash (not sales on credit). Cash also may flow into a business as a result of collection of receivables, capital injections, loans, etc. Cash flows out through cash payments (disbursements) for expenses like supplies, material, rent and loan payment.

Projections, forecasts and predictions are not always accurate. But they are better than no plan at all. Please refer to Self-Help Guide H for further discussion concerning estimating and projection preparation. Refer to Self-Help Guide B on things vs. dollars. Then apply these concepts when making a cash flow projection.

The cash flow financial tool emphasizes the times in the business calendar when money will be coming into and going out of your business. The advantage of knowing when cash outlays must be made is the ability to plan for those outlays. Therefore, you will not be forced to resort to unexpected borrowing to meet cash needs. Illiquidity is a killer, even for profitable businesses. Lack of profits (losses) won't kill a business as quickly as lack of cash. For instance, non-cash expenses on an income statement, such as depreciation, will only make your profit look negative (a loss). But a lack of cash to meet your trade and other payables will force a business into bankruptcy. Cash is needed to pay invoices, meet loan payables and so forth. If cash is not in the checking account, and a loan cannot be arranged, other people to whom you owe money will sue and force you into bankruptcy.

A cash flow projection for the future near term period will show the need for a loan or needed equity to meet future payments. An income statement will not show these cash needs. (See Self-Help Guide H for further discussion of the time period for a cash flow projection.) If you know of a potential problem in advance, you may be able to find ways to finance your business operations or minimize your credit needs to lower interest expense. Many of the advantages of studying the cash flow projection stem from timing: More options are available to you, at lower cost and with less panic, if a cash flow projection is prepared in advance.

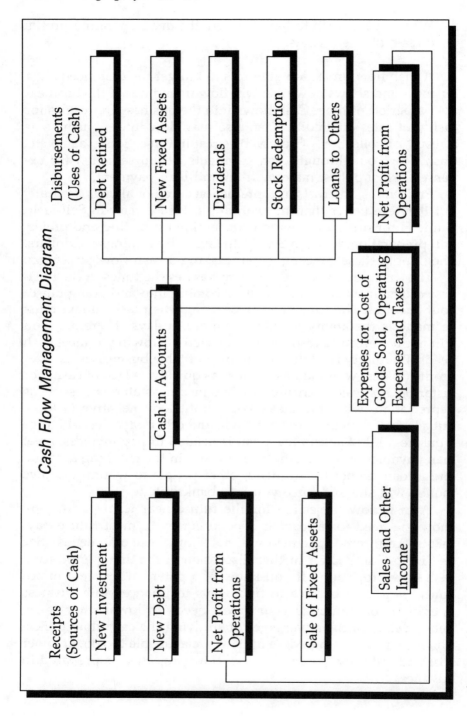

Cash Flow Management Diagram

Disbursements (Uses of Cash)

- Debt Retired
- New Fixed Assets
- Dividends
- Stock Redemption
- Loans to Others
- Net Profit from Operations

Cash in Accounts

Expenses for Cost of Goods Sold, Operating Expenses and Taxes

Receipts (Sources of Cash)

- New Investment
- New Debt
- Net Profit from Operations
- Sale of Fixed Assets

Sales and Other Income

In a start-up business, cash is injected into the business by the owners (equity) or by borrowing (as a loan). As the business operates, cash is generated primarily from sales as operating revenue. Yet sales can be for either cash or on credit. Perhaps your business has all cash sales (no sales on credit). On the other hand, all sales may not be cash sales. If you offer credit (charge accounts, term payments, trade credit) to your customers, you must have a means of knowing when those credit sales will turn into cash-in-hand. The shorter the time period from making a sale to getting paid, the better your situation will be. This concept is blurred in an income statement but made very clear by the cash flow projection.

Rapid inventory turnover is equally important to good cash flow. When goods are purchased for sale, the supplier must be paid. You, therefore, have made an investment of your cash in inventory that can only be replaced by collection of the money from your customer after the item has been sold.

Refer to Self-Help Guide H for further discussion of sales forecast techniques and incorporate assumptions as needed for the cash sales, credit sales and inventory in the cash flow projection. When sufficient cash cannot be generated from cash sales plus collections from credit sales, the business must borrow money, increase investment by the owners or sell assets for cash.

Certainly, a cash flow projection will be needed for large purchases. To purchase a large piece of equipment for cash requires many months spent building enough cash to make the purchase. If the equipment is to be financed, you must first save the cash down payment and also arrange the loan in advance of the date the equipment is needed. These are examples of typical cash flow management situations.

After it has been developed, a cash flow projection can be converted into a budget. If the cash outlay for a given item increases over the amount allotted for a given month, determine the cause and take corrective action as soon as possible. If the cash outlay is lower than expected, it is not necessarily a good sign. Maybe a bill wasn't paid. With this means, reviewing the movement of cash position will provide better control of your business.

Discrepancies between expected and actual cash flow are indicators of opportunities as well as problems. If cash sales and collections don't match the cash flow projection, look for the cause.

CASH FLOW ELEMENTS

CASH AT BEGINNING OF PERIOD

SOURCES	USES
ADD: CASH RECEIPTS	SUBTRACT: CASH DISBURSED

SOURCES — ADD: CASH RECEIPTS

1. Cash received from equity investment
2. Cash received from loans
3. Cash received from assets sold
4. Sales of products or services for cash (cash sales)
5. Receivables collected on prior sales made on credit
6. Miscellaneous cash received

USES — SUBTRACT: CASH DISBURSED

7. New inventory purchased for cash
8. Salaries & wages paid
9. FICA, federal & state withholding taxes
10. Fringe benefits paid
11. New equipment purchased for cash
    11.1 Processing equip.
    11.2 Office, sales equip.
    11.3 Trucks & cars
12. Insurance premiums
13. Fees
    13.1 Accounting
    13.2 Legal
14. Rent
15. Utilities
    15.1 Heat, light, power
    15.2 Telephone
16. Advertising
17. Principal & interest on debt
18. Transportation
    18.1 Oil, gas, etc.
    18.2 Vehicle maintenance
19. Freight
20. Taxes
    20.1 Income, federal, state
    20.2 Property
    20.3 Excise
    20.4 Sales tax
21. Dividends paid or drawn by owner

TOTAL: CASH RECEIVED   TOTAL: CASH DISBURSED

Formula

Cash At Beginning Of The Period (C_b) plus Total Cash Received (TC_r) minus Total Cash Disbursed (TC_d) equals Cash At End Of The Period (C_e).

$$C_b = TC_r - TC_d = C_e$$

Note: A cash flow statement operates like a checkbook or a coin purse; cash must be put in before cash can be taken out. Cash In is the amount of actual dollars that you receive. Cash Out is the amount of actual dollars that you pay out (disburse). Amounts do not include obligations that you incur now that will be received or paid at a future date.

Perhaps the projection was too low. Maybe you've opened a new market or introduced a new product that can be pushed even harder. The cash savings may indicate a new way of economizing.

Cash Flow Block Diagram

You can use the Cash Flow Block Diagram to make sure you don't omit any ordinary cash flow item. But be sure to add items that are peculiar to your business.

The level of detail you wish to provide is your decision. Depending on the value of the result, compare the time required to prepare a more detailed projection. You may want to provide more (or less) detail than is shown in the accompanying examples. For example, you might benefit from itemizing your cash flow into a series of cash flows, each representing a single product or service. This can be particularly handy if you have more than one source of revenue or if you are a manufacturer and need to prepare numerous bids. The accumulated information gained by several projections can help decide which bids are most important to you.

Cash flow projections are more easily prepared using a computer. Spreadsheet programs are valuable because you can use graphic displays to see the concepts more easily. Computers can link together several different financial statements. Furthermore, a computer allows you to develop "what-if" situations with much greater speed and accuracy.

Cash Flow Elements

Many of the elements required for making a cash flow projection are contained in the list of Cash Flow Elements. Review the items so that you understand the sources and uses of cash. Perhaps, keep the list handy when preparing your cash flow projection.

Finding Help for a Start-Up Small Business

There are several sources of help for small businesses. They include government agencies, not-for-profits, educational institutions, similar businesses, suppliers and customers, business associations, professionals and consultants. Each of these is discussed in detail in this self-help guide.

The services range from free counseling to for-fee consulting services. For example, the U.S. Small Business Administration and most states sponsor free counseling and publish low-cost self-help booklets. Educational institutions provide a broad array of low-cost courses that teach the fundamentals of small business management. Similar businesses and business associations may provide guidance in a specific field or industry. A for-fee professional or consulting service may be needed to resolve a difficult technical problem. Needless to say, the beginning entrepreneur must establish a good working relationship with the four professional areas discussed in Self-Help Guide K; namely, an attorney, an accountant, a banker and an insurance representative. However, for help beyond these professional sources, the start-up business person should investigate the free or low-cost services first. Later, consultants can be engaged after determining the value of the information sought.

More important than cost of the service is the type of service and the value of the information obtained. In some situations, a licensed professional may be the only alternative. In others, a high-priced specialist, completely knowledgeable on a specific technical subject, may provide the greatest return on your time or money. On the other hand, a free counselor may be able to provide the same depth of understanding. So, it is suggested that you search out and utilize the most knowledgeable sources at the least expense.

Governments

Each of the three levels of U.S. government—federal, state and local—provides programs that promote small business. Critical to your success in locating help are your dedication, your ability to search out programs that apply to your business situation and patience with any complications encountered. Governments help businesses grow because growing business will increase the tax base and create more jobs. But you need to be relentless in your pursuit. Most often, government employees will need to be led (pushed) to assist you. However, by continuously asking questions and following-up on the leads that develop, great amounts of help can be found. Try any or all of these leads. Local telephone numbers can be found in the blue pages (government) of your local telephone directory, your telephone company information assistance service or through the federal information center, 800-735-8004.

- **U.S. Small Business Administration**. Call or visit your local office or call the national answer desk, 800-827-5722.

- **Business Assistance Program**. Call the local office of the U.S. Department of Commerce or the business liaison office in Washington DC, 202-377-3176.

- **Federal Information Center**. Most larger cities have a telephone listing for the Federal Information Center in the blue pages of the telephone book. This service may help locate specific types of services that are available.

- **New Business Incubation Centers Referral Service**. Many cities, counties and towns provide assistance to start-up small businesses through an "incubator." The nearest incubator may be located in the telephone book, from your Chamber of Commerce or by calling 202-653-7880.

- **Enterprise Zone**. The federal government and some states provide a locality that has tax abatement and other lower-cost services to assist start-up companies. In particular, enterprise zones are often set up to encourage exports.

- **State Economic Development Commission.** Most states provide assistance to small start-up businesses. But it may be difficult to locate the source of the assistance needed because the knowledge about the service is located in the state's capital. In your state capital, locate the state government office that promotes economic development within the state.

- **County Economic Development Office.** Many counties provide an office that will help you search out assistance for starting a new business in your county.

- **City or Community Development Department.** Often cities will provide incentives to start a new business or help existing companies to stimulate economic growth in the city or community.

Not-For-Profits

A wide array of not-for-profit assistance exists on local, regional, national and international levels. They fall into two groups, government-sponsored and privately-sponsored. Contact with the government sponsored groups can be made directly or through the sponsoring government agency. Contact with private organizations may be accomplished by referring to the business section of the telephone book.

SCORE: The most important source of free counseling help for the start-up entrepreneur is the Service Corps of Retired Executives (SCORE). Across the U.S., 13,000 SCORE volunteers provide expert counsel for virtually every type of start-up business. Probably there are SCORE counselors near you. In a typical city, for instance, there may be as many as 100 volunteer counselors with a wide variety of business backgrounds. In a small town, perhaps 10 counselors may be within a short driving distance.

SCORE members are former small business owners and managers who volunteer their time for the self-satisfaction of helping other small businesses succeed. These men and women may have already overcome the problems you are facing, and their experience could be invaluable. The primary purpose of SCORE is to provide a community service, thus their guidance is free to the start-up company or anyone in small business. SCORE can provide the advice, guidance and counseling, but you must do the work necessary for success. This counseling can be obtained by telephone, computer modem or a visit to the SCORE chapter office located nearby. SCORE services include:

Counseling: The advice furnished by SCORE counselors may be basic start-up information, advice towards solving a particular problem or assistance in planning future growth. The counselor will meet with you as frequently and for as long as necessary to solve your particular problems.

Training: Broadly focused pre-start-up business workshops are offered periodically, as well as more specialized classes, seminars and conferences on topics of great value to specific segments of the business community. Subjects covered in specialized training courses include business organization, site selection, trade promotion, marketing, licenses, accounting, taxation and financing. A modest fee may be charged to cover the cost of materials, meeting room or other expenses. SCORE members who teach the courses are volunteers and receive no pay. So the fee charged is very low in comparison with other educational programs.

Information: Some SCORE chapters have amassed a large library of information and data available to small business owners. All you need to do is ask. But you must know the right questions to ask.

The nearest SCORE chapter can be located by several means. Call your Chamber of Commerce, call the nearest SBA office or sometimes SCORE can be located in the telephone directory. From anywhere in the United States, you can call the "SBA Answer Desk," 800-827-5722. In addition to a wide variety of recorded information about small businesses, you can obtain the location and telephone number of any SCORE chapter anywhere in the U.S. Written inquiries can be directed to the local SCORE chapter, to the nearest SBA office or to the National SCORE Office, Small Business Administration, Suite 5900, 409 3rd St. SW, Washington, DC 20024.

Besides SCORE there are several other not-for-profit organizations on federal, state and local levels. On a national level, these organizations include the Small Business Development Center (SBDC), Small Business Institute (SBI) and the Small Business Innovation Research (SBIR) program.

On the state level, the state university system often provides personnel who have small business and industry experience. Sometimes, this experience is provided through the university extension service

In your area, check with the Chamber of Commerce, the Better Business Bureau, Rotary, Lions, American Federation of Independent Businesses and the like. Many of these organizations provides information and/or assistance in small business start-ups and management.

Educational Institutions

Educational institutions like high schools, community colleges, junior colleges and universities provide adult and vocational education courses. Most frequently, these educational institutions increase knowledge about specific business functions vital to success. That is, educational institutions are very helpful in business functional areas such as common business law, accounting, interpreting financial statements, typing, office administration, practical marketing, applied marketing and theory.

Sometimes, courses are available to help a start-up in a particular field of business. In one city, for instance, a local community college offers help in starting a bed and breakfast, a restaurant, a book store, a consulting business, a beauty salon and a trucking business.

Since educational institutions offer academic theory as well as practical knowledge, be selective in the type of knowledge you seek to acquire. A course in international economic theory would usually provide less help for a start-up than bookkeeping fundamentals or interpretation of accounting statements.

Similar Businesses

Do you know somebody who is in a business similar to yours? Do you know the individual well enough to discuss your idea with him or her? Provided that you are not directly competing for customers, a similar business will often share the expertise it has gained.

Business owners are proud people. They are somewhat egotistical about their accomplishments. Therefore, they frequently will boast about (share) important detailed facts that are vitally important to success. If you do not know someone, search for a similar business in a locale where you will not directly compete. Make a cold call to them. Tell them your plans and ask for their guidance. The response may astound you. You may find the business person warm and friendly and willing to give you their complete cooperation and assistance.

Suppliers and Customers

Those businesses that sell to or purchase from your type of business can offer valuable information. Since they are both upstream and downstream from your business, they could provide a wealth of knowledge about the state of the business field.

The information derived from each source is fundamentally different in nature. From suppliers, you can learn who are the strong competitors as well as sources of customer contacts. You can also often obtain free hints about the state of affairs in the field, such as prevailing trends. Furthermore, the contact you make with the suppliers will establish a good basis for your continued business relationship after your business has been established.

From customers and potential customers, you can learn what they need and want, how much they are willing to pay, how their current sources of supply can be improved, why the market is structured in a particular way and other information that will assist with your marketing program. The means for obtaining information from customers is sometimes complicated and involved. A well-designed survey may be helpful.

Business Associations

If you do not know about the association or organization that exists for the business you wish to start, this fact should be a strong word of caution that you are not prepared to start the business. You should be familiar with this association. Otherwise, it implies that you are not technically knowledgeable about the business. To be successful, it is most important that you know more about the business than all your competitors.

Business associations are mentioned here because these groups often collect statistics about their members. Furthermore, they have a storehouse of specific knowledge in the field, and their mem-

Finding Help for a Start-Up Small Business 355

bers have already faced the challenges you are about to undertake. The association may provide the names of similar businesses that you can contact. The information obtained from these sources is very helpful in understanding your competition and in the formulation of your business plan.

For instance, if you are starting a general contracting company, you should know about the Association of General Contractors. Likewise, other associations exist, such as the American Soybean Association, American Waterways Operators, The Concrete Council, The Direct Marketing Association, Independent Computer Consultants Association, United Dairy Industry, Disc Jockey Association, Association of Candy and Tobacco Distributors, Beer Wholesalers, Cosmetologists Association and National Restaurant Association. Each association is very specific to a field. You must be acquainted with the association in your field.

In your telephone book yellow pages, you can usually find a list of associations. Sometimes the association for a specific business may not have an office in your city or the association exists and meets locally but does not have an office location with a telephone number. If there is an association in your city, this implies the competition is strong with several other profitable businesses already well established. Remember, the association exists only because of its dues paying members and for the benefits to its members.

In your local library, you should be able to locate a book that lists all the associations in the United States. The spectrum of these groups is very broad, but you should only be interested in the one or two organizations that specifically relate to your business line.

Often, trade magazines are available in specific business fields. You should regularly read the publications in your field so you are aware of trends and the actions of your competitors. In larger cities, a newspaper may exist that caters to the small business person.

Professionals

Self-Help Guide K is devoted entirely to the four main types of professional assistance that must be acquired by a start-up business. Mentioning these professionals here is to emphasize the necessity of acquiring this assistance. Do not try to start a business without a good relationship with each professional or with personal knowledge and understanding of each area.

Consultants

Often consultants provide specific and excellent guidance. Because they are usually professionals, they most often provide assistance only in their respective fields. That is, a consultant will provide technical assistance in a specific field, like financial management, not general start-up guidance. Other than the four main professionals mentioned in the previous section, consultants can usually be found in technical fields such as communications, education, engineering and training.

But these types of assistance are not usually of much value to the beginning start-up small business. Governments and not-for-profit organizations often provide better guidance for the start-up and at much less cost. Yet management consultants can sometimes be very effective in assisting a start-up.

Consultants are listed last in this list of places for help only because of the cost of their services. The cost of a consultant is usually very high relative to other forms of guidance.

Finding Professional Assistance

Starting a business requires an enormous amount of knowledge, energy and determination. So the start-up business person should seek the assistance of professionals in fields where personal knowledge is not sufficient. But identifying the best professional help for your small business may be very difficult.

These guidelines are provided to assist with the process of finding an attorney, an accountant, a banker and an insurance representative. It has been said that these four professionals are necessary for successful start-up of a new business. Furthermore, the start-up business person usually does not have adequate skills in these professions since many years of study and practice are necessary for attainment of excellence in each field.

Throughout the course of your business operation, each will provide skilled analysis and expert advice crucial to your firm's success or failure. Therefore, selection of the most appropriate firm or individual in each profession should be accomplished through a carefully prepared and well executed plan. Two sources of help: the U.S. Small Business Administration (SBA) or the Service Corps of Retired Executives (SCORE).

A word of caution: Since you will be buying a service, it is essential that you understand the basic principles of each service. This is necessary because you are ultimately responsible for all business decisions even if you follow the advice of the professional. Furthermore, you will understand much more fully the application of the professional advice to the operation of your business. It is your business success that will be affected by application of the advice; the risk is yours.

Sometimes, these professional services are very expensive to employ. Therefore, their use should be carefully evaluated prior to seeking the advice. You should understand exactly what you need to achieve before consulting the expert professional. Often, much of the preparatory work in each profession can be accomplished by less expensive means under your control then given to the professional for implementation.

Your Attorney

The first crucial advice you should get is from an attorney (lawyer) concerning your business structure. That is, should you be a sole proprietorship, a partnership or a corporation? Later, during the operation of your business, questions concerning contracts, legal and tax matters may arise wherein the advice of an attorney could be the determining factor in the results achieved. Each business situation is different but, also businesses are different. In fact, they are so different that one attorney may be much more helpful than another attorney simply because of his or her familiarity with that type of business. In your search for an attorney:

1. **Assess Your Need.** Determine whether you need assistance with a particular immediate problem or whether you need a continuous source of counseling to avoid problems over the future course of your business. Your approach might well be different depending on your need.

   In order to get good legal representation for a particular problem, it is mandatory to know the facts in order to make a good selection of an attorney. Yet, one of the most important services of an attorney is the advice to avoid legal problems. The old saying "An ounce of precaution is worth a pound of lawsuits" is absolutely true in the legal profession. Surely, the avoidance of a lawsuit is much more cost effective than defending a lawsuit. So, evaluation of a problem by a professional attorney may be money well spent.

2. **Local Bar Association.** Locate the Bar Association from the local telephone book. Most large city metropolitan areas operate a lawyer referral service organized so you and a legal professional first interview to evaluate your need. Then you are offered the names of a few attorneys who are knowledge-

able in your field and whom you can interview individually. The Bar Association supervises the operation of the service and sets restrictions that govern the attorneys under the program.

3. **Legal Directory**. Most areas publish such a directory, listing fields of practice and biographical information on the individual lawyers and law firms. Search for this publication in a local law library, a university law library or the public library. The librarian will usually be able to assist in your search.

4. **Other Sources**. Discuss your need with others in businesses similar to yours. Contact the local trade association for your type of business. Try the nearest law firm in your neighborhood. Ask your librarian for the name of one or more books that provide guidelines for selecting an attorney. Ask for referrals from friends or relatives who are in business. Collect the suggestions and narrow your search to the few who offer the most promise of fulfilling your need.

5. **Screen, Interview, Analyze and Select**. Methodically narrow your choices. Then interview those attorneys who might fill your need most successfully. Be prepared with a list of questions that you have developed during your search and screening. Does the lawyer consult primarily in your field? Will the lawyer provide a few references of other clients he or she represents? In each case, find out how the firm charges for services. Try to get a flat fee or at least an estimate. Determine who will handle your work, a partner or an associate? After all the interviews are complete, evaluate the results and make the selection of the attorney who will handle your situation.

Accounting Services

In recent years, the sophistication of accounting procedures and the complexity of tax laws have increased the need for professional accounting services. For instance, knowing the precise definition of an employee as opposed to an independent contractor could permit your business to avoid serious tax complications. Also, penalties for late submittal of tax deposits are severe. The facts speak for themselves. Failure of small businesses is generally the result of two situations: insufficient cash flow and lack of business management expertise by the small business owner. For these two reasons alone, a small business owner should consider employing a professional accounting service. Consider the following in your approach to accurate and effective financial management:

1. **Segregation of Work.** Determine if you intend to perform all (most) accounting activities at the company premises by employees or whether you will take the job to the place of business of the accounting professional. Generally, there are three levels of knowledge associated with people who handle accounting matters: Bookkeeper, Accountant or Certified Public Accountant (CPA). Choose the most appropriate and competent person for each assignment.

2. **Your Bookkeeping System.** Assess your need for financial information. Obtain professional advice about setting up the books, recordkeeping procedures, interpreting the firm's records, and providing financial advice based on interpretation of the data. Analysis of the data must be accomplished in an efficient and a timely manner. The availability and accuracy of these data are vital to your success.

3. **Searching for Assistance.** Follow a procedure similar to that outlined for an attorney. Contact the local accounting association or the American Institute of Certified Public Accountants (AICPA). There may be an accounting referral service in your area, although these are more rare than lawyer referral services. Contact other businesses similar to your business and inquire at the association in your field. Your banker may also be able to suggest an accounting firm that specializes in your field of business. Screen, interview, analyze and make a selection of the financial assistance you need for your business.

A recent addition to the specialized accounting field is the payroll processing firm. You should investigate such firms' services, effective benefits and cost. These firms stay abreast of payroll tax law changes and advise when tax deposits are due. Many small businesses have found that a payroll processing firm can provide the service more accurately and at less cost than they could in-house.

Banking Services

A good bank can be one of your best business friends. But all banks are not the same. Some banks handle commercial (business) accounts, while other banks may handle only personal accounts. Contact the Small Business Administration in your area to obtain a list of banks that handle commercial accounts. In a larger city, there may even be banks that specialize in firms similar to yours. Determine the services that each bank can provide to your business. For instance, you may want a bank that establishes a post office box for your business, makes your collections, deposits the cash into your account immediately and provides a daily listing of transactions. This eliminates lost interest due to processing and float time.

Determine several banks that you will interview. Narrow the list of banks to the few most likely to offer banking services you need then interview each bank. Obtain a list of services that are provided. Compare the list of services and schedule of fees charged by each bank. Since every business usually needs additional capital, evaluate the loan policy before selecting the bank for your business. This is important, whether or not you need to borrow start-up financing. If you need a loan later, your bank can provide the loan. Select the most appropriate bank considering all the factors.

When approaching the bank, try to get an introduction to the president or senior loan officer first. Of course, if you already do your personal banking at this bank, you may already be acquainted. This personal contact will build credibility and trust that go beyond the impersonal paper facts. Furthermore, these individuals may make the loan decisions and can often waive policies that otherwise would prevent making the loan.

Insurance Representative

Financial protection for risks that you cannot pay from company cash requires insurance protection. Yet the risks of your business are peculiar to a particular type of business operation. So careful selection of an insurance representative and insurance company is important. They must be familiar with the coverage that you need. You should evaluate the means by which your claim will be settled to your satisfaction in the event of a loss.

As a new business, you may have difficulty obtaining insurance protection. This is because the insurance company and its representative lack knowledge about you and your business. Therefore, follow the procedure below for a thorough assessment of your needs during selection of your insurance representative.

Evaluate your insurance protection needs. A good method of evaluating your insurance protection needs is to categorize the losses. Three levels of loss risk are suggested:

a. Events that will force you out of business.

b. Serious losses after which you could still stay in business, but it would be a struggle to survive.

c. Losses you can meet out of current company financial resources.

For each potential loss category and for each identified risk, determine the limits of coverage desired:

a. Unlimited loss protection.

b. Maximum loss protection for cash value or replacement value.

c. Deductible or floor amount of insurance protection.

If you lease from someone else, review the owner's policy for the protection he or she might provide for your business property. You don't want to pay for protection already provided free.

1. **Business Insurance Types**. There are many types of insurance that cover small businesses. Some of the most common that you should consider are workers' compensation, general liability, product liability, automobile, truck, fidelity bond, surety bond, crime, contracts, credit, transportation, business interruption, key person, business owners, business continuation

and rental. A complete list should be discussed with your insurance representative.

2. **Employee Benefits**. In your analysis of insurance needs, include the employee benefits you need or want to carry. Some benefits have almost become accepted norms for employing others. For example, a hospitalization plan is necessary for families today. Consider the jeopardy you impose on employees and their families if they do not have medical insurance. So you must consider medical and hospitalization insurance, workers' compensation insurance, disability insurance, group life insurance, a retirement plan and the like.

3. **Obtain Estimates**. A new small business may have difficulty obtaining adequate insurance protection. What track record do you have? What financial risks do you pose for the insurance company? In many business fields, only a few insurance companies carry business liability insurance. So submit your list of insurance protection needs to three firms and get three bids for consideration. Insurance companies sell policies to businesses through:

   a. *Insurance agent*. An agent works for only one insurance company and represents only that company.

   b. *Insurance broker*. A broker represents several different insurance companies and can, theoretically, select the best company for protection against each of your business risks.

   c. *Insurance pool*. Available but expensive, a pool is a collection of insurance companies that agree to share the risk for new unknown applicants. Each new applicant is assigned to an insurance company in a random order. In this situation, your company may be assigned to an agent or a broker with which you make arrangements for your insurance needs.

4. **Analysis and Selection**. Compare the bids and other information which were obtained. Often, a chart will help with the evaluation. In one column, list each type of insurance protection by category as well as the limits and floor of protection needed. In the three other columns, list the premium amounts charged by

the insurance companies. Make the final selection considering the protection provided and the premiums required.

It is sometimes important to check the integrity and financial strength of the insurance company. Determine the record of claims payment by the insurance company. These concerns are especially important if you are considering a small unknown insurance company.

Over the years, as your business grows, your needs for insurance also increase. Periodically, reevaluate and reconsider the insurance protection needed by your business.

Code of Ethics for a Small Business Person

Integrity, morals and ethics exist in the individual or they do not exist at all. They must be upheld by individuals or they are not upheld at all. In order for integrity, morals and ethics to be characteristics of your company, they must be present in you and each of your employees. These three characteristics are necessary for the establishment of trusting business communication. It is through trust and consistent reliance on trust in others that the business community is able to achieve prosperity and growth. You and each of your employees must be:

- Honest and trustworthy in all relationships.

- Truthful and accurate in what you say and write.

- Fair and considerate in treatment of employees, associates, customers and suppliers.

- Law abiding in all activities.

- Committed to accomplishing all tasks in a superior manner and to providing the highest quality products and services.

- Respectful of the integrity and dedication of others with whom you are in contact.

Your company image is the reflection of people's perception of you or your employees. You, as the owner, must set an example of integrity and character. Demand the same from each employee.

What image does your customer have from contact with the company? Who do they contact? It is always a person. This individual person and the communication with that person are what the customer remembers. That individual contact with that single person forms their impression of your entire company.

Integrity leading to high standards of ethics and moral conduct requires hard work, courage and difficult choices. These characteristics do not happen by chance. Rather, they are achieved through consistent application of integrity and honest communication with others.

Maintaining a high standard of ethics, morals and integrity may sometimes require you to for go a business opportunity. In the long run, however, you will be better served by doing what is right rather than what is expedient. To demonstrate your commitment to integrity and ethics, become a member of the Chamber of Commerce, the Better Business Bureau, Trade Associations, and similar organizatonis in your community as well as those in your business field.

Start-Up Checklist
for Small Businesses

This checklist is located at the back of this book for ease of reference by the start-up small business person. However, the checklist is the place to begin for you to analyze your ability and capacity to start a new business or to buy an existing business.

Borrowed in part from a pamphlet published by the U.S. Small Business Administration, this checklist contains a comprehensive and practical list of all the areas that must be considered by the start-up business person. You can use this checklist to evaluate a completely new venture proposal or an apparent opportunity in your existing business.

When you consider starting your business, it is very important that you consider all aspects of being in business. This checklist will help you determine if your idea is a real business opportunity. Do you have the entrepreneurial spirit? Do you really know what you are getting into? Is owning your own business the ultimate panacea that has been professed by some people? Will you be your own boss? Can you do what you want, when you want? Will you make lots of money? Etc.

Starting a business is usually a very demanding task. Often it involves long hours, dedicated pursuit of detail and observation of all conditions that can cause failure or success. Therefore, thorough preparation is necessary for success. If you leave out an item, or you don't fully consider an item, that item may be the very most important element to success or, for that matter, to failure.

Perhaps the most crucial problem you will face is determining the feasibility of your idea. Getting into the right business at the right time is simple advice. But this advice is very difficult to implement. The high failure rate of new businesses indicates that few ideas result in successful ventures. Often, failures result from entrepreneurs who strike out on a business venture so convinced of the merits that they fail to thoroughly evaluate its potential for success or failure. Most of all, the people who fail in business have failed to evaluate the probability of failure.

Dedicate the time necessary to perform this analysis thoroughly and completely. The checklist is designed to help you screen out ideas likely to fail before you invest extensive time, money and effort. Would you rather learn the outcome now, or after investing large amounts of your time, money or effort?

Important ingredients to success include: the feasibility of the idea, your personal demeanor and your personal entrepreneurial spirit. An entrepreneur must have a unique combination of vision, aggressiveness, drive, creativity, energy, endurance, stamina and cleverness. Most of all, you must possess the self-determination to make it work because nobody else will do it. You must do it. If you have the idea that small business owners who work for themselves don't have to listen to anybody else and make a lot of money with little effort, you are dead wrong. You are kidding yourself! A small business person must be a loner to the extent that everyone else will tell you what to do and how to do it, but the real test is, Can you do it?

To determine the feasibility of going into business, you must gather information. Write down the facts and analyze them so that you can evaluate the merits of the information to answer the question: Should I go into this business? First analyze yourself then analyze the merits of your business idea.

Personality Introspection: YES   NO

1. Do you have the personal and personality
    characteristics so that you can both adapt to
    and enjoy small business ownership?   ____   ____
2. Do you like making your own decisions?   ____   ____
3. Do you enjoy competition?   ____   ____
4. Do you have willpower and self-discipline?   ____   ____
5. Do you plan ahead?   ____   ____
6. Do you set goals for yourself?   ____   ____

7. When you set a goal for yourself, do you
   make it happen? Do you achieve the goal? ____   ____
8. Can you delegate authority to others and set
   goals and incentives for them? ____   ____
9. Do you have a good perception of how
   things will happen, before the things occur? ____   ____
10. Do you get things done on time without
    prodding? ____   ____
11. Are you adaptable to changing conditions? ____   ____
12. Can you be a self-starter, motivator and
    innovator? ____   ____
13. Can you take criticism? ____   ____
14. Can you rebound from failure-prone
    situations? ____   ____
15. After Questions #2 - #14, read question #1
    again. Did you answer question #1
    truthfully and fairly? ____   ____

Physical, Emotional and Financial Strains: YES   NO

16. Are you willing to work 10 to 15 hours
    per day, perhaps 6 days each week and
    maybe even holidays and without vacations? ____   ____
17. Do you have the physical stamina to handle
    extreme business stress? ____   ____
18. Can you withstand intense emotional strain? ____   ____
19. Are you prepared to lower your standard of
    living if business conditions are tough? ____   ____
20. Are you prepared to lose your savings and
    any other investment in the business? ____   ____
21. Do others depend on you emotionally or
    financially, i.e., family, spouse, children
    or parents? ____   ____
22. Are these family members willing and
    capable of withstanding the emotional and
    financial strain, perhaps even a lower
    standard of living? ____   ____
23. Can you withstand the emotional and
    financial demands from them if conditions
    are tough? ____   ____

24. If relatives, business associates or friends
    invest or work in your business, are you pre-
    pared to face them in the event of failure or
    the loss of their investment in your business? ____   ____

25. After Questions #16 - #24, read Question #1
    again. Did you answer Question #1
    truthfully and fairly?   ____   ____

Your Knowledge of Business/Product/Service: YES   NO

26. Have you worked in this business long
    enough to fully understand the forces that
    drive success?   ____   ____

27. Have you worked in this business long
    enough to fully understand the forces
    that contribute to failure?   ____   ____

28. By your colleagues, are you considered
    an expert?   ____   ____

29. You personally must have training, ex-
    perience and superior technical skills in the
    type of business you start. Do you have the
    technical knowledge to conduct this business
    on your own, by yourself?   ____   ____

30. Should you go to work for somebody else
    in order to learn the basic technical skills?   ____   ____

Business Planning Ability: YES   NO

31. Do you have the ability to perform all as-
    pects of a feasibility study? Are you objective? ____   ____

32. Do you have the time to perform a
    feasibility study?   ____   ____

33. Will you personally perform the
    feasibility study?   ____   ____

34. Will you devote the time and knowledge
    necessary to perform a comprehensive
    feasibility study?   ____   ____

35. Will you inquire, consult with and listen to
    other professional experts concerning
    important elements of the feasibility study?   ____   ____

36. Do you have the money to hire someone
    to perform a feasibility study for you?   ____   ____

37. If someone else studies the business's feasibility for you, will you make the critical decisions and will you take ownership of the feasibility study results? ____ ____

38. Will you comprehend and fully understand the study report when it has been prepared for you? ____ ____

39. When a reviewer or a lender asks questions about the feasibility study that was prepared, will you be forced to answer, "That is what the study says," without understanding why the study says it? ____ ____

40. Will you personally collect the results of the feasibility study into a business plan? ____ ____

41. Questions #31 to #37 were designed to emphasize the point that few people can claim expertise in all phases of feasibility assessment and business planning. You should realize your personal limitations and seek appropriate assistance where necessary (i.e., legal, marketing, financial). Yet you must take ownership of the result? This is very important? So did you honestly and fairly answer Questions #38, #39 and #40? ____ ____

42. Question #37 should tell you that you are solely responsible for the feasibility study. Will you be responsible and accountable for the preparation? ____ ____

43. Questions #38 and #39 should tell you that you must understand what you are doing. Will you fully understand? ____ ____

44. Question #40 should tell you that you must plan the key elements of your success. Will you plan? ____ ____

45. Will you personally prepare a business plan before you start your business? ____ ____

Business Plan Information:

46. Briefly describe the business you want to enter.

_____

47. List the product/service you want to sell.

_____

_____

48. Describe who will use your product/service.

_____

_____

49. Explain why someone would buy your product/service.

_____

_____

50. Describe the business location needed, i.e., type of neighborhood, zoning, traffic count, nearby firms, accessibility, size, etc.

_____

_____

51. List suppliers of products/services that are needed.

_____

_____

52. List the labor and staff needed to provide your product/service.

_____

_____

53. List your major competitors, those who sell or provide similar product/service.

_____

_____

54. Describe your customer. Be specific!

_____

_____

55. Explain the factors that will motivate buyers who will buy from you.

_____

_____

Requirements for Success: YES   NO

56. Did you complete all the information requested by Questions #46 through #55?   ____   ____

57. Does this information describe a viable and successful business?   ____   ____

58. Do you feel good about the information you have written about your business in response to Questions #46 through #55?   ____   ____

59. Does your business/product/service serve a presently unfulfilled need?   ____   ____

60. Does your business/product/service serve an existing market in which demand exceeds supply?   ____   ____

61. Can your business/product/service successfully compete with existing competitors because of an "advantageous situation," such as better performance, higher quality, price, location or other key characteristic?   ____   ____

62. To determine whether your idea meets with the basic requirements for a successful new venture, you must be able to answer "YES" to at least one of the questions numbered 59 through 61. Did you answer #59, #60, and #62 honestly and fairly?   ____   ____

63. Do you offer a lower price, better quality or a better performing product or service?   ____   ____

64. Do you offer a lower price than your competitors?   ____   ____

65. Do you offer better quality than your competitors?   ____   ____

66. Do you offer better product performance than your competitors?   ____   ____

67. Because of the advantages of your
business/product/service, will customers
stop buying from their present supplier
and begin buying from you?   ____   ____
68. Why will existing customers change and
buy from your business?

_____

_____

Potential Major Flaws: YES   NO

69. Are there causes (i.e., restrictions, monopolies
or shortages) that make any required factors
of production unavailable (i.e., unreasonable
cost, scarce skills, energy, material, equip-
ment, processes, technology or personnel)?   ____   ____
70. Are there potential detrimental environ-
mental effects?   ____   ____
71. Are there factors that prevent effective
marketing?   ____   ____

Professional Relationships: YES   NO

Every business should establish working relationships with four
specialized professional business areas that can be called upon for
professional advice as needed.

72. Attorney: An attorney can help form the
business and handle business forms, leases,
contracts, partnership agreements, buy/sell
agreements, government regulations,
litigation, etc. Will you engage the services
of an attorney?   ____   ____
73. Bank: Is your personal banking relationship
with your bank in good standing?   ____   ____
74. Can you set up a business bank account
based on your good personal banking record? ____   ____

75. Accountant: Financial and tax reporting have become extremely complex. Most entrepreneurs require detailed professional knowledge in this field. Much of your book-keeping work can be done by employees, but professional financial and tax advice are essential. Do you have an accountant?   ____   ____

76. Insurance: A business cannot operate without insurance protection. Do you have an insurance representative? Locate a good insurance representative in your field of business. Can you consult with this person for advice on financial protection against risks you cannot meet from current working capital?   ____   ____

77. Do you have a good relationship with each of these important professional service providers? Do you have access to specialized advice in these areas or the knowledge yourself?   ____   ____

Money/Capital/Financing Needs: YES   NO

Answer only one of the questions numbered 78, 79, 80 or 81. Answer "yes" only for the greatest amount of money that you will invest in the business. If you have less than 30% of the money needed to start the business, be sure to answer Questions #84 and #85.

78. Will you invest 100 percent of the money needed?   ____   ____

79. Will you invest more than 50 percent of the money needed?   ____   ____

80. Will you invest 30 to 50 percent of the money needed?   ____   ____

81. Will you invest less than 30 percent of the money needed?   ____   ____

It takes money to start a business.

82. Are capital requirements excessive for entry into this business or for continuing operations? ____ ____

83. Is adequate financing hard to obtain? ____ ____

84. If you have less than 30 percent of the money needed, can you get gifts or personal loans from relatives, friends, business associates, suppliers or customers to increase your equity to more than 30 percent of the amount needed? ____ ____

85. Do you have 30 percent of the equity needed, and can you arrange to borrow the remainder? ____ ____

Final Exam—"The Business Plan":   YES   NO

86. Do you have a business plan already prepared? ____ ____

87. Did you/will you prepare the business plan only because the lender or someone else requires it? ____ ____

88. Do you have an excellent knowledge of this business? Can you implement the factors that will demand your success in this business? ____ ____

89. Do you understand the physical, emotional, personal and personality strains on you and your loved ones? ____ ____

90. Will you seek help and assistance in areas where you are lacking in knowledge or experience? ____ ____

91. Do you personally have sufficient equity to start the business? ____ ____

92. Are you honest with yourself and were you honest with your answers on this test? ____ ____

93. Did you pass or fail this test? ____ ____

If you feel unsure of your probability for success, set this questionnaire aside for 30 days or more. Study areas of deficiency or go to work in the field of your business before starting the business. Then reread, update and modify your business plan. Answer Questions #46 through #55 again. Make the changes that are necessary.

After a suitable waiting period, take this test again.

94. Now, do you feel good about the prospects
      for success of this business?   ____   ____
95. Do you pass or fail this test now?   ____   ____

Good Luck To You!

Scoring Your Start-Up Small Business Potential

Adding the scores for the various test questions will provide an assessment of your ability to start a small business. A score is counted only for each YES answer. A NO answer does not have an effect on your ability to start a small business, except as noted in the scoring section.

Each question is weighted as to its importance to the total for an overall score. Count the weighting factor for each YES answer. Note that some questions have negative values and points should be deducted for YES answers to these questions.

Have you answered each question fairly, honestly and critically?

Score your ability to start this business by entering the weight for each question in "your score" column in the scoring table. The maximum possible score is 290 points (335 positive point answers and 40 negative point answers).

Total your score by summing the totals in columns 1, 2 and 3. Don't forget to subtract negative point questions. If you answered YES to a question with a note on the scoring table, read the explanation. Now consider your ability to start your business by comparing you score with the grading categories listed below.

Scoring Table

COLUMN #1				COLUMN #2				COLUMN#3		
QUESTION NUMBER	WEIGHT	YOUR SCORE		QUESTION NUMBER	WEIGHT	YOUR SCORE		QUESTION NUMBER	WEIGHT	YOUR SCORE
1	1			36	1			71	-5	
2	2			37	3			72	3	
3	3			38	5			73	4	
4	2			39	-5			74	1	
5	2			40	5			75	2	
6	2			41	10			76	2	
7	1			42	10			77	10	
8	1			43	5			78	15	
9	3			44	5			79	10	
10	1			45	10			80	5	
11	1			46	0			81	Note 1	
12	3			47	0			82	Note 2	
13	3			48	0			83	5	
14	3			49	0			84	-5	
15	10			50	0			85	-5	
16	2			51	0			86	10	
17	2			52	0			87	-5	
18	2			53	0			88	20	
19	1			54	0			89	8	
20	1			55	0			90	3	
21	-3			56	1			91	10	
22	3			57	1			92	20	
23	3			58	1			93	10	
24	3			59	3			94	Note 3	
25	10			60	3			95	Note 3	
26	5			61	3			YOUR #3 TOTAL =		
27	5			62	5					
28	2			63	5					
29	10			64	5					
30	Note 1			65	5					
31	2			66	5					
32	2			67	1					
33	3			68	0					
34	3			69	-10					
35	3			70	-2					
YOUR #1 TOTAL =				YOUR #2 TOTAL =						
				ADD TOTALS FROM COLUMN 1 + COLUMN 2 + COLUMN 3 =						

Note 1	If YES, stop ... Do not start a business now without experience in the field and 30% captial.
Note 2	Be very cautious about starting a business without your own captial. If YES, add 5 points.
Note 3	No points, considering that you honestly answered all the questions again.

Greater Than 260 Points: If your score was more than 260 points, it is likely that you were not honest with yourself while answering the questions. Take the test again. Be more honest, fair and critical of your perceptions of yourself and your ability to start a business.

230 to 259 Points: If your score was more than 230 points, you will be one of the best and most successful small businesses that was ever started. Or, you may have falsified your answers. It is very difficult to score 230 points as a start-up entrepreneur.

180 to 229 Points: A score of 180 to 229 means you have a good chance of being successful. Hopefully, you were honest with all your answers. You probably have what it takes to start the business. Congratulations! If you were very critical of your perceptions of yourself and your ability to start a business, go for it.

120 to 179 Points: If your score was between 120 and 179 you must work harder than the average new small business person to be successful. However, all may not be lost. Determination is one of the most important characteristics of a small business person. Begin studying and learning the key elements for success in your industry. Brush up on the weak areas or start the business later.

Less Than 120 Points: If your score was less than 120, forget about starting a small business.

Explanations Concerning Your Answers

Q1—A small business person must be self-starting, hard working, adaptable, aggressive, competitive, accountable, perceptive, decisive and a doer rather than someone who expects others to do for them. Do you have willpower to do what you think is right and then do it? If you answered NO to this question, forget about starting a business.

Q2—You will be making every decision that determines the success or failure of the business.

Q3—Competition is the name of the small business game. A small business person must compete with others in his or her own industry. In addition, the small business person must compete with every other opportunity customers have to spend their money elsewhere.

Q4—A small business person cannot be lazy or a procrastinator. You will not have the luxury to relax, lie in bed or do whatever is easy to avoid work. When you do not work, the business stops!

Q5—You must intuitively understand what will cause people to buy. Then create the conditions necessary to cause them to give their money to you for that thing. You must plan for this to happen. If you write this down on paper, it makes the ideas more clear to you and makes them easier to explain to others.

Q6—Goals are a part of the planning process. You must be able to set goals for sales and other activities. Then you must achieve the goals.

Q7—It is not enough to dream that people will buy your idea. You must aggressively pursue the activity that causes them to give their money to you for the idea that you have.

Q8—If you have employees, these employees will earn money for you only if you create an environment that causes them to do the things that result in sales for the small business.

Q9—In your personal life, a good realistic outlook is important to enjoyment. This includes anticipating things that could happen in the future then seeing those things become a reality. In your small business, you perceive sales and profits. The real question is, "Is your profit-making idea realistic?"

Q10—In your small business, who will make the sales from which the business will profit? That person is you. Nobody else!

Q11—The habits and tastes of people are constantly changing. Your small business must be able to quickly adapt to new trends in your industry. Does this constant change rattle you? Are you able to change direction quickly?

Q12—Did you answer no to this question? If you do not have these characteristics, who in your business will have them?

Q13—Everyone else will tell you what you must do to be a success in your small business. Often this can be perceived as criticism. If you collapse and cannot be effective in overcoming this adversity, your small business will not succeed.

Q14—A successful small business constantly struggles to stay alive. This often involves recovery from a decision to go in a particular direction, yet the market conditions changed. Many people call the early decision, "a bad decision"; the small business person must look at this environment as "an opportunity."

Q15—If you answered no, stop now. Do not go into this business.

Q16—Do you think small business owners have an easy time working and being their own bosses? Is the main activity carrying money to the bank? Think again!

Q17—Can you handle the necessary physical activity? If you do not make the business go, who will make the business into a success? If you get sick; no sick pay? If you go on vacation; no paid vacation!

Q18—When things get tough, the tough get going.

Q19—In the early years of a new small business, things may not go as planned (or fantasized). Do you have the physical, emotional and financial strength to make it through these tough times? Will your family suffer unbearably?

Q20—Before you start, consider the worst—the business may fail. If the business fails, is it OK with you that you lost the amount of money you put into the business?

Q21—No is good in this situation because only you can lose. Otherwise, if you are the head of the household, and everything depends on you as the breadwinner, the pressure from others may be unbearable to you.

Q22—If the family members cannot withstand the pressure, they will exert more pressure on you. Perhaps they do that now in other ways.

Q23—You must be a pillar of inner strength to be successful in the face of suffering loved ones.

Q24—If you lose your money, that is one thing. But to waste someone else's money in addition to your money is wrong. That person had trust in you and expected to earn a profit. They may never forgive you.

Q25—If you answered no, stop now. Do not go into this business.

Q26—If the business succeeds, it will succeed primarily because you are smarter and quicker than your competition. If you have only a surface knowledge of the details of the business, go to work for someone else in this business to learn the fundamentals.

Q27—What not to do is sometimes more important than knowing what you could do. Think very hard about what can go wrong to cause your business to fail before you invest time, money and energy.

Q28—You do not have to be an expert. But you must have the confidence in your ability to say to your self, "My colleagues respect my knowledge and ability in this business."

Q29—You do not have to be an expert. But you must totally understand and be able to explain those things important to the operation of the business. You personally must have training, experience and superior technical skills in the type of business you start. Otherwise, you must depend on others to perform these vital, success-impacting functions. Most frequently, you cannot hire a person who has key experience that you lack in the hope that this knowledge will make the business go. You must thoroughly and completely understand this type of business. Often, you can learn the supporting skills, such as business management. But it is much more difficult to learn the technical aspects while you are starting a business. You must have the skills and expertise which are critical to success. You must know what things need to be done and how things are done. You must select the best location for the business. You must know who are your competitors. You must know why your business will be more successful than your competitors. You must fully understand why you want to start the business. If you do not now have the technical skills necessary for the business, go to work for someone else until you have mastered these skills.

Q30—What is the turnover, how do you order, from whom do you order, what do customers like about the product or service, what do customers dislike? Thousands of these questions exist. You must know or guess the answers.

Q31—Is this a feasible idea? Do you know how to write down the important elements that determine if the idea is feasible?

Q32—If you do not take the time to determine the feasibility of your idea, who will determine its feasibility?

Q33—Your best approach is for you to perform the feasibility study yourself. If you pay someone else to study the feasibility for you, will that person may not tell you all the problems that may occur. Or will they give you a nicely typed document that looks good and be happy to take your money to *their* bank.

Q34—If you have the knowledge to perform a feasibility study and you have the time, commit to doing the study. After you have completed the study, you will know that you have accomplished a major step in determining your business potential.

Q35—Do not be a know-it-all. Be a good listener and remember what you hear.

Q36—If you have the money, perhaps your best action is to save it. Then do the feasibility study yourself so you will understand what is important and what is not important.

Q37—Who is to blame if the business fails? Is it you? Or, is it the person whom you hired to do the feasibility study? What matters is, it is your business. You own the business.

Q38—If you know the technical aspects of the business, you should understand the study report. If you do not have the business knowledge, take classes to learn it.

Q39—If you cannot explain the study report, do you think others will have confidence in your potential for success?

Q40—Business plan, business plan, business plan! The plan does not have to be fancy. But the planning must be done.

Q41—Perhaps you had some "no" answers here. That is OK. In fact a few "no" answers demonstrate that you don't think you know everything and are willing to learn from others. Yet the answer to question #41 must by yes for you to succeed.

Q42—If you are not responsible for the study, the plan and the execution of the plan, why do you think you can be responsible for conducting a business that is solely dependent on you, your management of the business and your drive to make it successful? Who, then, is responsible and accountable for the plan for your business? Nobody else but you is responsible for the plan for your business.

Q43—If you don't understand, you are headed for failure!

Q44—Lack of planning leads to failure.

Q45—Good! Don't worry about fancy prose with lots of words. Just write down the essential elements of what you plan to do, what you plan to avoid and how you plan to accomplish both of these goals. The plan should document the objectives you want to attain with your business, what goals you intend to accomplish, when you will reach the goals and how you plan to avoid problems that could cause failure. This planning performs two necessary functions: 1) forces you to consider all aspects that may be encountered and help solve these situations before they occur, and 2) provides a guide during business operation to measure progress and helps develop an understanding of areas where you do not meet expectations.

Q46 through Q55—Answers to these questions must be completed as fundamental information for your business plan. If you already have the business plan, you can skip these questions unless they remind you of a part of the plan that must be revised or improved.

Q56—If no, did you skip this section because it was too long and cumbersome? But this information is essential to understanding your business: These answers will be the foundation for your success. If your answer to the question was yes, good. You have done your homework and have most of the information at hand to write the business plan.

Q57—By the time you answer this question yes, you surely have confidence in the success you expect from the business. If you answered no, what does that tell you about your probability for success?

Q58—If you answered yes, you are probably an entrepreneur.

Q59—Reread your plan. Does the plan describe the unfulfilled need? Make revisions as necessary.

Q60—Reread your plan. Does the plan describe the demand and the supply? Make revisions as necessary.

Q61—Reread your plan. Does the plan describe the competition? Make revisions as necessary.

Q62—If no, stop. You must be honest and truthful in this analysis. Yet, all "yes" answers may show over-confidence or optimism beyond reality. On the other hand, one or two hesitant no answers demonstrate honesty in yourself. Keep working on your idea until all the answers are yes.

Q63—If your answer is no, why will someone buy your product or service? Reasonable assurance should be evident that there is a need to offer the product or service or that a demand can be developed through advertising to provide a profitable return on your time and money. You must understand your market and the customers who will buy what you offer for sale. This is necessary to convince them to cancel their present provider of the product or service. Then those customers must switch suppliers so that they buy those items from you. Remember, customers make calculated value judgment decisions for purchases made. They want to get the best performance and highest quality at the lowest price.

Q64—If your answer is no, then you must offer significantly better quality and significantly better performance in your product/ service. If your answer is yes, do you understand why your price is less than your competitors? Is your pricing structure carefully thought out or will hidden costs cause you to lose money? Low price alone, without high performance and good quality, usually will not produce a successful business.

Q65—Customers want better quality and better performing products at the same cost as inferior products. If you answered no, do you have an advantage over competitors? What quality advantages?

Q66—Customers want better quality and better performing products at the same cost as inferior products. If you answered no, do you have an advantage over competitors? What performance advantages?

Q67—Read that question again. Do you comprehend the implication of what action your customer must take? Regardless of your answer, you must understand this concept.

Q68—On this line, you should have written a commanding statement about why customers will beat down all obstacles to buy your product/service from you.

Q69—To answer this question yes, you must fully understand all the technical aspects of your product or service, including the marketplace, the competitors and the need for your product or service.

Q70—People are becoming more aware of environmental hazards. Laws have been enacted to restrict many business activities. Do you understand these limitations?

Q71—One factor might be lack of understanding by your customer about what your product or service can do for him or her. Another may be insufficient finances for marketing. Marketing is most important to educate prospects to become buyers.

Q72—The answer should be yes? True, a business can be started without an attorney. But the dangers are great. An attorney is trained to foresee potential legal dangers and prevent them from occurring.

Q73—If your answer is no, you must first get your personal financial affairs in order before you can be trusted with the financial affairs of a business.

Q74—The answer must be yes! You cannot do business without a business bank account. If your business bank account will be located in the same bank as your personal bank account, establishing rapport with the bank may be easier because bank personnel know you. However, some banks specialize in small business transactions and can provide a wider variety of services. Set up the business bank account and establish a good working relationship with a bank that can handle your business transactions in a location convenient to the business.

Q75—The answer should be yes! Payroll accounting and tax laws have become very complex. A good accountant should keep you out of much trouble in this area. One missed tax deposit could cancel a year's worth of profit.

Q76—The answer should be yes! Engage an insurance representative who understands the type of business in which you will be dealing. If you didn't answer yes, you do not understand the need for insurance.

Q77—You confirmed your confidence in business success by answering yes to questions #72 through #76.

Q78—If you answered yes, financial worries are at a minimum concerning the amount of money needed to start the business. Yet you should still worry about losing your own money.

Q79—You are lucky to have sufficient resources to start your small business.

Q80—Most small businesses start with this amount of the owner's investment into the business. You should be confident.

Q81—If your answer was no, do not start this business unless the answer to questions #84 and #85 is yes.

Q82—You may not be able to start a business requiring significant investment that you do not possess. Often, other investors cannot be convinced of the merits.

Q83—Lenders and investors must be convinced of the venture before they will invest. To invest, they must be assured they will get their investment money back plus a reasonable profit on the investment.

Q84—These individuals may lend money to you on trust, without collateral. You must repay the money. Their personal loan to you may give the boost in your equity needed to start the business.

Q85—It takes money to start a business. To borrow money is possible but only if you have sufficient funds of your own in cash, inventory or equipment to provide a reasonable equity for loan consideration. Sufficient funds should be available to buy fixed assets, equipment, supplies, labor and materials, meet overhead, take advantage of discounts and provide the ability to arrange credit and thus eliminate immediate financial problems and worry. Ensure there is enough working capital for your needs. Your personal financial stability is essential to establishing a trusting and effective working relationship with a bank or other lender.

Q86—If yes, continue. If no, write the plan before you proceed.

Q87—A yes answer denotes your lack of understanding of the need for a business plan.

Q88—Congratulations to your yes answer! You must be confident of your knowledge and your ability to start this business. Go for it!

Q89—Congratulations to your yes answer! You must possess the personal characteristics that will breed success into your business.

Q90—If yes, have you decided what help you need? If no, apparently you are undertaking more than you can bear.

Q91—If yes, continue. If no, stop; do not try to start a business.

Q92—If yes, continue. If no, stop; do not try to start a business.

Q93—If yes, continue. If no, stop; do not try to start a business.

Q94—If yes, continue. If no, stop; do not try to start a business.

Q95—If yes, continue. If no, stop; do not try to start a business.

Resources for Small Businesses

Upstart Publishing Company, Inc. Publications on proven management techniques for small businesses are available from Upstart Publishing Company, Inc., 12 Portland St., Dover, NH 03820. For a free current catalog, call (800) 235-8866 outside New Hampshire, or 749-5071 in state.

The Business Planning Guide, 6th edition, 1992, David H. Bangs, Jr. and Upstart Publishing Company, Inc. A manual that helps you write a business plan and financial proposal tailored to your business, your goals and your resources. Includes worksheets and checklists. (Softcover, 208 pp., $19.95)

The Market Planning Guide, 1990, David H. Bangs, Jr. and Upstart Publishing Company, Inc. A manual to help small-business owners put together a goal-oriented, resource-based marketing plan with action steps, benchmarks and time lines. Includes worksheets and checklists to make implementation and review easier. (Softcover, 160 pp., $19.95)

The Cash Flow Control Guide, 1990, David H. Bangs, Jr. and Upstart Publishing Company, Inc. A manual to help small-business owners solve their number one financial problem. Includes worksheets and checklists. (Softcover, 88 pp., $14.95)

The Personnel Planning Guide, 1988, David H. Bangs, Jr. and Upstart Publishing Company, Inc. A 176-page manual outlining practical, proven personnel management techniques, including hiring, managing, evaluating and compensating personnel. Includes worksheets and checklists. (Softcover, 176 pp., $19.95)

The Start Up Guide: A One-Year Plan for Entrepreneurs, 2nd edition, 1994, David H. Bangs, Jr. and Upstart Publishing Company, Inc. This book utilizes the same step-by-step, no-jargon method as *The Business Planning Guide*, to help even those with no business training through the process of beginning a successful business. (Softcover, 176 pp., $19.95)

Managing by the Numbers: Financial Essentials for the Growing Business, 1992, David H. Bangs, Jr. and Upstart Publishing Company, Inc. Straightforward techniques for getting the maximum return with a minimum of detail in your business's financial management. (Softcover, 160 pp., $19.95.)

Building Wealth, 1992, David H. Bangs, Jr. and the editors of *Common Sense*. A collection of tested techniques designed to help you plan your personal finances and how to plan your business finances to benefit you, your family and employees. (Softcover, 168 pp., $19.95)

Buy the Right Business—At the Right Price, 1990, Brian Knight and the Associates of Country Business, Inc. Many people who would like to be in business for themselves think strictly of starting a business. In some cases, buying a going concern may be preferable—and just as affordable. (Softcover, 152 pp., $18.95)

Borrowing for Your Business, 1991, George M. Dawson. This is a book for borrowers and about lenders. Includes detailed guidelines on how to select a bank and a banker, how to answer the lender's seven most important questions, how your banker looks at a loan and how to get a loan renewed. (Hardcover, 160 pp., $19.95)

Can This Partnership Be Saved? 1992, Dr. Peter Wylie and Dr. Mardy Grothe. The authors offer solutions and hope for problems between key people in business. (Softcover, 272 pp., $19.95)

The Complete Guide to Selling Your Business, 1992, Paul Sperry and Beatrice Mitchell. A step-by-step guide through the entire process from how to determine when the time is right to sell to negotiating the final terms. (Hardcover, 160 pp., $21.95)

The Complete Selling System, 1991, Pete Frye. This book can help any manager or salesperson, even someone with no experience, find the solutions to some of the most common dilemmas in managing sales. (Hardcover, 192 pp., $21.95)

Creating Customers, 1992, David H. Bangs, Jr. and the editors of *Common Sense*. A book for business owners and managers who want a step-by-step approach to selling and promoting. Techniques include inexpensive market research, pricing your goods and services and writing a usable marketing plan. (Softcover, 176 pp., $19.95)

Export Profits, 1992, Jack S. Wolf. This book shows how to find the right foreign markets for your product, cut through the red tape, minimize currency risks and find the experts who can help. (Softcover, 304 pp., $19.95)

Financial Troubleshooting, 1992, David H. Bangs, Jr. and the editors of *Common Sense*. This book helps the owner/manger use basic diagnostic methods to monitor the health of the business and solve problems before damage occurs. (Softcover, 192 pp., $19.95)

Financial Essentials for Small Business Success, 1994, Joseph Tabet and Jeffrey Slater. Designed to show readers where to get the information they need and how planning and record keeping will enhance the health of any small business. (Softcover, 272 pp., $19.95)

From Kitchen to Market, 1992, Stephen Hall. A practical approach to turning culinary skills into a profitable business. (Softcover, 208 pp., $24.95)

The Home-Based Entrepreneur, 1993, Linda Pinson and Jerry Jinnett. A step-by-step guide to all the issues surrounding starting a home-based business. Issues such as zoning, labor laws and licensing are discussed, and forms are provided to get you on your way. (Softcover, 192 pp., $19.95)

Keeping the Books, 1993, Linda Pinson and Jerry Jinnett. Basic business recordkeeping both explained and illustrated. Designed to give you a clear understanding of small business accounting by taking you step-by-step through general records, development of financial statements, tax reporting, scheduling and financial statement analysis. (Softcover, 208 pp., $19.95)

Marketing Your Invention, 1992, Thomas Mosley. This book dispels the myths and clearly communicates what inventors need to know to successfully bring their inventions to market. (Softcover, 232 pp., $19.95)

The Small Business Computer Book, 1993, Robert Moskowitz. This book does not recommend particular systems but rather provides readers with a way to think about these choices and make the right decisions for their businesses. (Softcover, 190 pp., $19.95)

Steps to Small Business Start-Up, 1993, Linda Pinson and Jerry Jinnett. A step-by-step guide for starting and succeeding with a small or home-based business. Takes you through the mechanics of business start-up and gives an overview of information on such topics as copyrights, trademarks, legal structures, recordkeeping and marketing. (Softcover, 256 pp., $19.95)

Target Marketing for the Small Business, 1993, Linda Pinson and Jerry Jinnett. A comprehensive guide to marketing your business. This book not only shows you how to reach your customers but also gives you a wealth of information on how to research that market through the use of library resources, questionnaires, demographics, etc. (Softcover, 176 pp., $19.95)

On Your Own: A Woman's Guide to Starting Your Own Business, 2nd edition, 1993, Laurie Zuckerman. *On Your Own* is for women who want hands-on, practical information about starting and running their own business. It deals honestly with issues like finding time for your business when you're also the primary care provider, societal biases against women and credit discrimination. (Softcover, 320 pp., $19.95)

Problem Employees, 1991, Dr. Peter Wylie and Dr. Mardy Grothe. Provides managers and supervisors with a simple, practical and straightforward approach to help all employees, especially problem employees, significantly improve their work performance. (Softcover, 272 pp., $22.95)

The Restaurant Planning Guide, 1992, Peter Rainsford and David H. Bangs, Jr. This book takes the practical techniques of *The*

Business Planning Guide and combines it with the expertise of Peter Rainsford, a professor at the Cornell School of Hotel Administration and restaurateur. Topics include establishing menu prices, staffing and scheduling, controlling costs and niche marketing. (Softcover, 176 pp., $19.95)

Successful Retailing, 2nd edition, 1993, Paula Wardell. Provides hands-on help for those who want to start or expand their retail business. Sections include strategic planning, marketing, market research and inventory control. (Softcover, 176 pp., $19.95)

The Woman Entrepreneur, 1992, Linda Pinson and Jerry Jinnett. Thirty-three successful women business owners share their practical ideas for success and their sources for inspiration. (Softcover, 244 pp., $14.00)

Index

Is a Definition Missing from
The Language of Small Business?

Can you add a definition?

Can you improve a definition?

Can you help expand small business knowledge for the benefit of others?

Please suggest improvements to the author on the form below.

As you use *The Language of Small Business* you may discover terms, words, phrases, idioms, acronyms or abbreviations peculiar to the small business in your industry or area. Please use the form below to submit these definitions to the author for consideration in future editions or for inclusion in an on-line database dictionary.

Use additional sheets if necessary and mail to:

Author, The Language of Small Business
Upstart Publishing Company, Inc.
12 Portland St.
Dover, NH 03820

Date: _____

Submitted by: _____

Address: _____

City/State/Zip: _____

I submit the following definition(s) to the author of *The Language of Small Business* for consideration:

Term #1 _____

Definition _____

_____

_____

Term #2 _____

Definition _____

_____

_____

"Carl Trautmann's *The Language of Small Business* is an exceptionally complete, pertinent and useful addition to entrepreneurial literature. It should be on the shelves of all public, corporate and academic libraries."
—Gustav Berle, Small Business Owner
and author of 12 small business books

"This book is excellent source information for the international small business person who must translate business from another language into English. Since English is becoming the small business language throughout the world, understanding American and English business terms is necessary."
—Dr. Peter Minderjahn,
Ridder & Minderjahn, Stolberg, Germany

"As the executive director of an international organization that has as its mission the advancement of the practice of entrepreneurship worldwide, I believe that *The Language of Small Business* will greatly improve the level of understanding of English business terms by its comprehensive, yet concise definitions."
—Robert H. Brockhaus, Ph.D.
Coleman Foundation Chair in Entrepreneurship

"This book is a guide for small business in making the right decision, no matter whether finance, marketing or management which is the heart of business. In my point of view, this book is a very valuable book to own. In addition, business is expanding all over the world. Each country has its own business language; however, international business is necessary using the same business language. *The Language of Small Business* is a beneficial tool not only for the American owner, but also for foreign business."
—T. Surapol and Supamas
Chaichareon Company, Ltd., Bangkok, Thailand